Editors: Gary Groth & Jason T. Miles
Production & Design: Jason T. Miles & Tony Ong
Associate Publisher: Eric Reynolds
Publishers: Gary Groth & Kim Thompson

Fantagraphics Books
7563 Lake City Way NE
Seattle, Wa 98115.

Distributed in the U.S. by W.W. Norton and Company, Inc. (800-233-4830)
Distributed in Canada by Canadian Manda Group (800-452-6642 x862)
Distributed in the U.K. by Turnaround Distribution (44 020 8829-3002)
Distributed to comic book specialty stores by Diamond Comics Distributors
(800-452-6642 x215)

To receive an illustrated catalog of fine comics and books, call 1-800-657-1100
or visit fantagraphics.com

ISBN 978-1-60699-509-9
Printed in Hong Kong

A CELEBRATION of HUMAN WEAKNESS

folly

The CONSEQUENCES of INDISCRETION

Comics by
HANS RICKHEIT

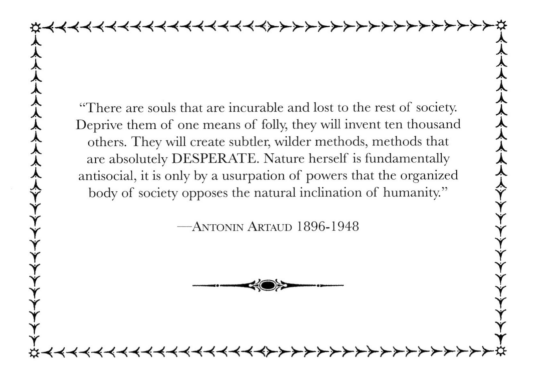

"There are souls that are incurable and lost to the rest of society. Deprive them of one means of folly, they will invent ten thousand others. They will create subtler, wilder methods, methods that are absolutely DESPERATE. Nature herself is fundamentally antisocial, it is only by a usurpation of powers that the organized body of society opposes the natural inclination of humanity."

—ANTONIN ARTAUD 1896-1948

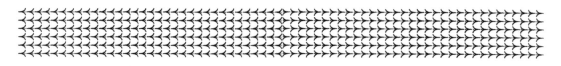

VOCABULARY

FOR THE BENEFIT OF YOUNG PEOPLE

accouchement a period of confinement during childbirth.

adoxography the rhetorical exercise in which praise is applied to things trivial, ugly, useless, ridiculous, dangerous, vicious, and without honor. In ancient Greece, practitioners of this skill praised gout, blindness, deafness, old age, negligence, adultery, flies, gnats, bedbugs, smoke, and dung.

deliquescence 1. the melting away of. Dissolving via absorption of atmospheric fluid. **2.** growing forth of multiple branches.

folly may refer: to an extravagantly overdone, minimally functional piece of architecture erected to suit a fanciful taste; to absurdity, daftness, dottiness, escapade, exorbitance, extravagance, farce, flapdoodle, fling, foolishness, foppery, frolic, fuckwaddery, gag, idiocy, imbecility, impracticality, imprudence, inadvisability, lewdness, lunacy, madness, monkeyshines, prank, obliquity, preposterousness, prodigality, profligacy, profusion, rashness, recklessness, rib, roguery, rollick, romp, senselessness, shenanigans, silliness, spree, stunt, stupidity, trick, triviality, unsoundness, vagary, vice, waste, wildness, witlessness, and zanyism; or to the prestigious edition you now fondle with your foolish appendages.

guileless sincere and without pretense. A right dinkum.

haecceity a person's or object's defining qualities of "this-ness."

interregnum an interlude definable by the absence of order.

lacuna a space holder or extended silence in place of the linguistically untranslatable.

nonpareils 1. things beyond compare, having no equal. **2.** Tiny, multicolored confectionery pellets.

numinous 1. evoking a sense of transcendent awe. [Carl Sagan was known to be fond of both the word and concept.]

peremptory an imperative command that forbids possibility of refusal.

pulchritudinous characterized by great physical beauty.

quiddity the inherent essence of a person or thing. The "is-ness."

The Underbrain flows through all such conduits as it may.

FRIENDS
YOU ARE
WELCOMED

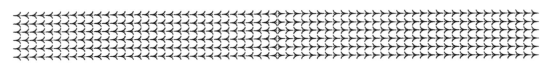

AN INTRODUCTION
by E. STEPHEN FREDERICK

Oh... folly, folly, folly... Now, let's try this on for size again, shall we? And so, we find ourselves in the same position as we once were. It is familiar; yet not as comfortable as we had remembered. Perhaps if we arrange this part here and here, and... Well, that's still not especially comfortable now, is it? Oh... folly, folly, folly. And as you might expect, a preamble of this sort is always dry, boring rubbish, hardly worth unmooring a boat for a stoat or for a walk in the woods. One might as well skip ahead to the point where you first imagine you have consciousness and are living in a universe which, even for a beginner such as yourself, should

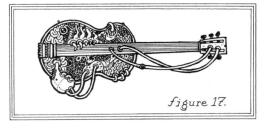

figure 17.

be neither an especially difficult nor an entirely undemanding misconcep-tion. GOOD! So here we are. Again. Welcome. If this is your first time, and you are not already familiar with the adoxography* of Hans Rickheit, this volume is an impeccable avenue of ingress, initiating you to the caress of The Under-brain. Continuing upon the presumption that this is your first conscious encounter with Hans Rickheit's work, some introduction is in order. In the world of literature at large, Hans is best known for his two critically acclaimed autobiographically-tinged graphic novels, *The Squirrel Machine* and *Chloe*. But within the circles of creators and connoisseurs of zines, Hans Rickheit's name has been well recognized since the 1990s. His work has been compared to such comic book luminaries as Robert Crumb, Chris Ware, Jim Woodring, Geof Darrow, and early comics pioneer Winsor McCay.

In 1790, the English poet and mystic William Blake wrote that "If the fool would persist in his folly he would become wise." By this measure, Hans epitomizes the marrow of wisdom. And by this same measure, this compendium is the apotheosis of a decade of visceral persistence. Its contents were drawn between 1999 and 2009, while Hans was working on the aforementioned graphic novels. These interregnum works offer short, sweet pre-measured doses of obsessive gratification to the reader. folly marks the first mass-published compilation of Hans' shorter works. Portions of folly have previously appeared in periodicals such as *Blurred Visions*, *Hoax*, *Kramer's Ergot*, *Legal Action Comics*, *Paper Rodeo*, *Paradigmino*, *Proper Gander*, *Reglar Wiglar*, *The Stranger*, and *Typhon*, but until now, many of these perplexing parables were available only in the form of rare, hand-stapled editions of *Chrome Fetus Comics*. Expect no discernable narrative uniting these brief autonomous excursions. As you proceed, various characters will become known to you. In the titular adventure, "folly," you will observe a hero of sorts, with avian inclination, who resolvedly overcomes obstacles to achieve a goal of questionable merit. You'll be introduced to the tyrannical, tricycle-riding Jeffrey (it's worth noting, for historical context, that "HAIL JEFFREY" was originally drawn in 2004). There will be multiple appearances by the solitary bear-headed gentleman, whom Hans refers to only as "the unnamed protagonist." And of course, you'll witness the ongoing misadventures of the pulchritudinous Cochlea and Eustachia. These identical masked nymphs are compelling to behold, from their bulbous heads down to their sturdy feet. Like many denizens of The Underbrain, Chochlea and Eustacia have a propensity for examining orifices and ambiguous devices, but the guileless zeal with which this duo probes their environment assures their status as two of Hans' most adored characters. Their existence begs to be replicated as animated cartoons, feature films, and action figures. But waste no more attention here on third-hand, vicarious epiphanies. Instead, consider that while you sleep, the cosmos economizes by allowing disparate variants of your very quiddity to borrow

---

*In 2010 Hans Rickheit was appointed to the coveted position of "Adoxographer of the Decade."

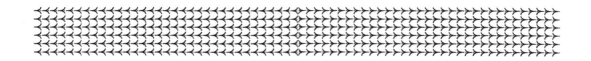

the mortal lacuna you call your body, and you are content to wander aimlessly into the deliquescence of the great forgetting. But Hans remains ever vigilant. Poor Fool though Hans may be, in sleep he accumulates unmatched wealth, and upon waking, labors anew to record and disseminate these Underbrain nonpareils for your edification. Please accept this offering and give thanks that you need not duplicate his accouchement.

Now, imagine a starry sky wrapped around a summer night. The numinous summer darkness encompasses a wide grassy lawn. On the grassy lawn, a child whirls in circles, gazing up into the deep apex of pivoting night. But it is the child who is motionless while the stars are spinning. Eventually the child collapses, dizzy in the folly of having spun the entire universe, heavy in the fullness of containing the haecceity of Summer and Night. The stars are childless and the motion is spinning. Forget not that causality works forward and backward and you have no choice but to capitulate to the weight of the uncertain future you are already heir to. It has always ended and begun thus.

This peremptory obfuscation provided courtesy of E. Stephen Frederick, caretaker of
The Empire S.N.A.F.U. Restoration Project.

figure 8.

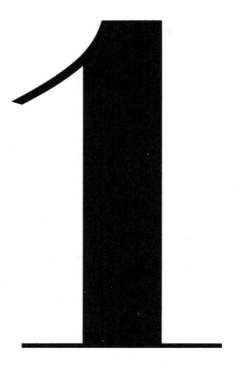

Important Questions that Children Ask

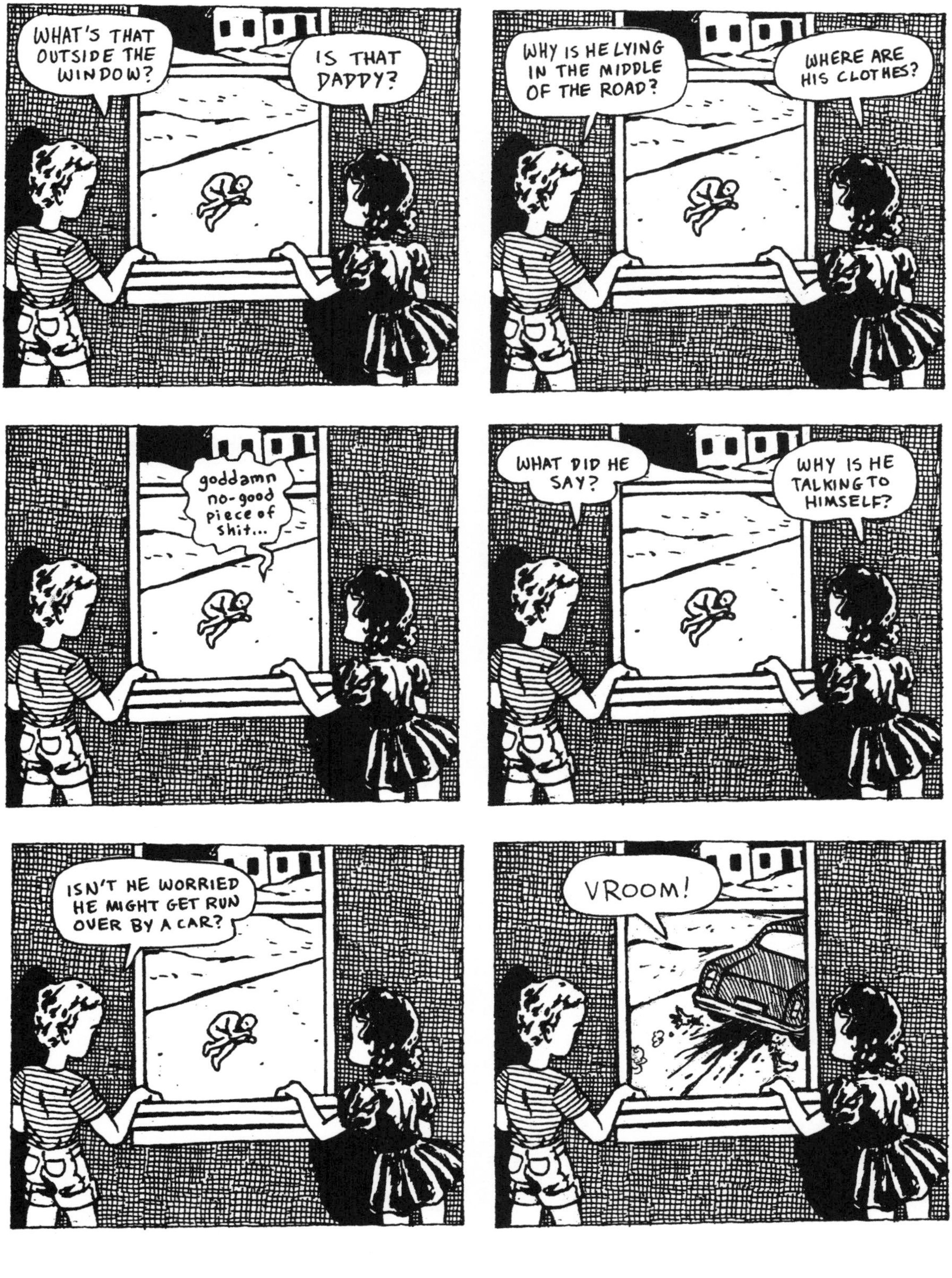
WHAT'S THAT OUTSIDE THE WINDOW?
IS THAT DADDY?
WHY IS HE LYING IN THE MIDDLE OF THE ROAD?
WHERE ARE HIS CLOTHES?
goddamn no-good piece of shit...
WHAT DID HE SAY?
WHY IS HE TALKING TO HIMSELF?
ISN'T HE WORRIED HE MIGHT GET RUN OVER BY A CAR?
VROOM!

CHROMEFETUS COMICS

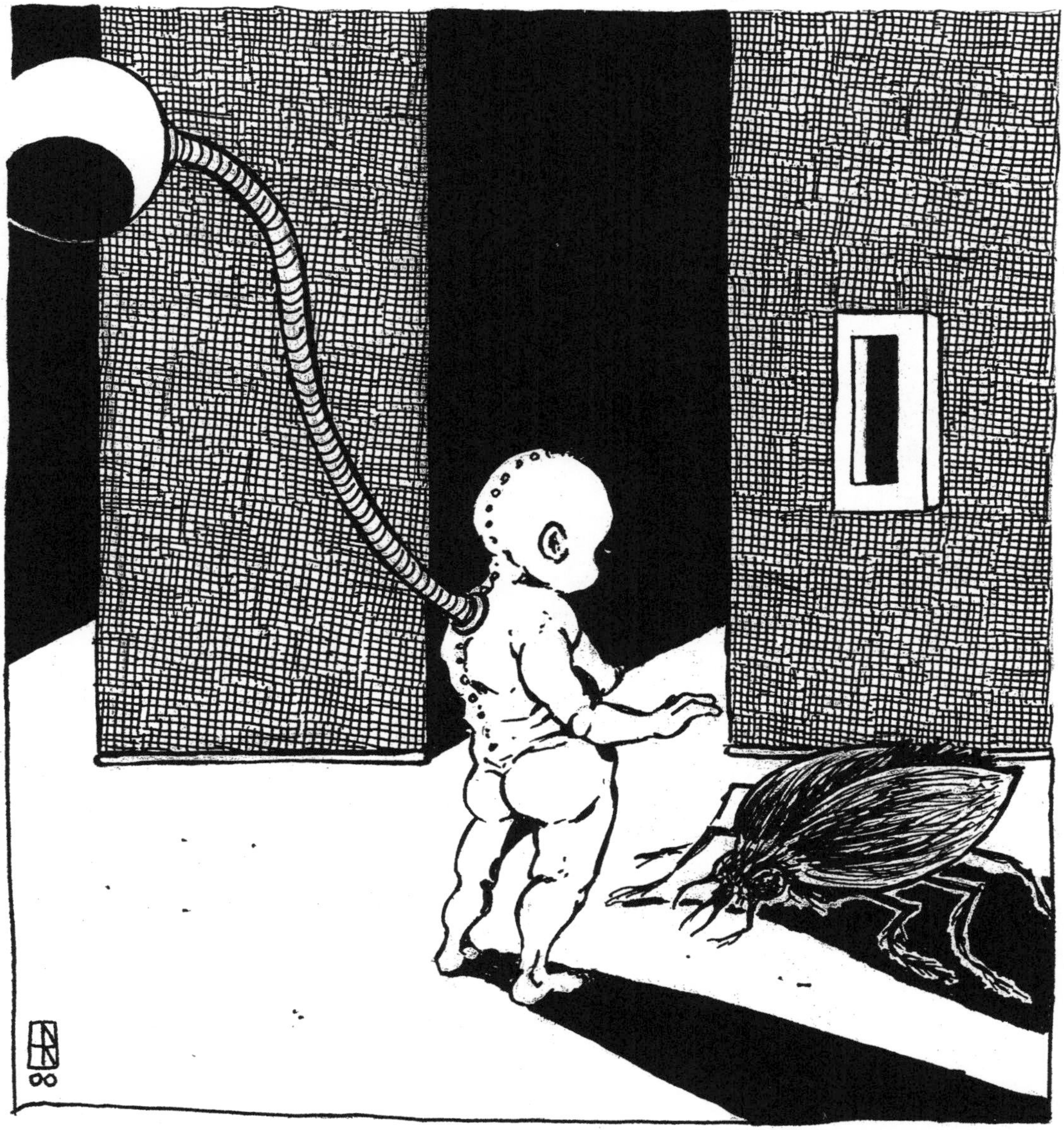

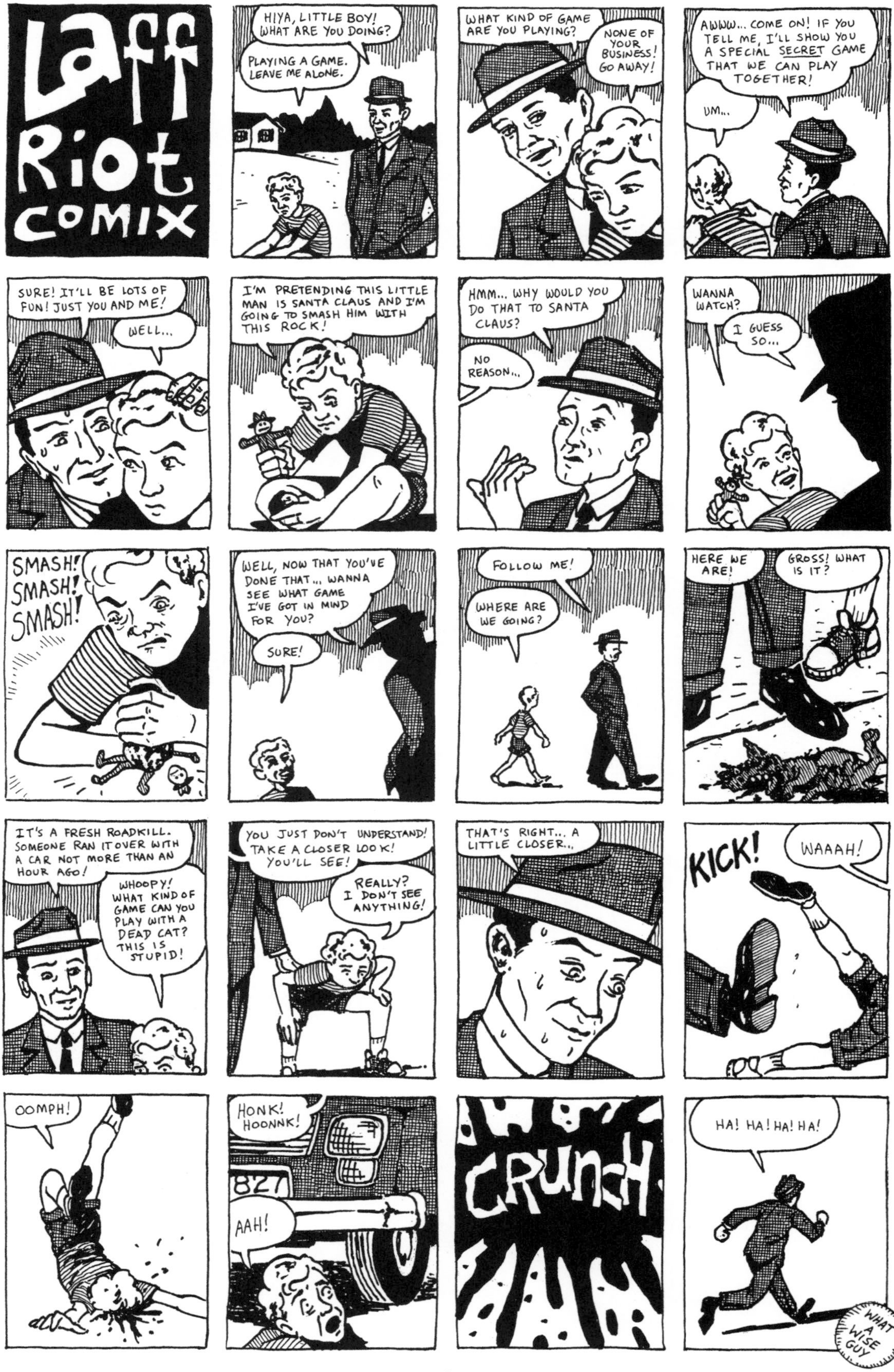

LAFF RIOT COMIX
HIYA, LITTLE BOY! WHAT ARE YOU DOING?
PLAYING A GAME. LEAVE ME ALONE.
WHAT KIND OF GAME ARE YOU PLAYING?
NONE OF YOUR BUSINESS! GO AWAY!
AWWW... COME ON! IF YOU TELL ME, I'LL SHOW YOU A SPECIAL SECRET GAME THAT WE CAN PLAY TOGETHER!
UM...
SURE! IT'LL BE LOTS OF FUN! JUST YOU AND ME!
WELL...
I'M PRETENDING THIS LITTLE MAN IS SANTA CLAUS AND I'M GOING TO SMASH HIM WITH THIS ROCK!
HMM... WHY WOULD YOU DO THAT TO SANTA CLAUS?
NO REASON...
WANNA WATCH?
I GUESS SO...
SMASH! SMASH! SMASH!
WELL, NOW THAT YOU'VE DONE THAT... WANNA SEE WHAT GAME I'VE GOT IN MIND FOR YOU?
SURE!
FOLLOW ME!
WHERE ARE WE GOING?
HERE WE ARE!
GROSS! WHAT IS IT?
IT'S A FRESH ROADKILL. SOMEONE RAN IT OVER WITH A CAR NOT MORE THAN AN HOUR AGO!
WHOOPY! WHAT KIND OF GAME CAN YOU PLAY WITH A DEAD CAT? THIS IS STUPID!
YOU JUST DON'T UNDERSTAND! TAKE A CLOSER LOOK! YOU'LL SEE!
REALLY? I DON'T SEE ANYTHING!
THAT'S RIGHT... A LITTLE CLOSER...
KICK!
WAAAH!
OOMPH!
HONK! HOONNK!
827
AAH!
CRUNCH
HA! HA! HA! HA!
WHAT A WISE GUY

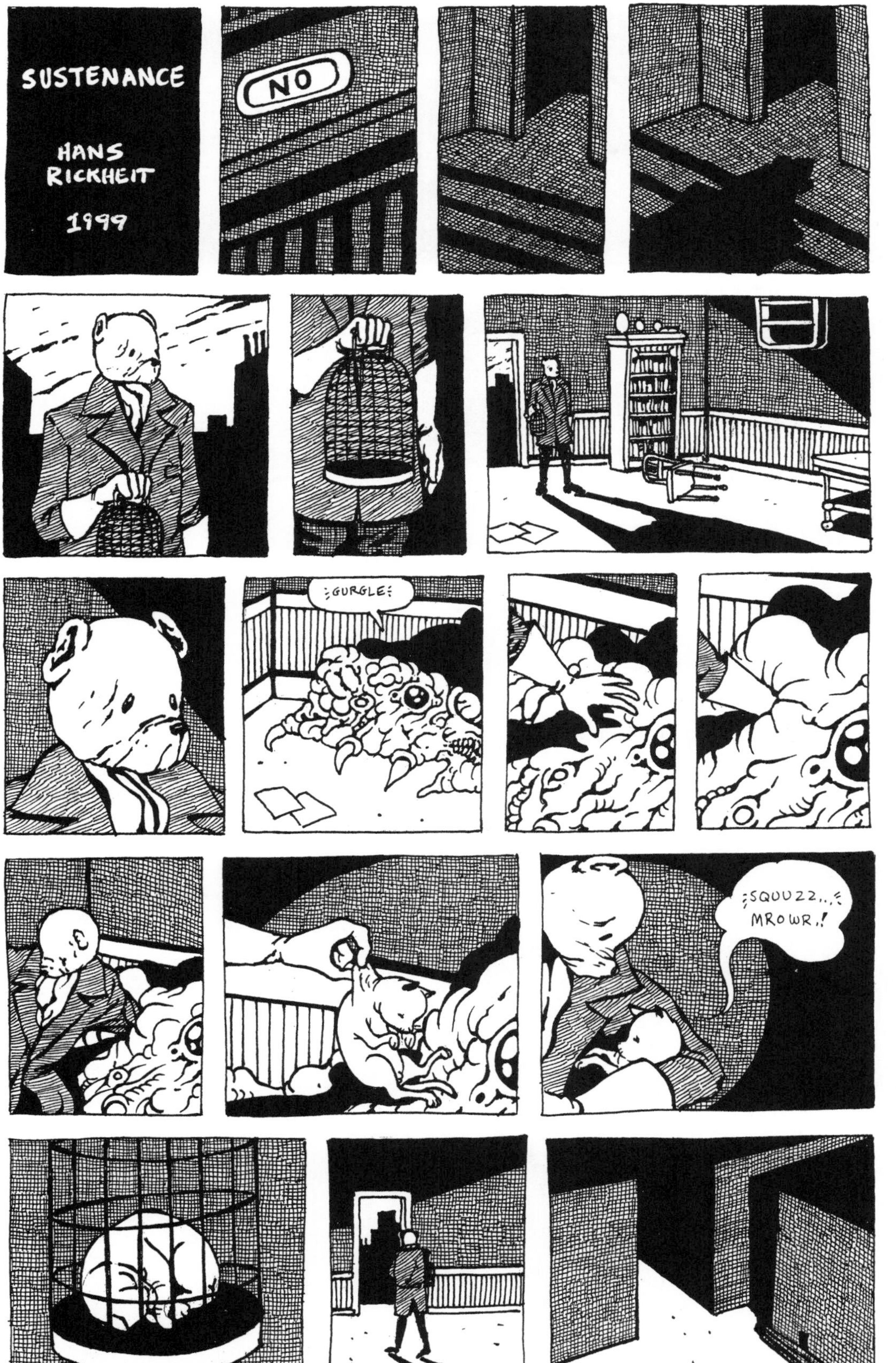
SUSTENANCE
HANS RICKHEIT
1999
NO
GURGLE
SQUUZZ..
MROWR!

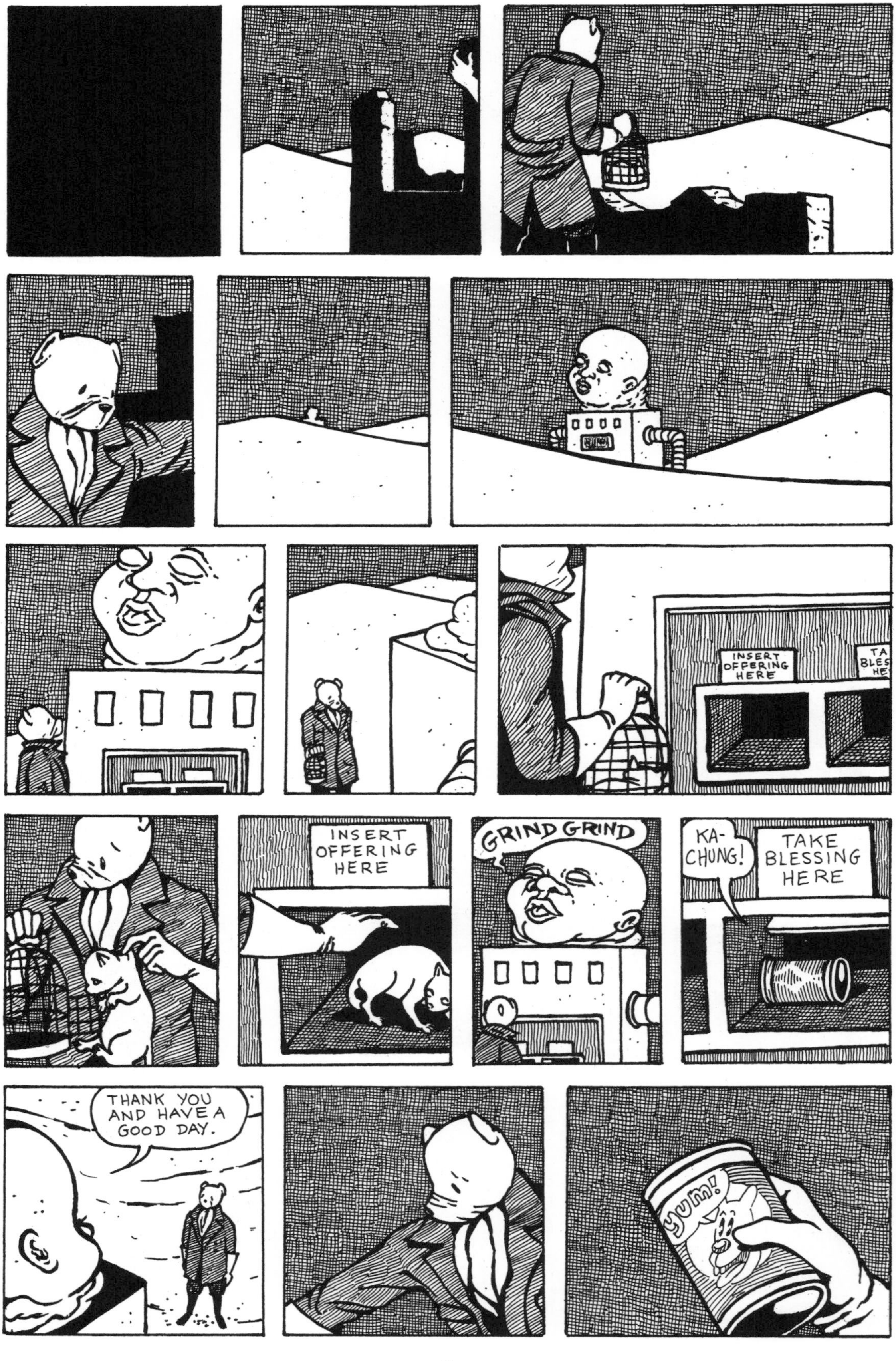
INSERT OFFERING HERE
TA BLES HE
INSERT OFFERING HERE
GRIND GRIND
KA-CHUNG!
TAKE BLESSING HERE
THANK YOU AND HAVE A GOOD DAY.
yum!

YUM!
CREAK
BLUG
SQUIK
POK
LADIES AND GENTLEMEN OF THE JURY, I HEREBY SUBMIT THIS AS FINAL EVIDENCE IN MY DEFENSE AGAINST THESE ALLEGATIONS...
BEEP! CLICK! MIGHT I REMIND THE COURT THAT FOR OVER TWENTY YEARS I HAVE BEEN A MODEL CITIZEN IN THIS COMMUNITY WITHOUT A BLEMISH ON MY RECORD, AND FURTHERMORE...
BLOG

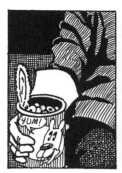

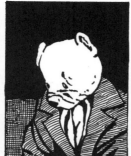

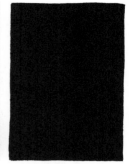

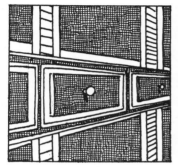

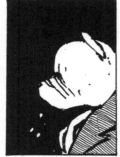

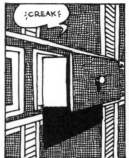

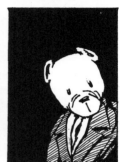

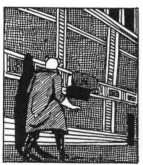

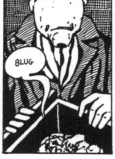

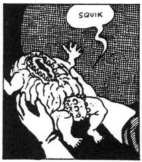

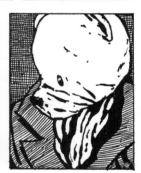

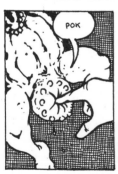

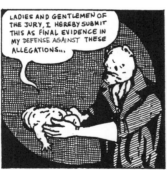

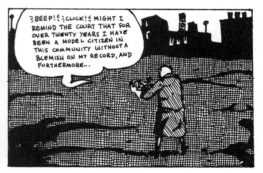

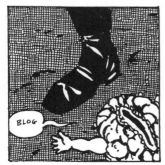

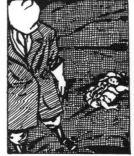

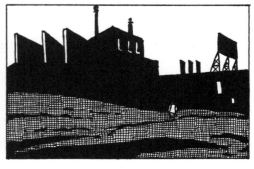

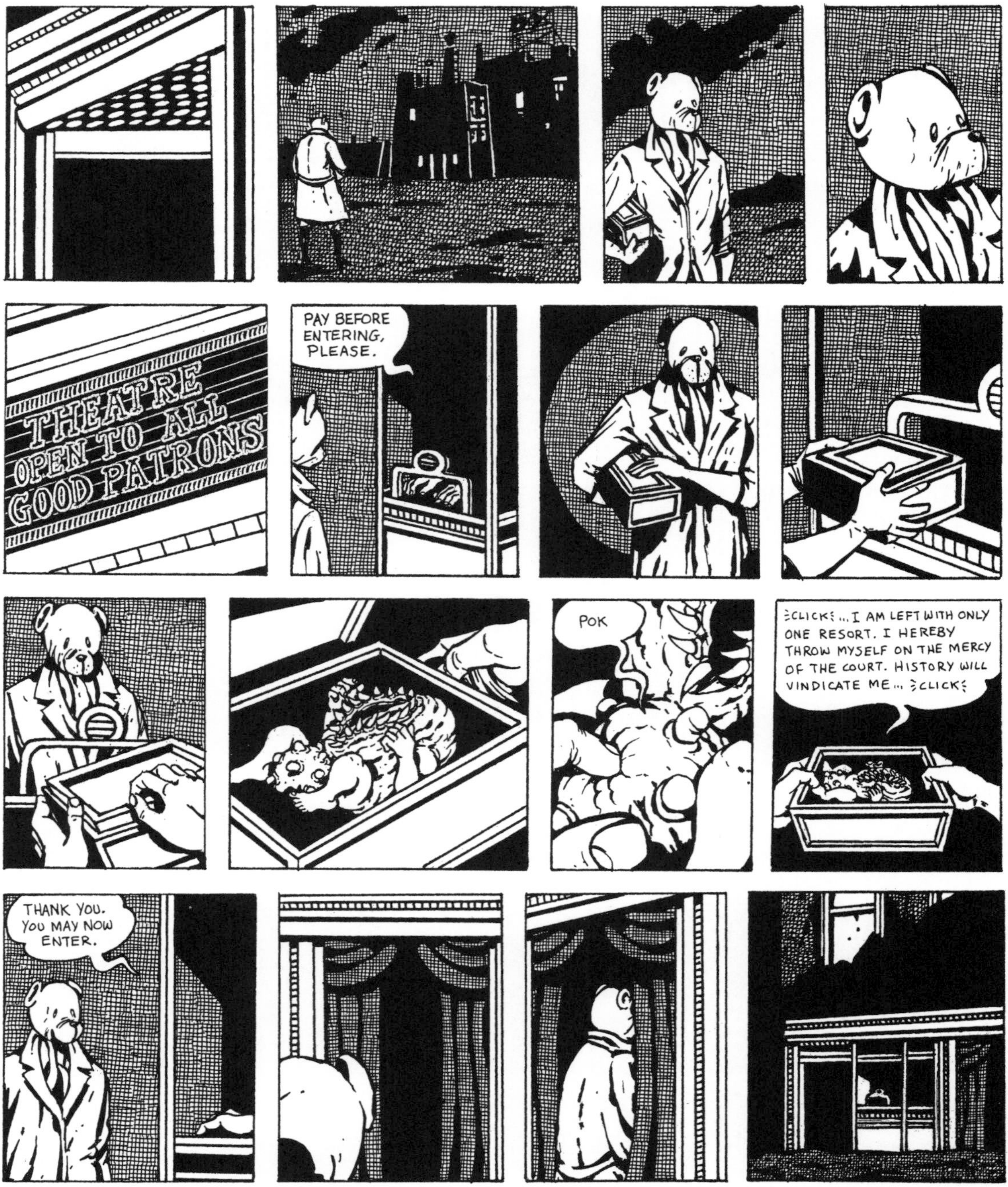
THEATRE
OPEN TO ALL
GOOD PATRONS
PAY BEFORE ENTERING, PLEASE.
POK
⁝CLICK⁝ ... I AM LEFT WITH ONLY ONE RESORT. I HEREBY THROW MYSELF ON THE MERCY OF THE COURT. HISTORY WILL VINDICATE ME ... ⁝CLICK⁝
THANK YOU. YOU MAY NOW ENTER.

EXIT
WHEN WILL IT END?
EXIT

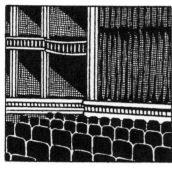

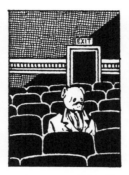

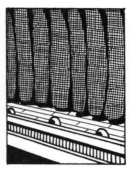

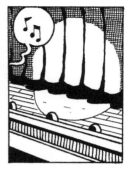

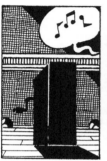

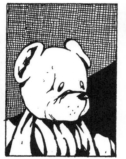

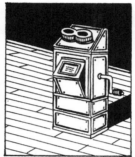

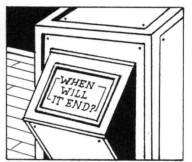

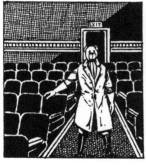

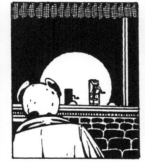

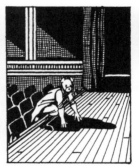

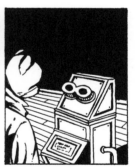

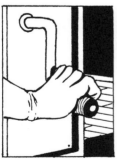

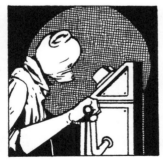

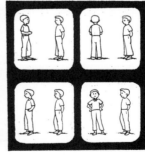

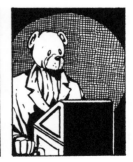

EXIT
EXIT
To View The Exhibit
PRESS THE BUTTON
PING!
TTON
GURGLE
SQUEE!!
A.
B.
I'M TIRED
I'M NOT!
GLAHHHHH

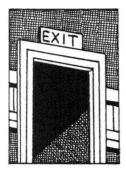

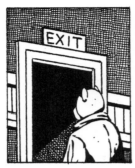

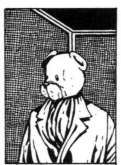

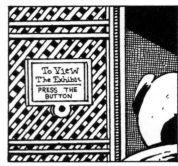

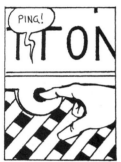

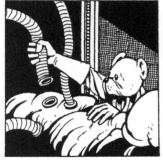

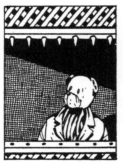

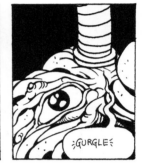

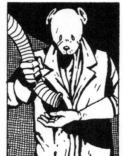

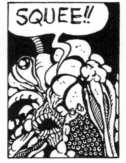

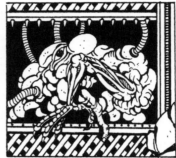

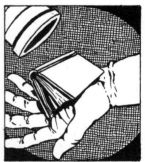

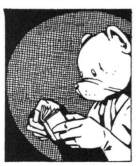

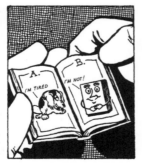

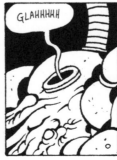

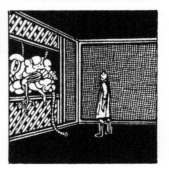

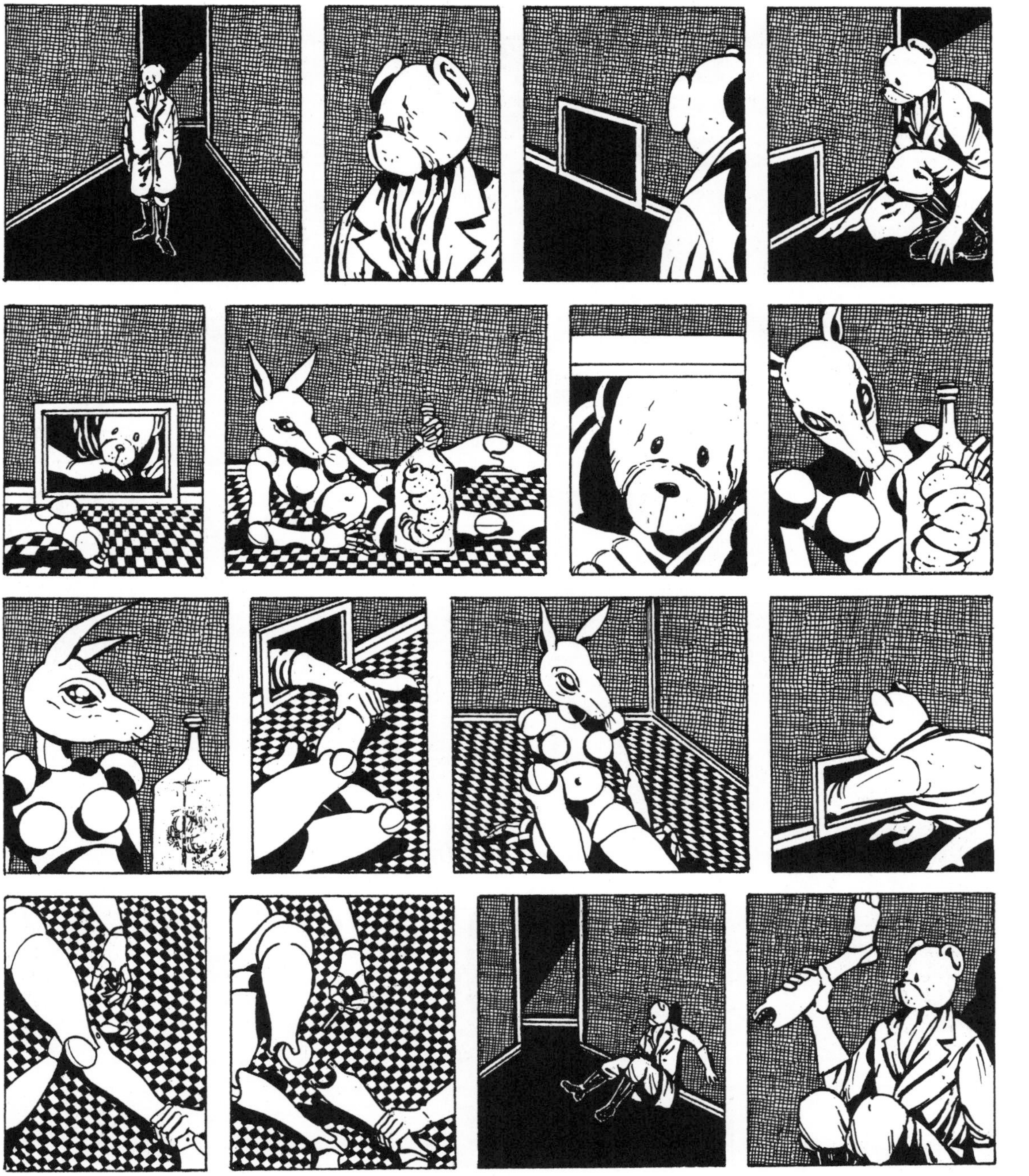

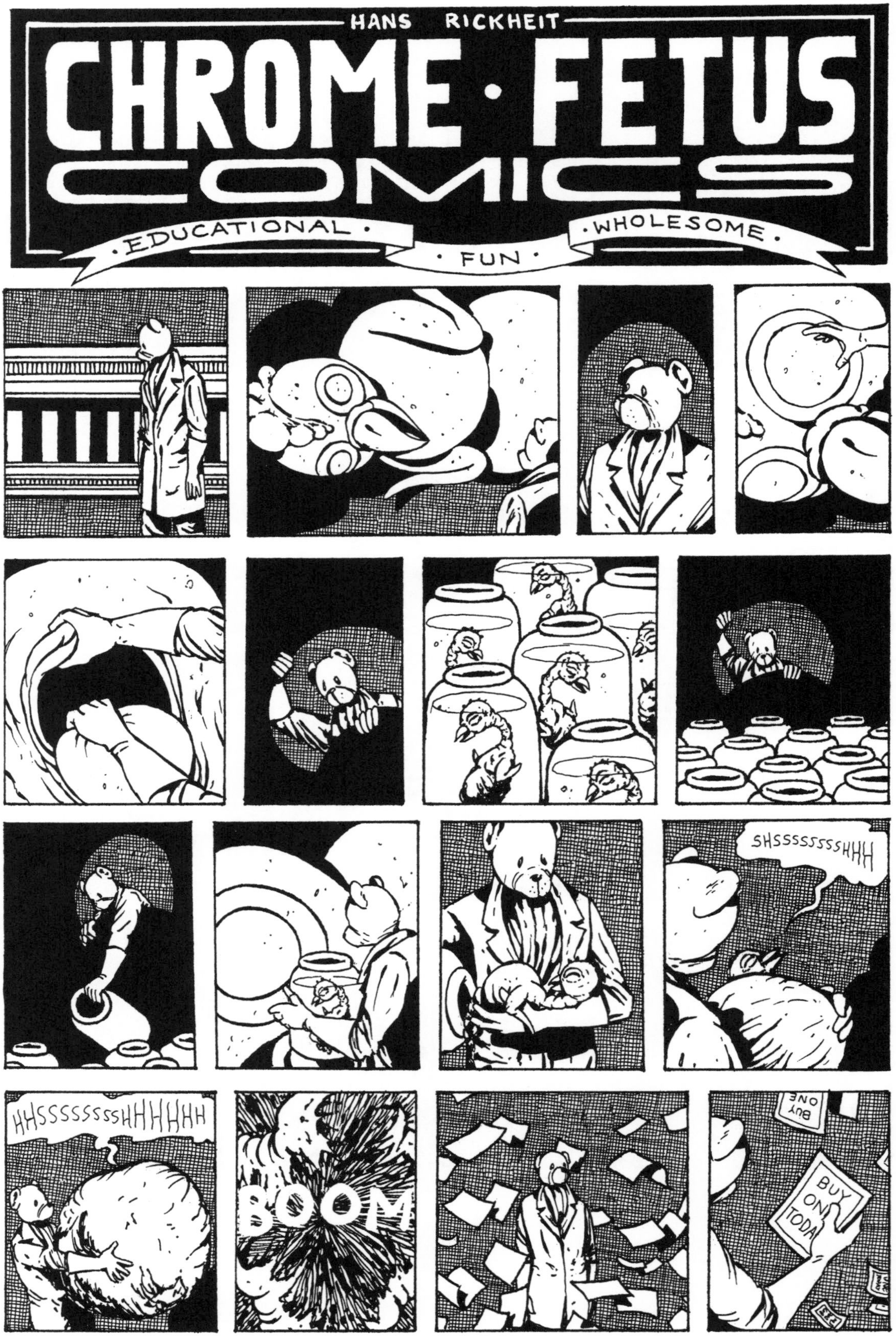
HANS RICKHEIT
CHROME · FETUS
COMICS
· EDUCATIONAL ·
· FUN ·
· WHOLESOME ·
SHSSSSSSSSSHHH
HHSSSSSSSSSHHHHHH
BOOM
BUY ONE
BUY ON TODA

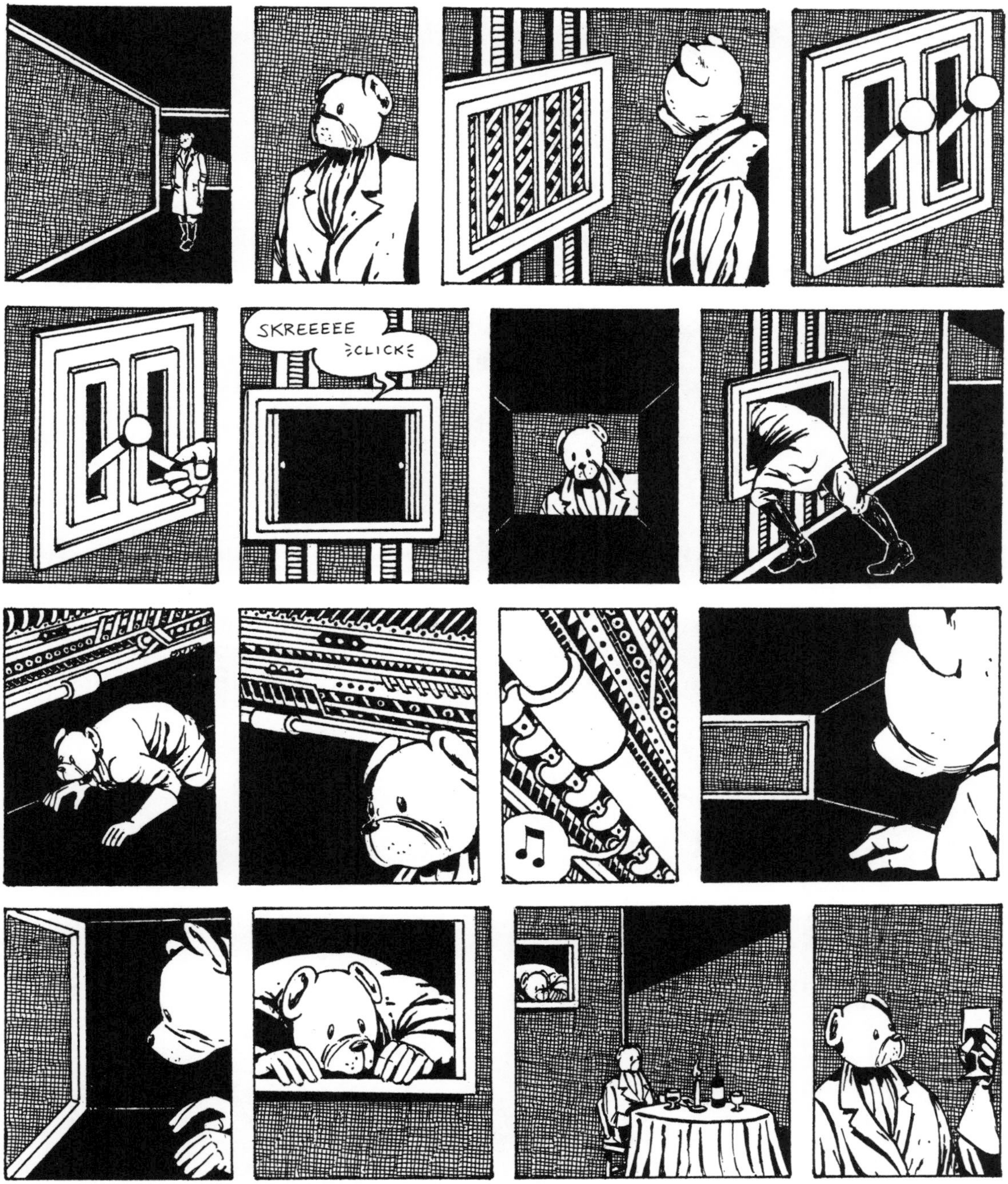
SKREEEEE
CLICK

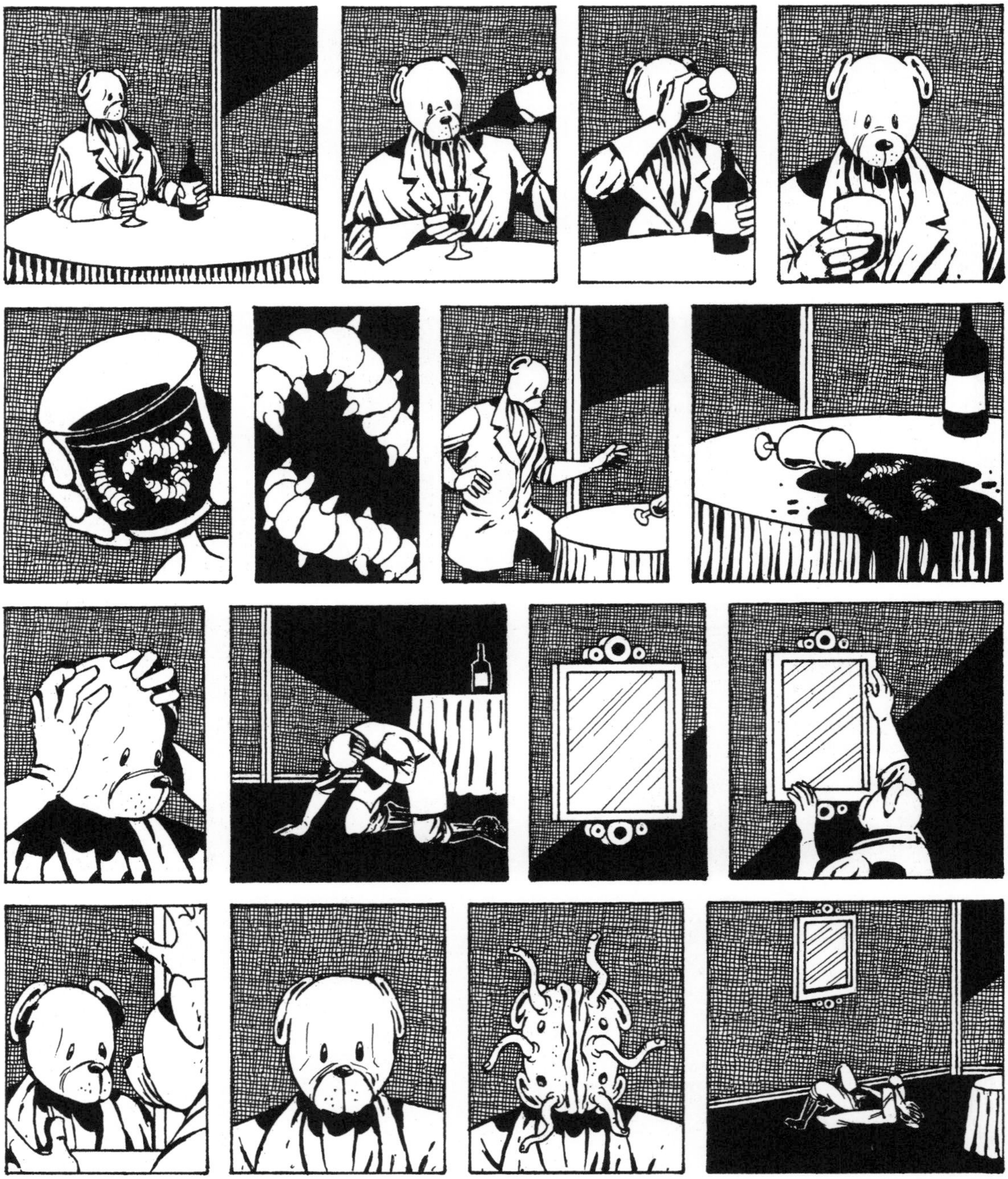

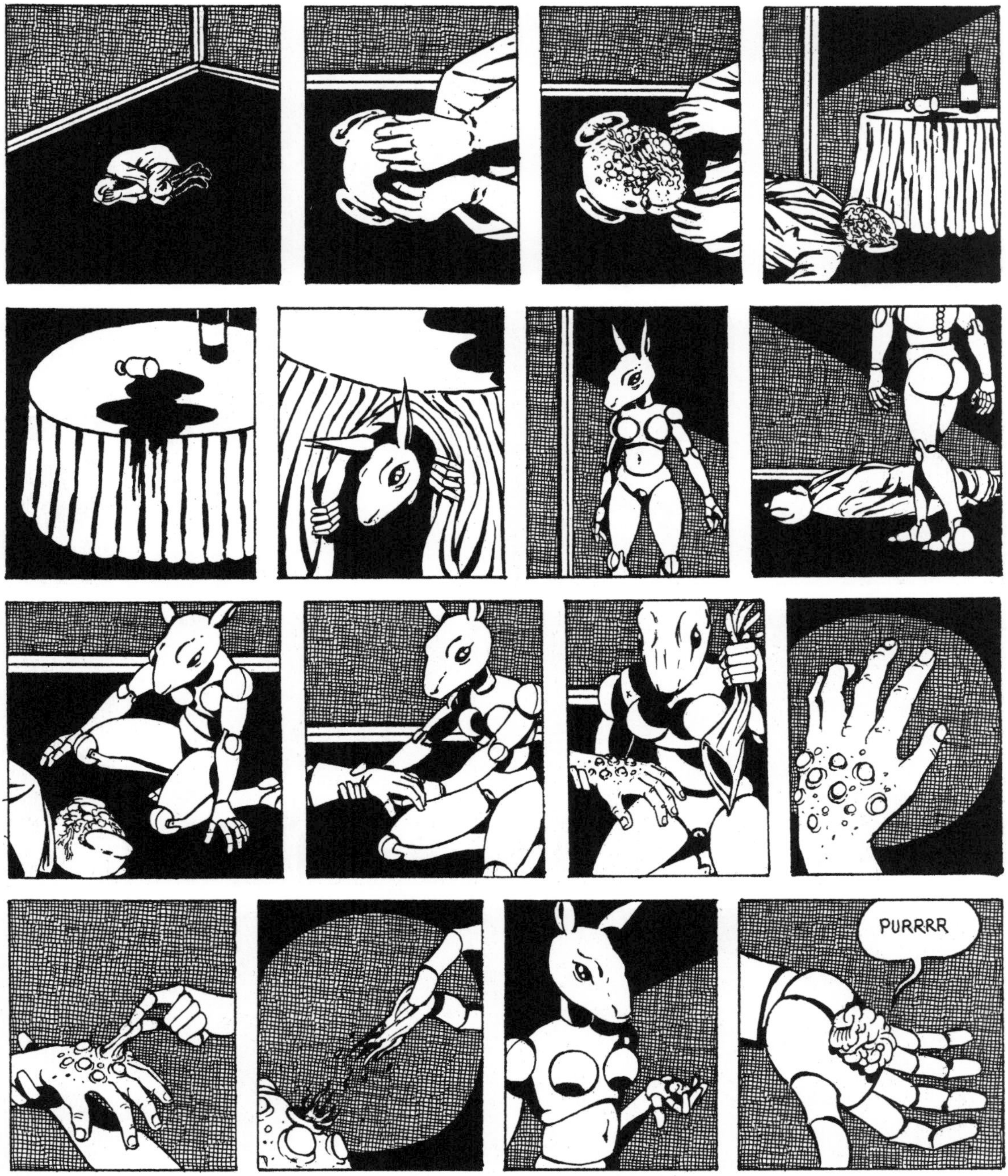
PURRRR

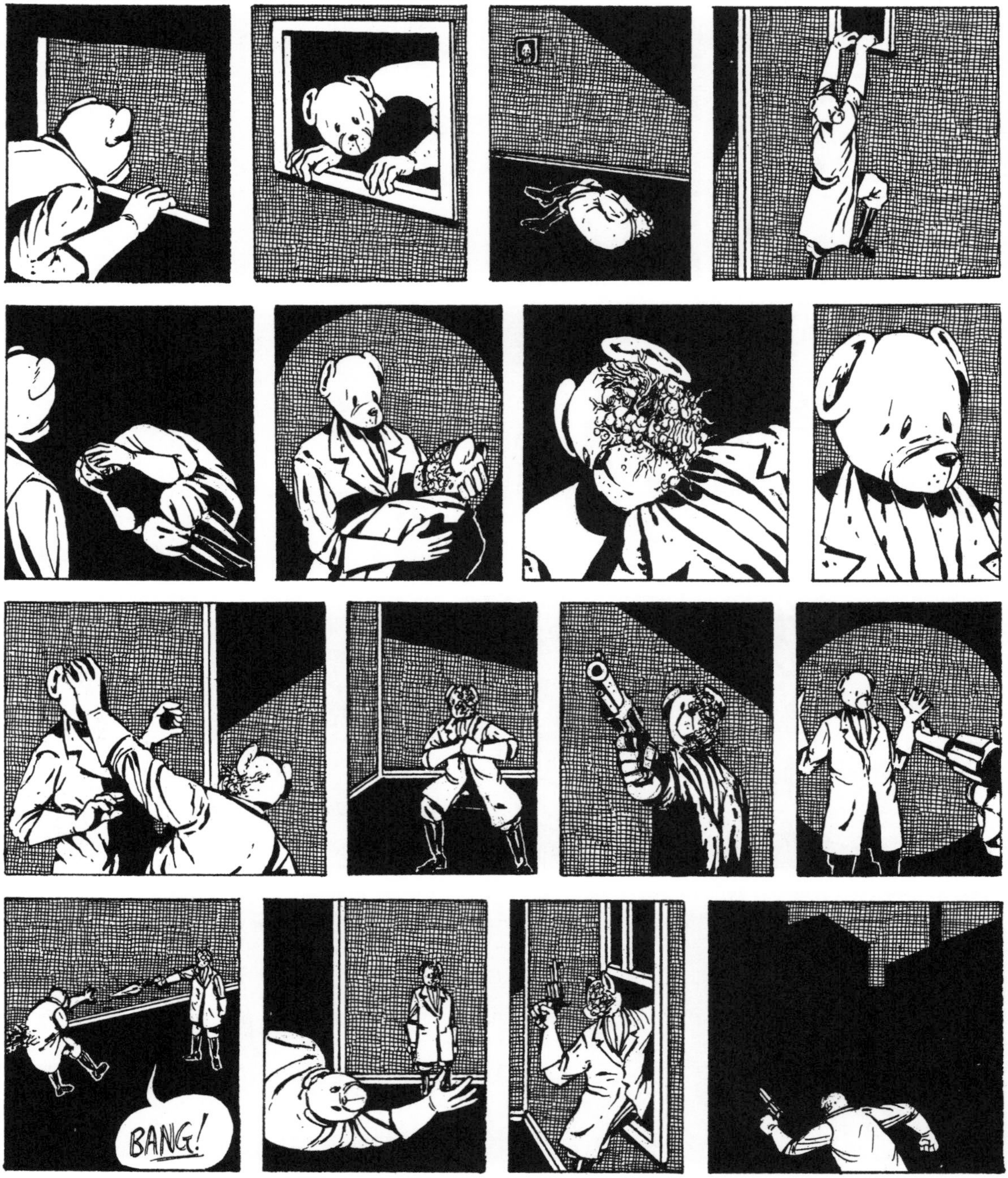
BANG!

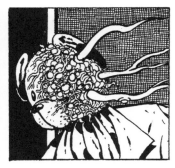

I THINK IT IS SICK.

YES.

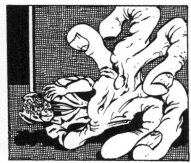

IT IS SEEING THINGS THAT ARE NOT REAL.

YES.

SHOULD WE TAKE IT WITH US?

YES.

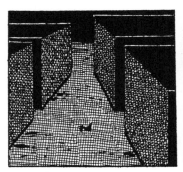

IT'S HEAVY!

BE SILENT.

WE'LL SET IT BY THE CORNER.

THIS THING IS EVIL.

BE CALMED... WE WILL NOT HARM YOU.

BRING ME THE TOYS.

THERE.

THE EVIL HAS BEEN REMOVED.

IT NOW HAS A FRESH SOUL TO TARNISH.

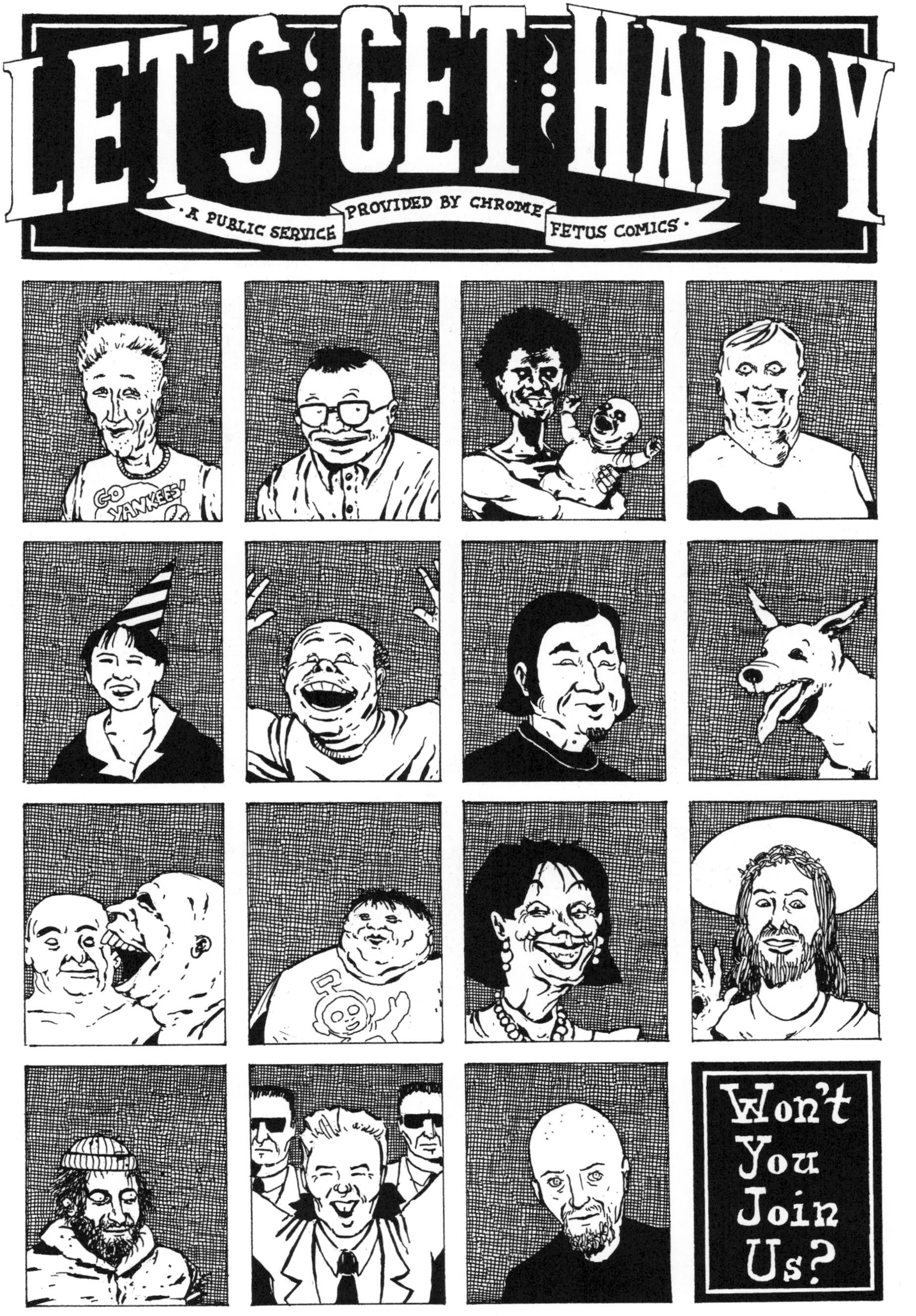
LET'S GET HAPPY
A PUBLIC SERVICE PROVIDED BY CHROME FETUS COMICS
GO YANKEES!
Won't You Join Us?

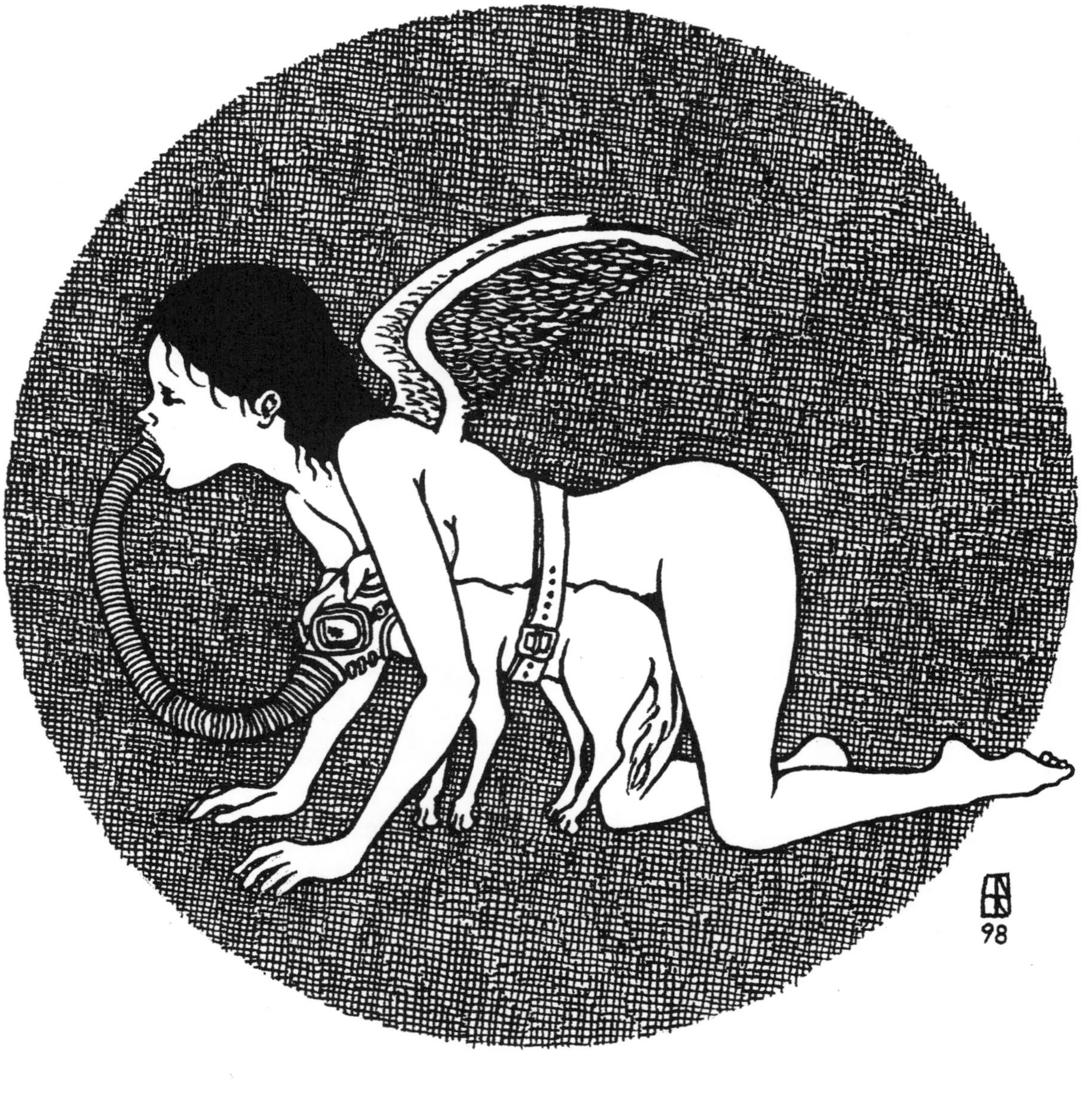
98

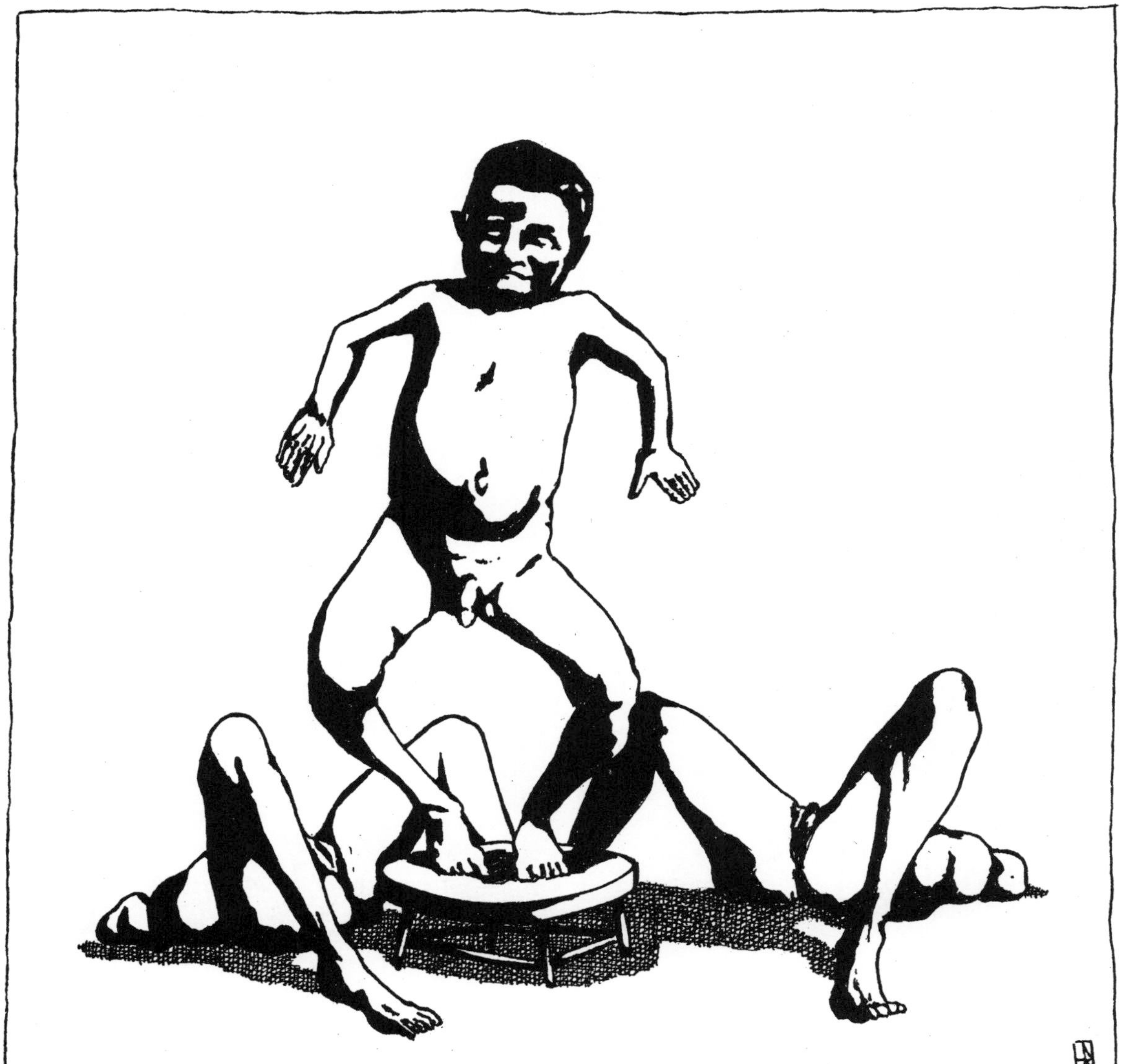

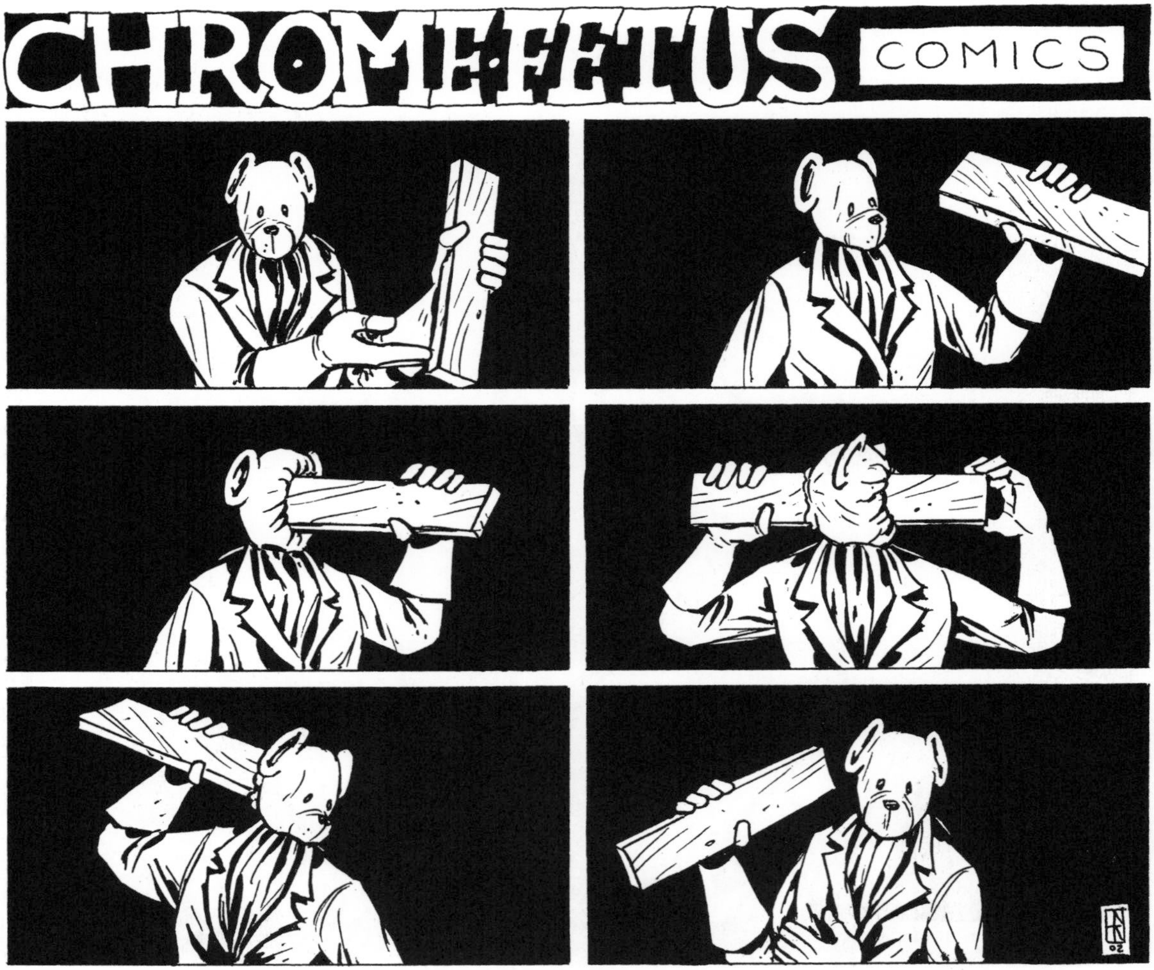
CHROME-FETUS
COMICS

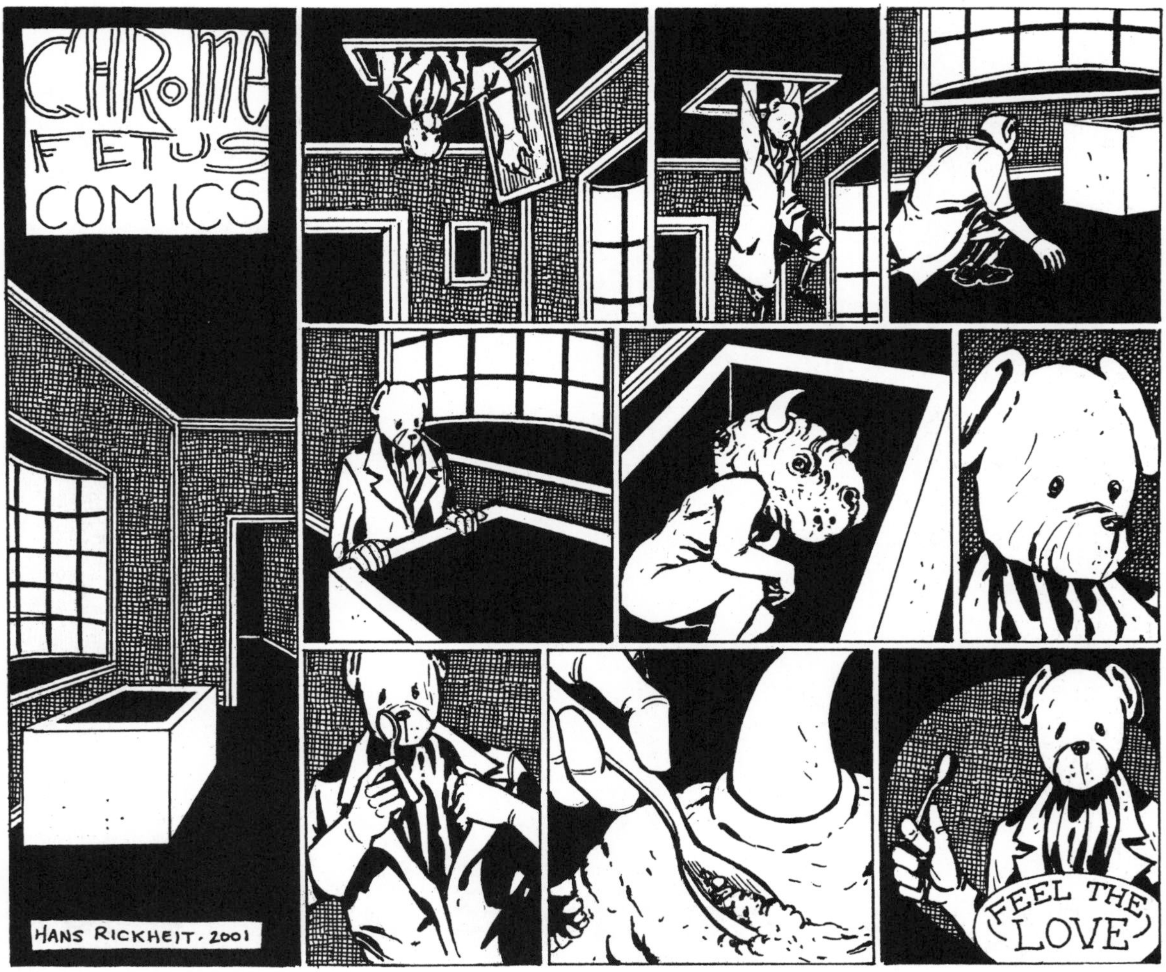
CHROME FETUS COMICS
HANS RICKHEIT · 2001
FEEL THE LOVE

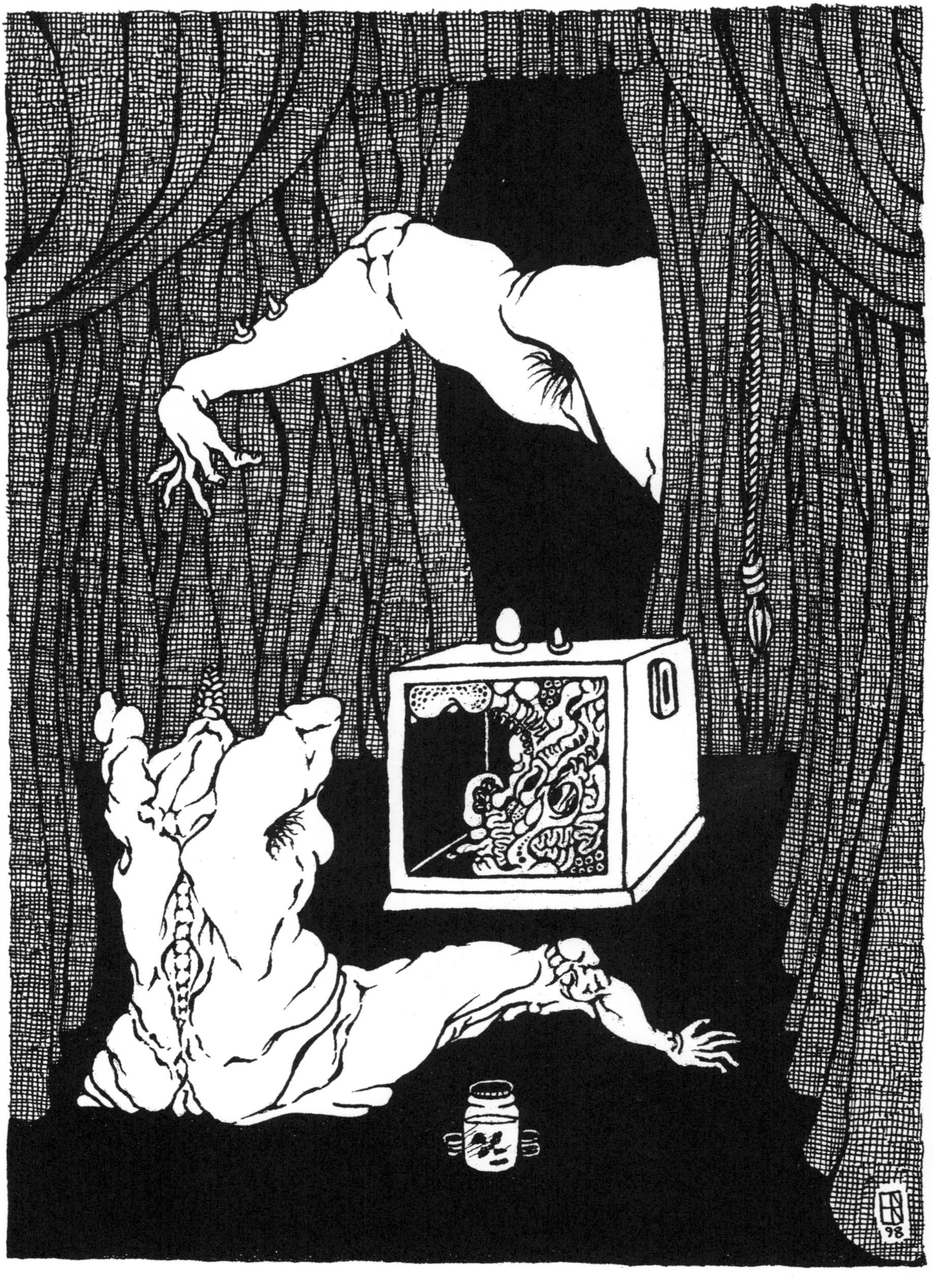

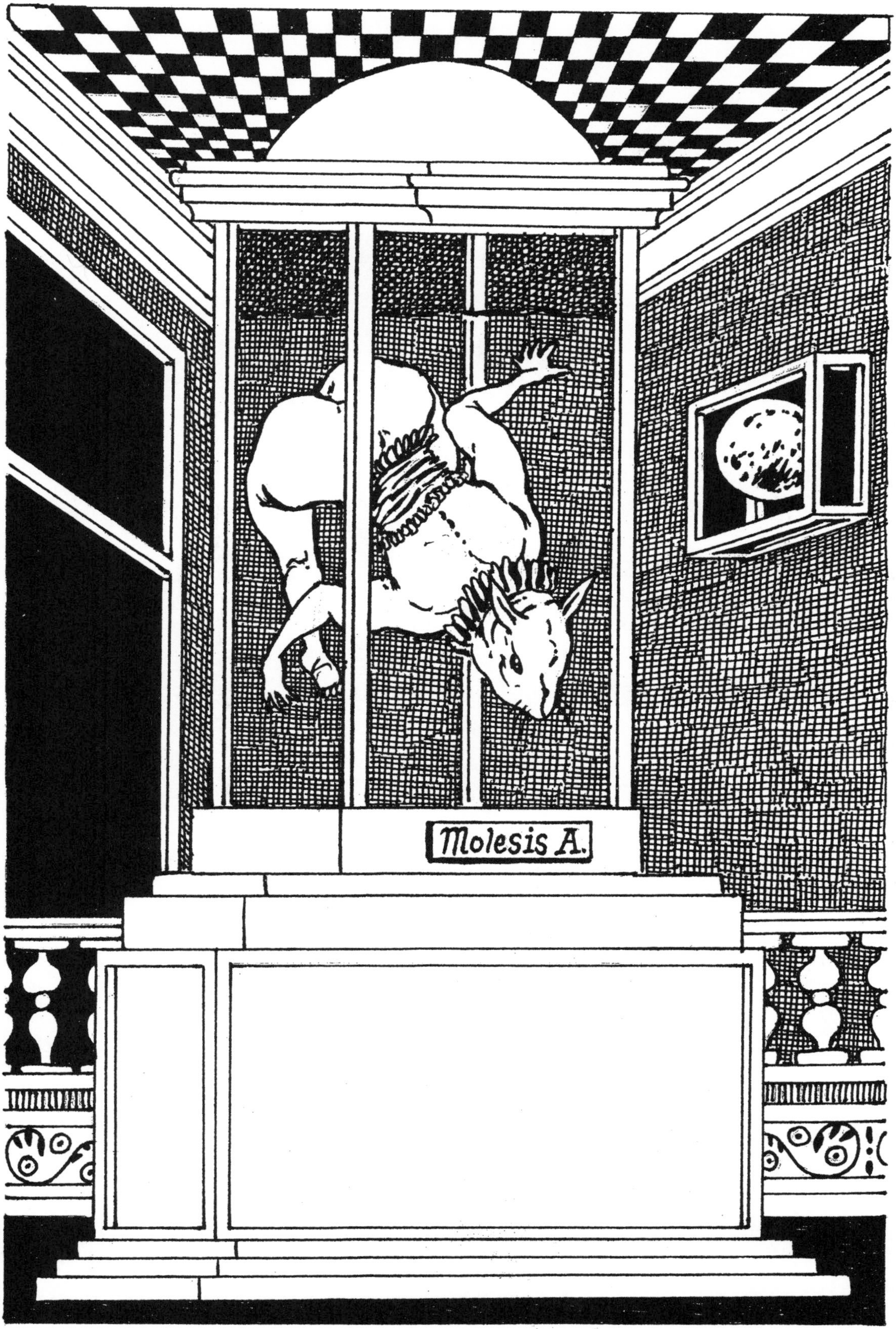
Molesis A.

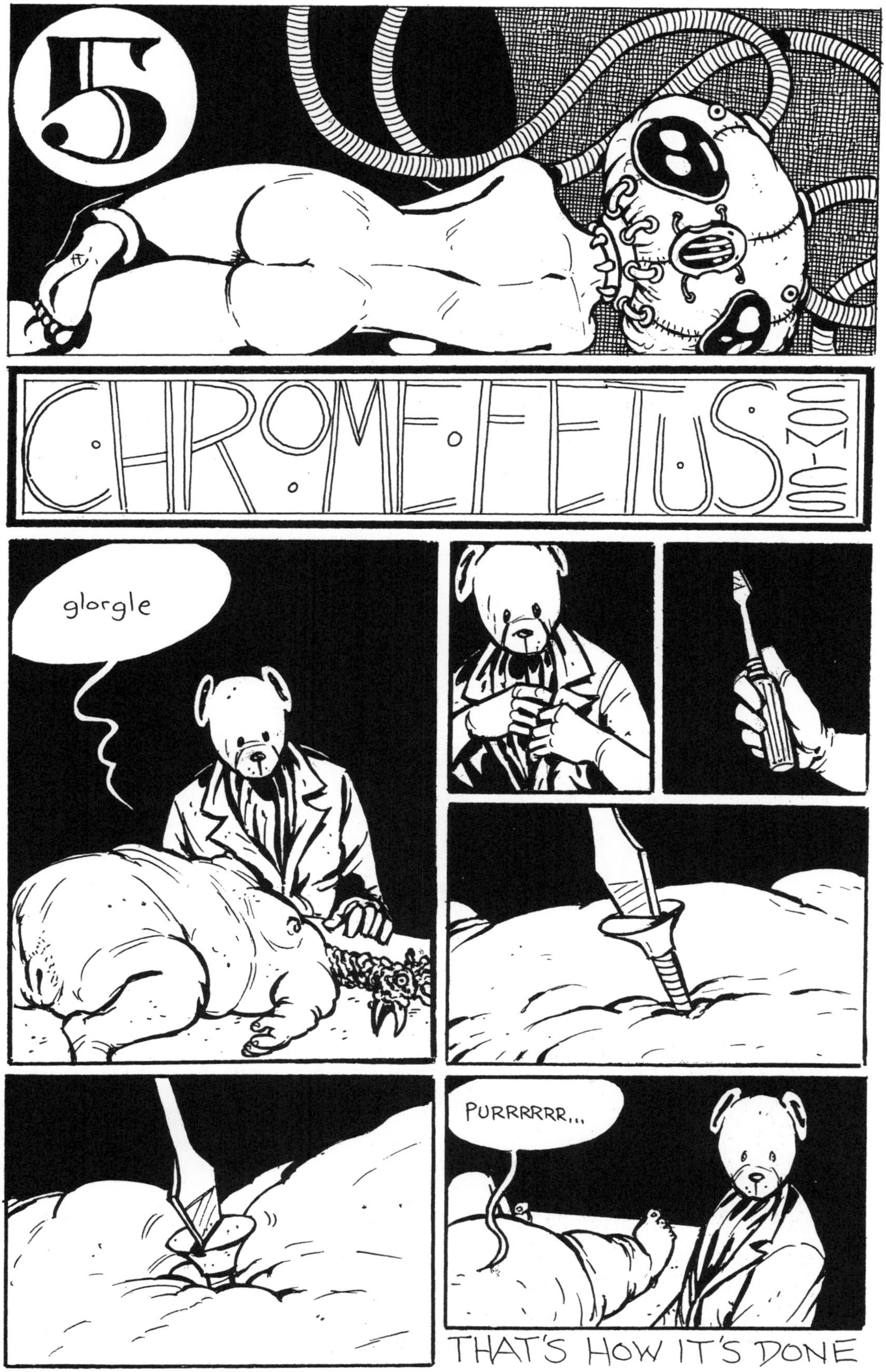
5
CHROME FETUS COMICS
glorgle
PURRRRRR...
THAT'S HOW IT'S DONE

MEANDER.

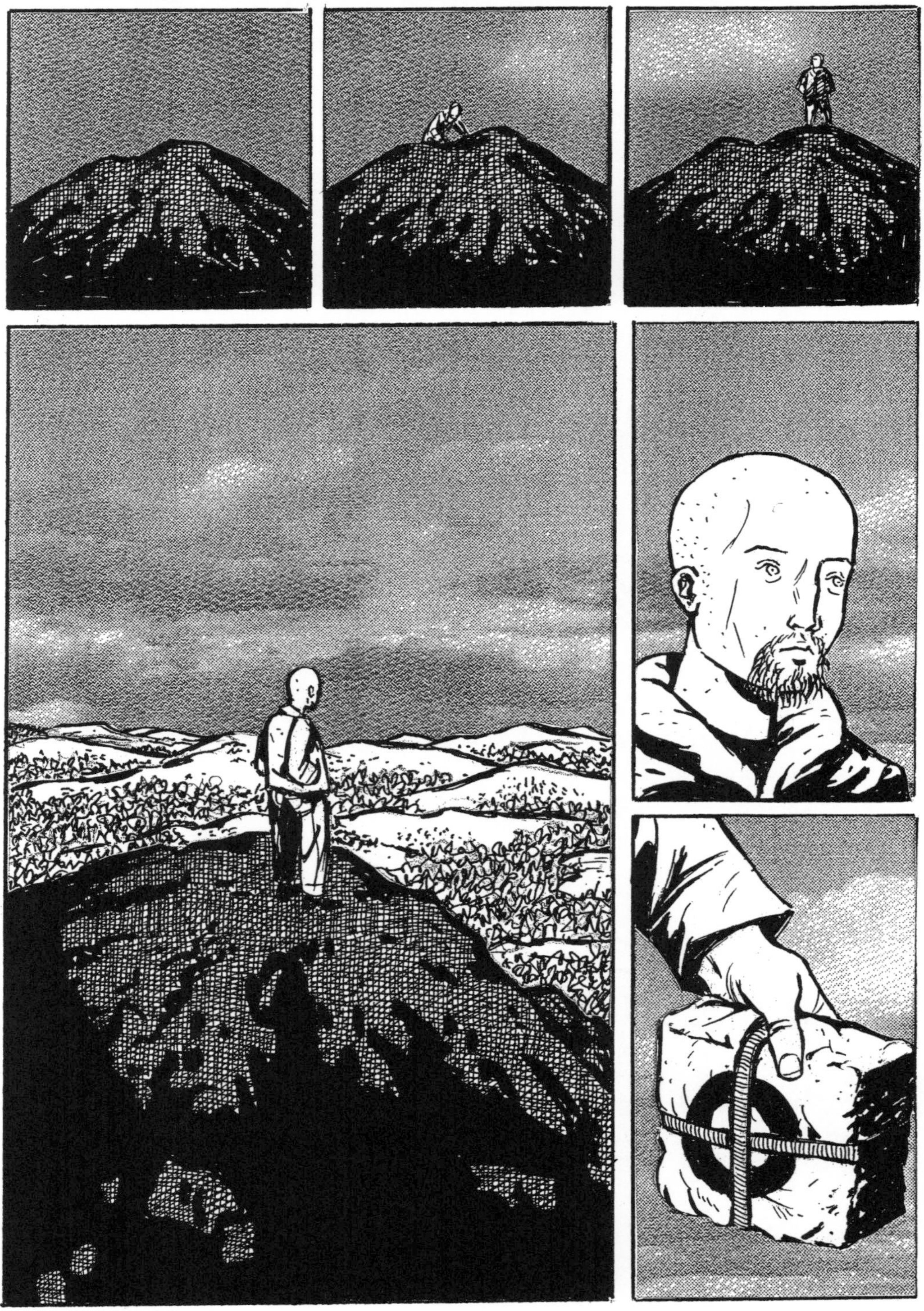

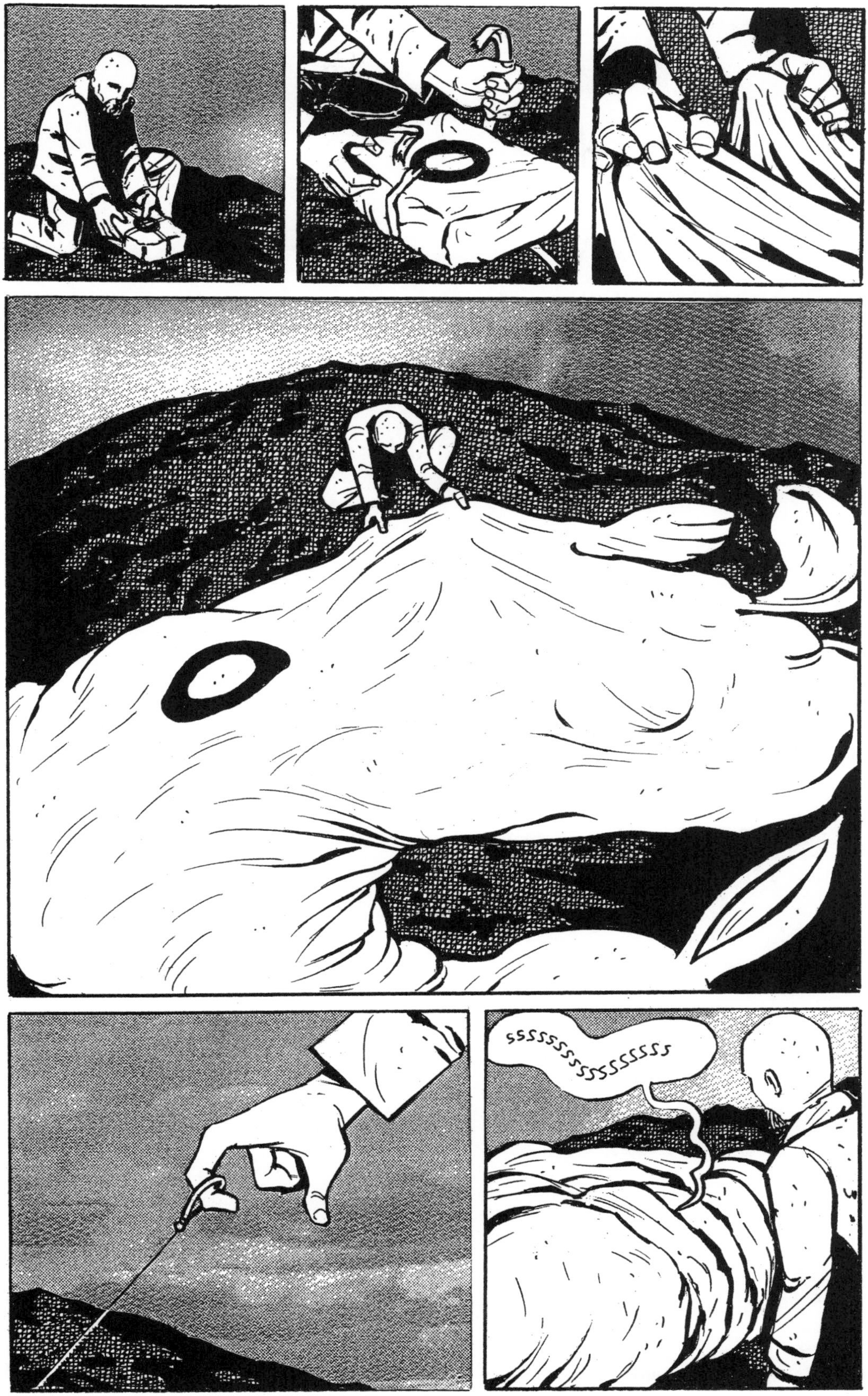
SSSSSSSSSSSSSSSSSSS

SSSSSSSSSSSSSSS

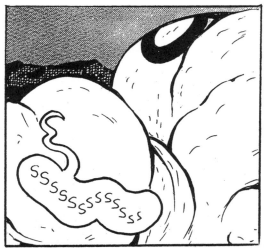

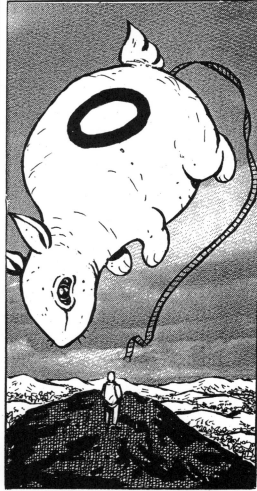

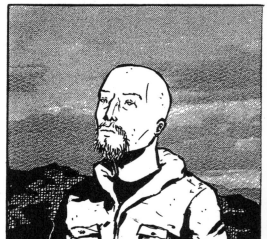

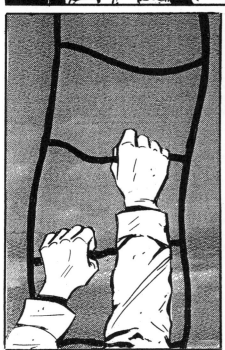

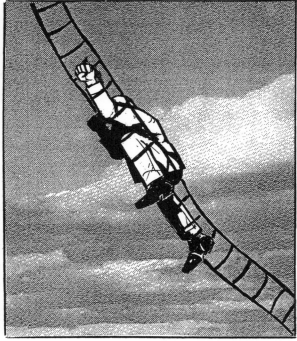

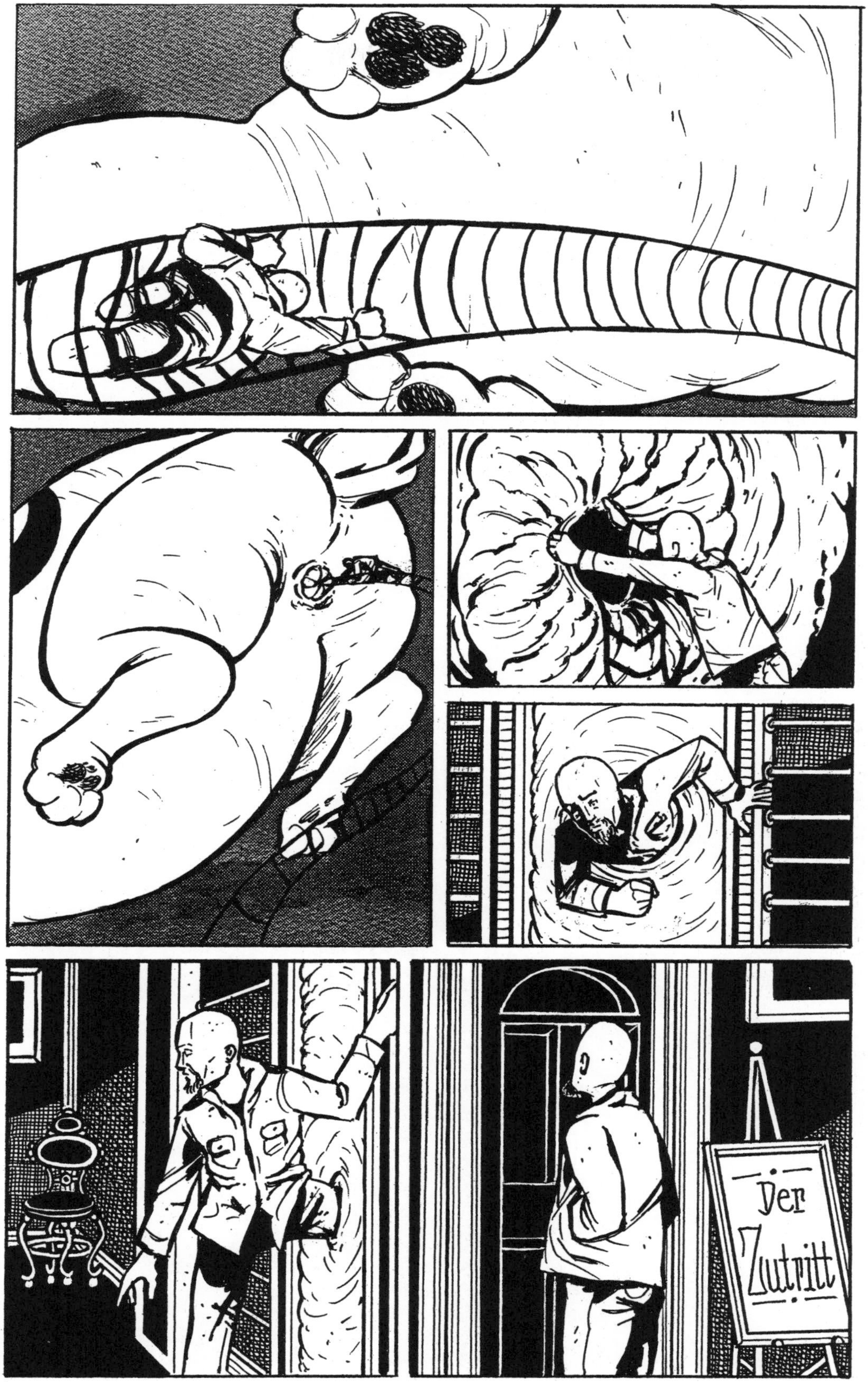
Der
Zutritt

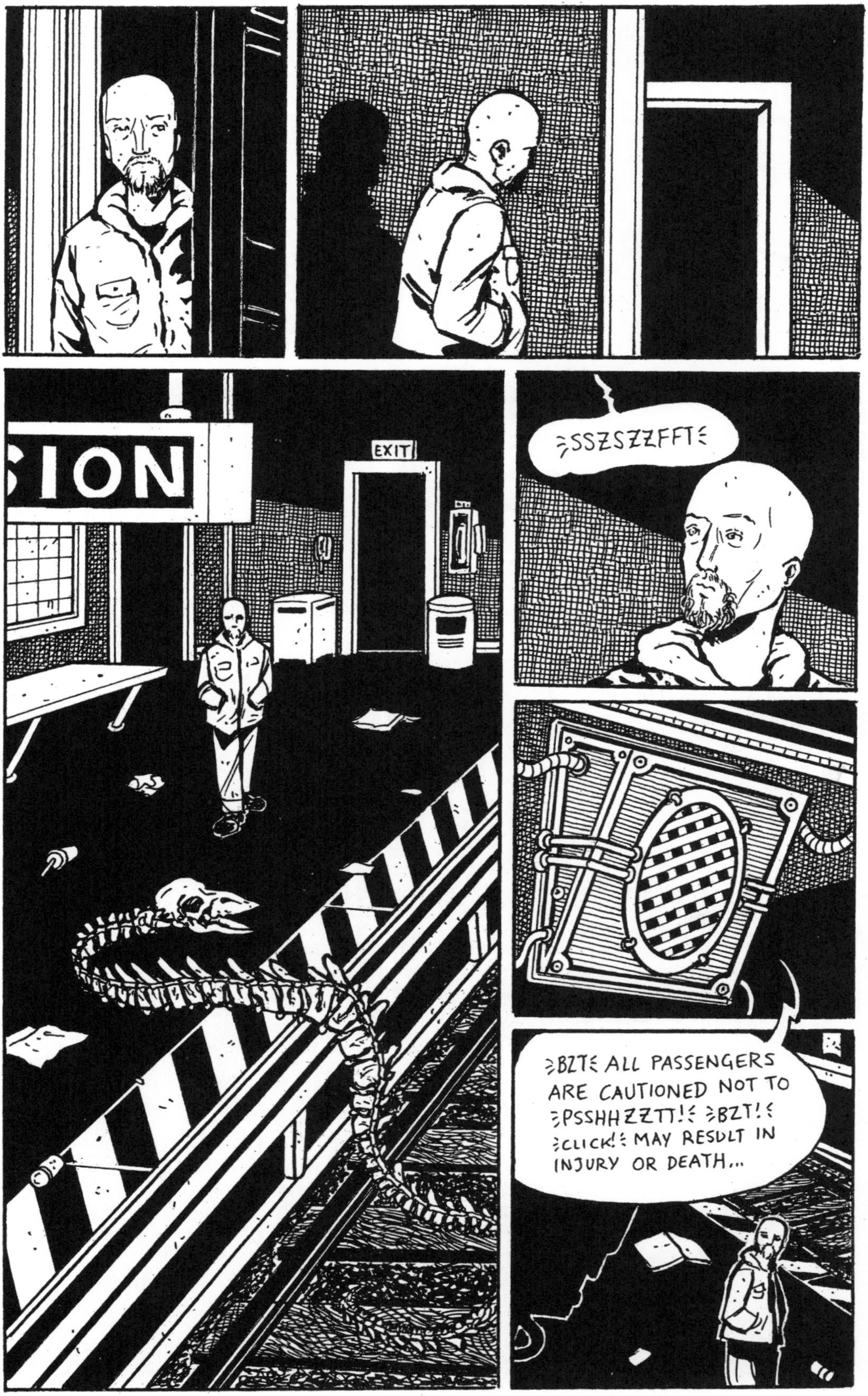
SION
EXIT
≷SSZSZZFFT≷
≷BZT≷ ALL PASSENGERS ARE CAUTIONED NOT TO ≷PSSHHZZTT!≷ ≷BZT!≷ ≷CLICK!≷ MAY RESULT IN INJURY OR DEATH...

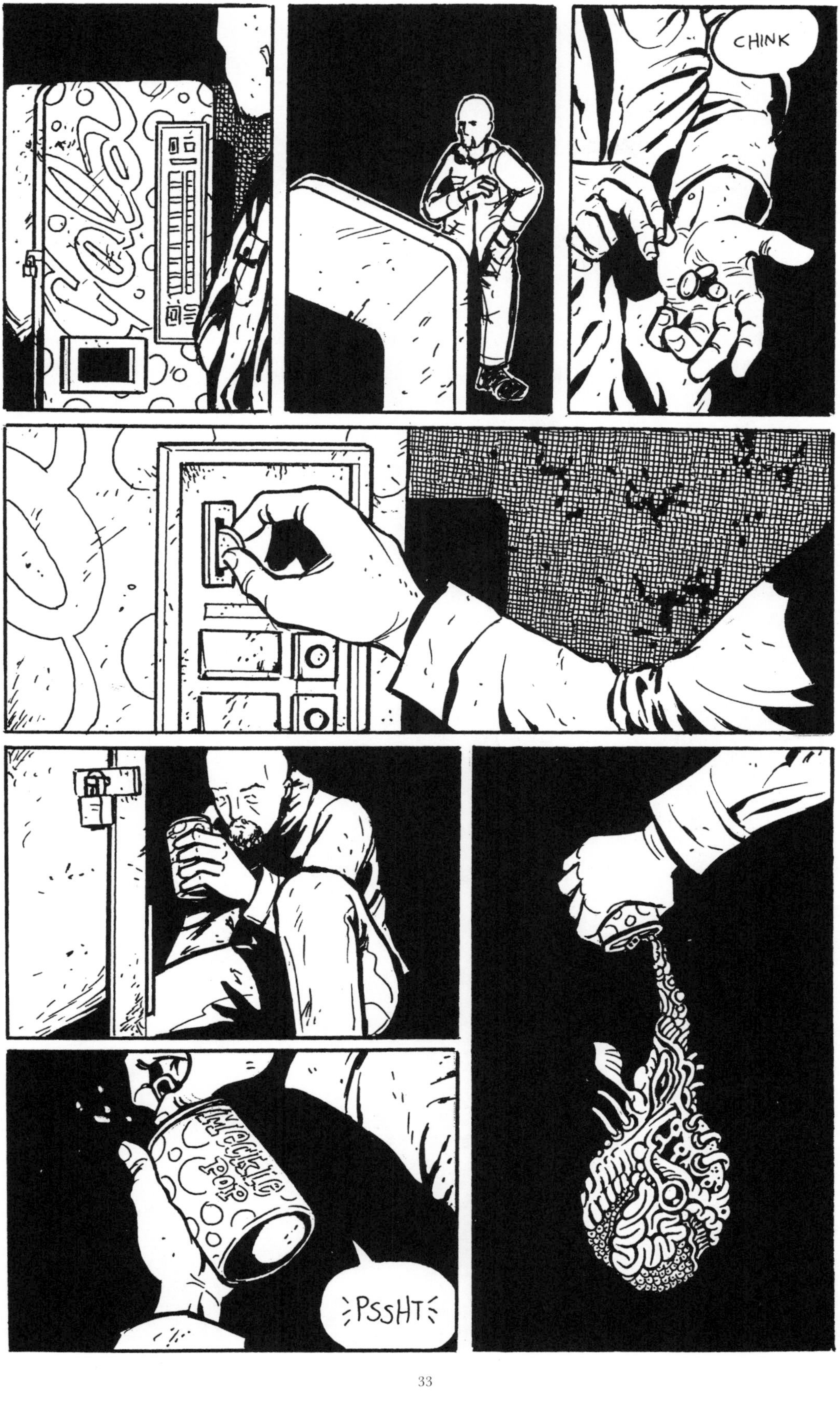
CHINK
PSSHT

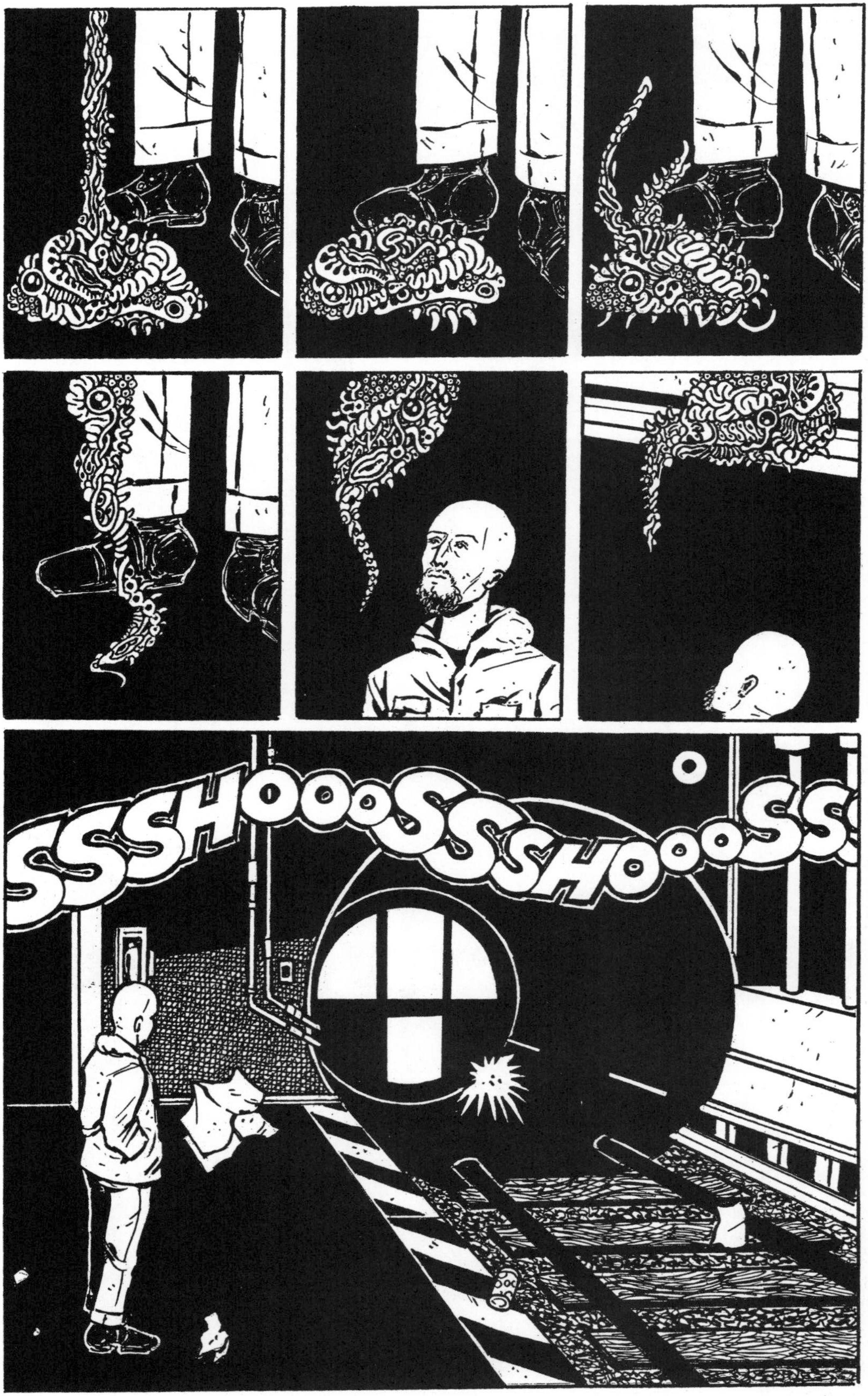
SSSHOOOSSSHOOOSSS

SHOOO
SSHOOS

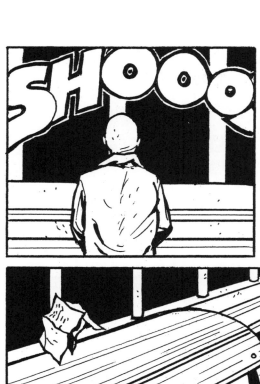

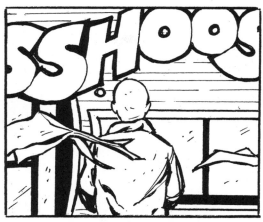

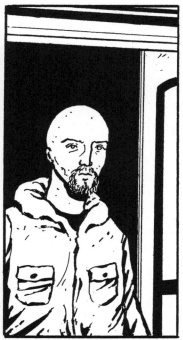

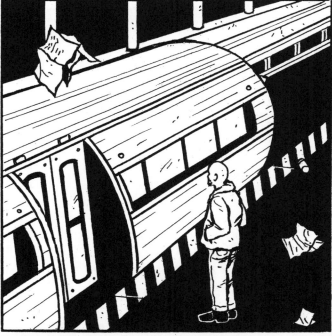

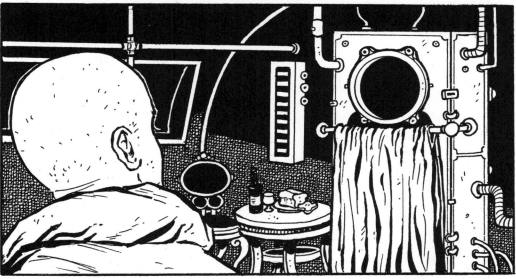

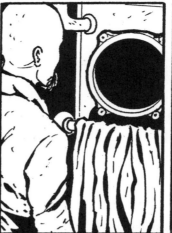

click

PWEEEE

"IT IS AT THIS POINT THAT THE SEXUAL EXCITATION REACHES THE CRITICAL PHASE."

"THE PENIS, FULLY ENGORGED WITH BLOOD, IS NOW READY TO ENTER THE VAGINA."

"THE FEMALE ORIFICE SHOULD BE THOROUGHLY LUBRICATED FOR MAXIMUM PENETRATION."

"BEGINNING WITH SLOW, GENTLE REPETITION, THE PENIS THRUSTS INTO THE VAGINA WITH GRADUAL INCREASE IN SPEED..."

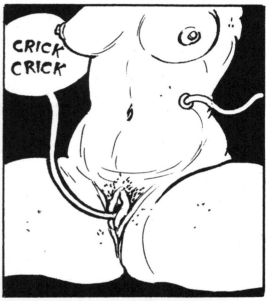

CRICK CRICK

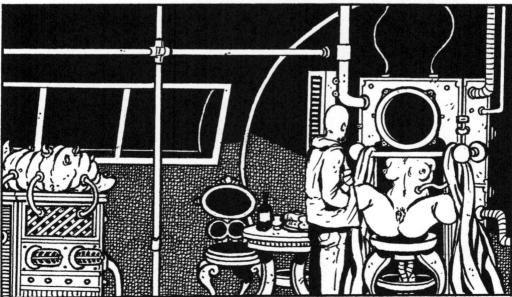

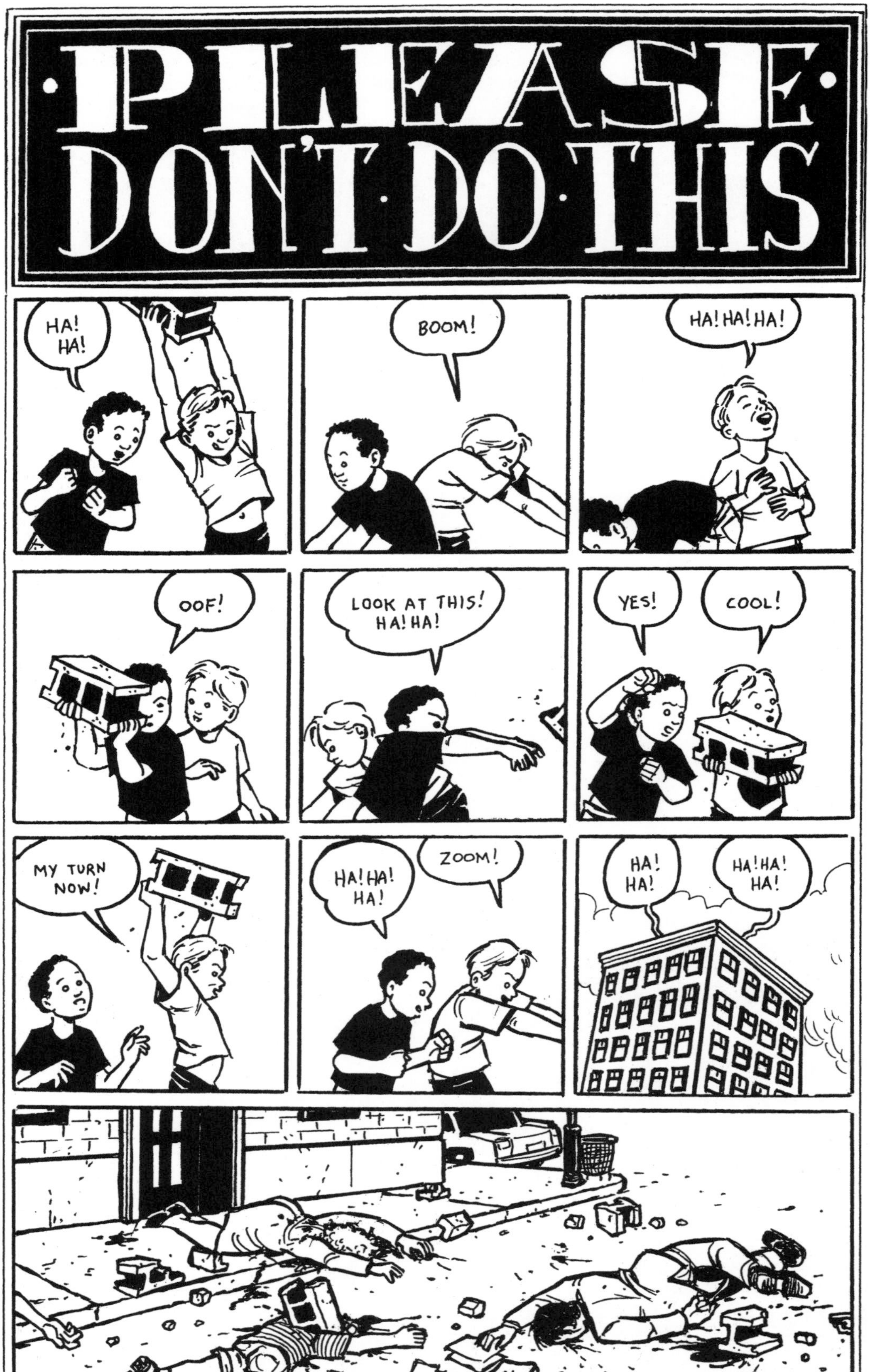
PLEASE DON'T DO THIS
HA! HA!
BOOM!
HA! HA! HA!
OOF!
LOOK AT THIS! HA! HA!
YES!
COOL!
MY TURN NOW!
HA! HA! HA!
ZOOM!
HA! HA!
HA! HA! HA!

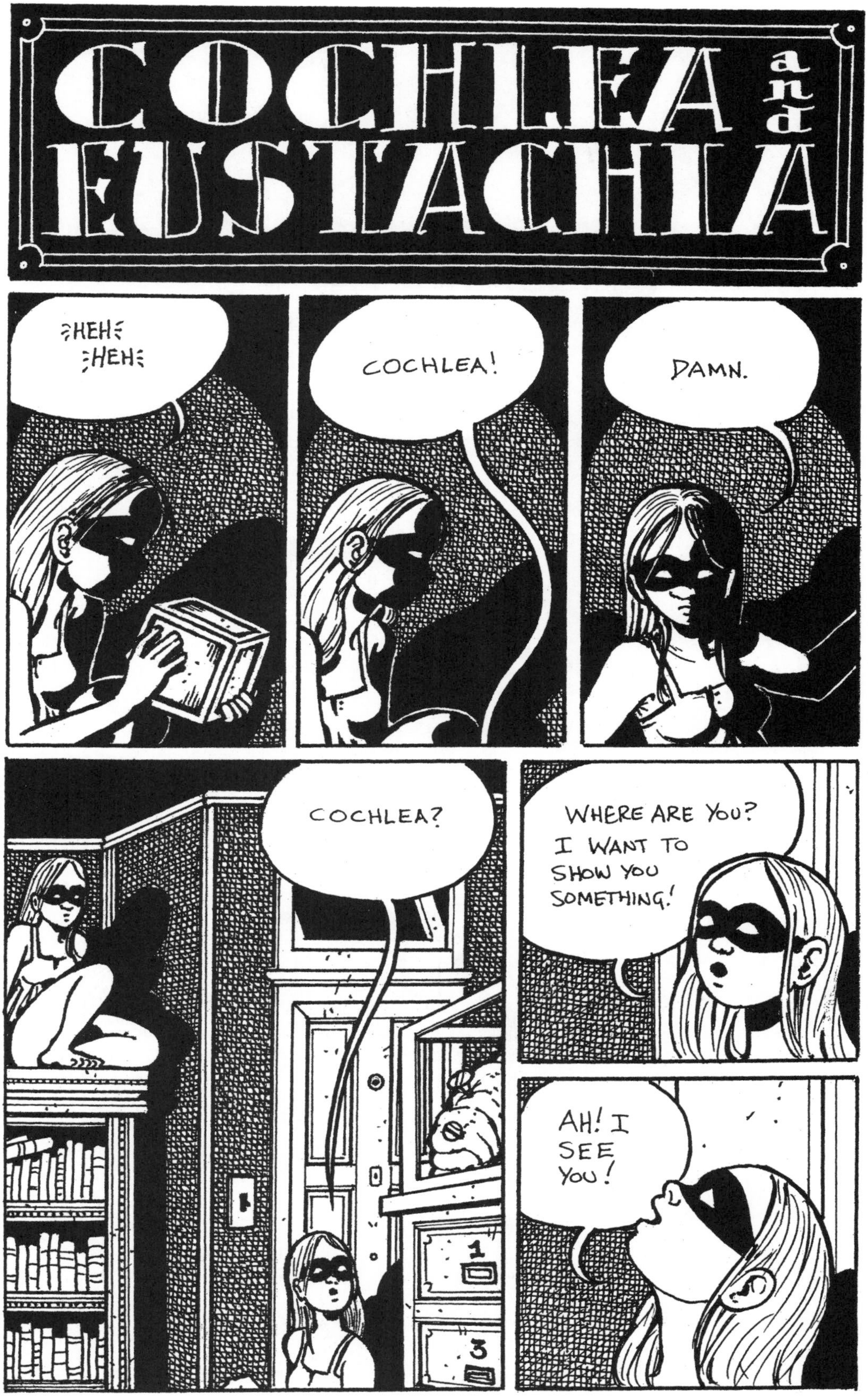
COCHLEA and EUSTACHIA
HEH HEH
COCHLEA!
DAMN.
COCHLEA?
WHERE ARE YOU? I WANT TO SHOW YOU SOMETHING!
AH! I SEE YOU!
1
3

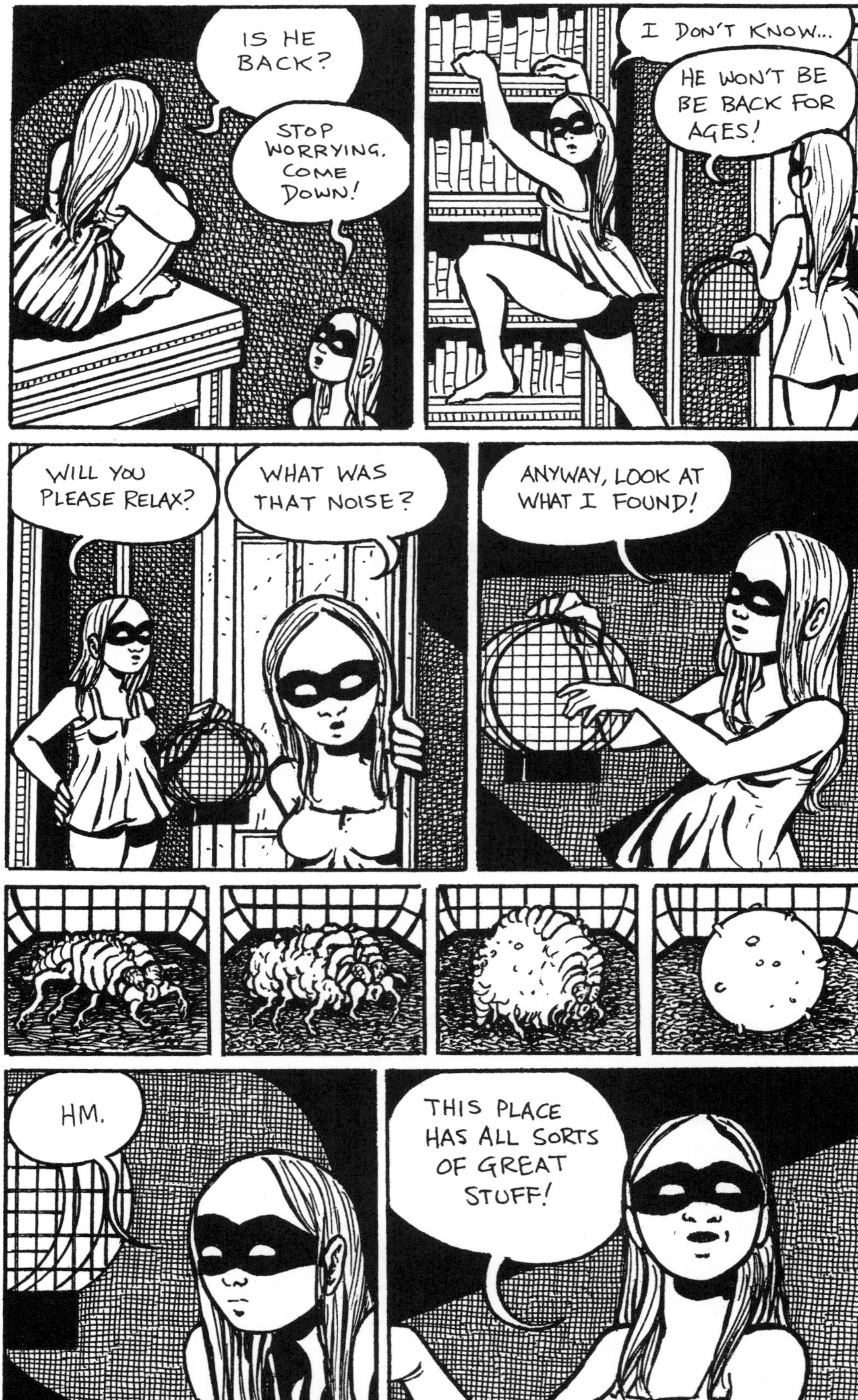
IS HE BACK?
STOP WORRYING. COME DOWN!
I DON'T KNOW...
HE WON'T BE BE BACK FOR AGES!
WILL YOU PLEASE RELAX?
WHAT WAS THAT NOISE?
ANYWAY, LOOK AT WHAT I FOUND!
HM.
THIS PLACE HAS ALL SORTS OF GREAT STUFF!

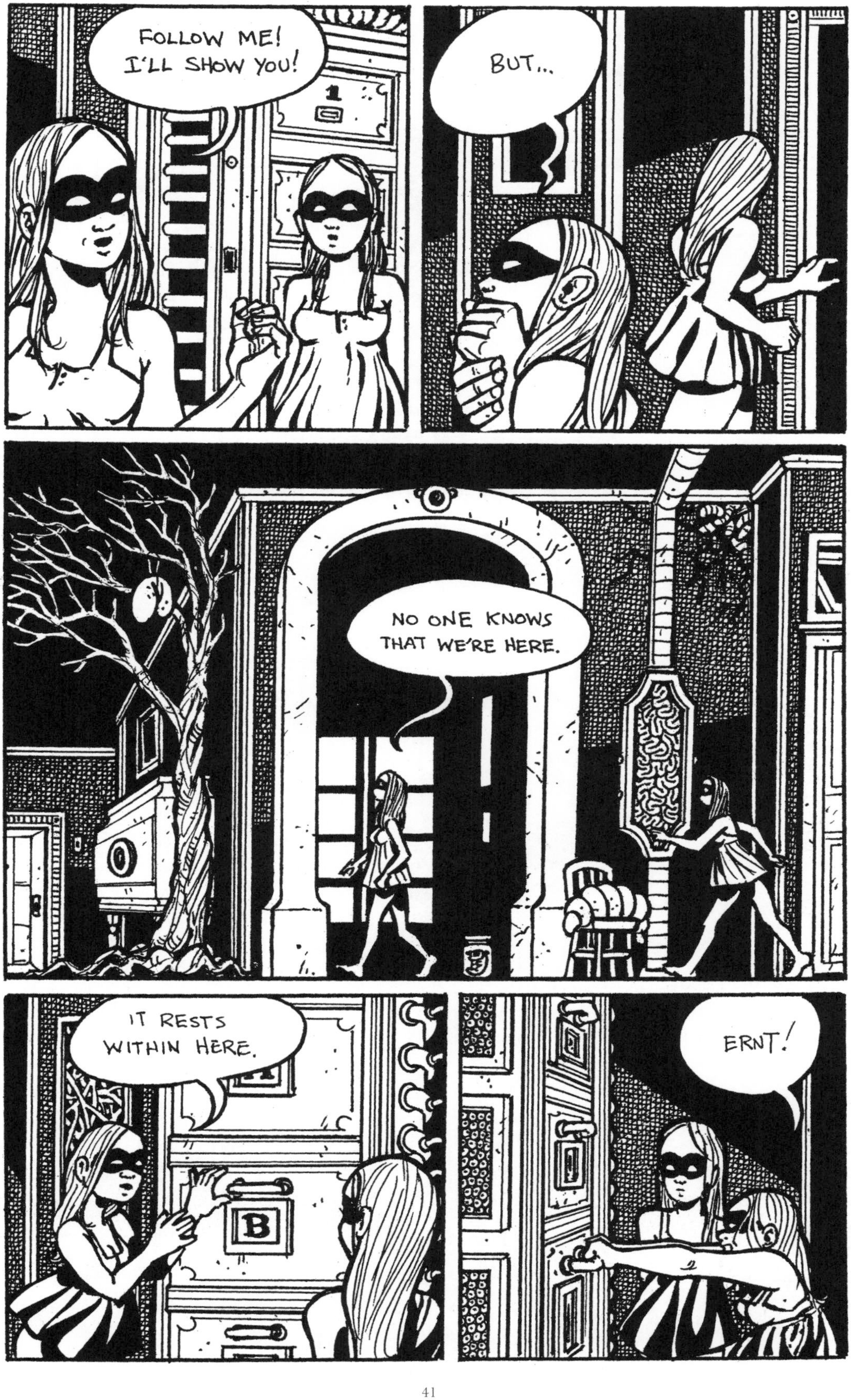
FOLLOW ME! I'LL SHOW YOU!
BUT...
NO ONE KNOWS THAT WE'RE HERE.
IT RESTS WITHIN HERE.
ERNT!

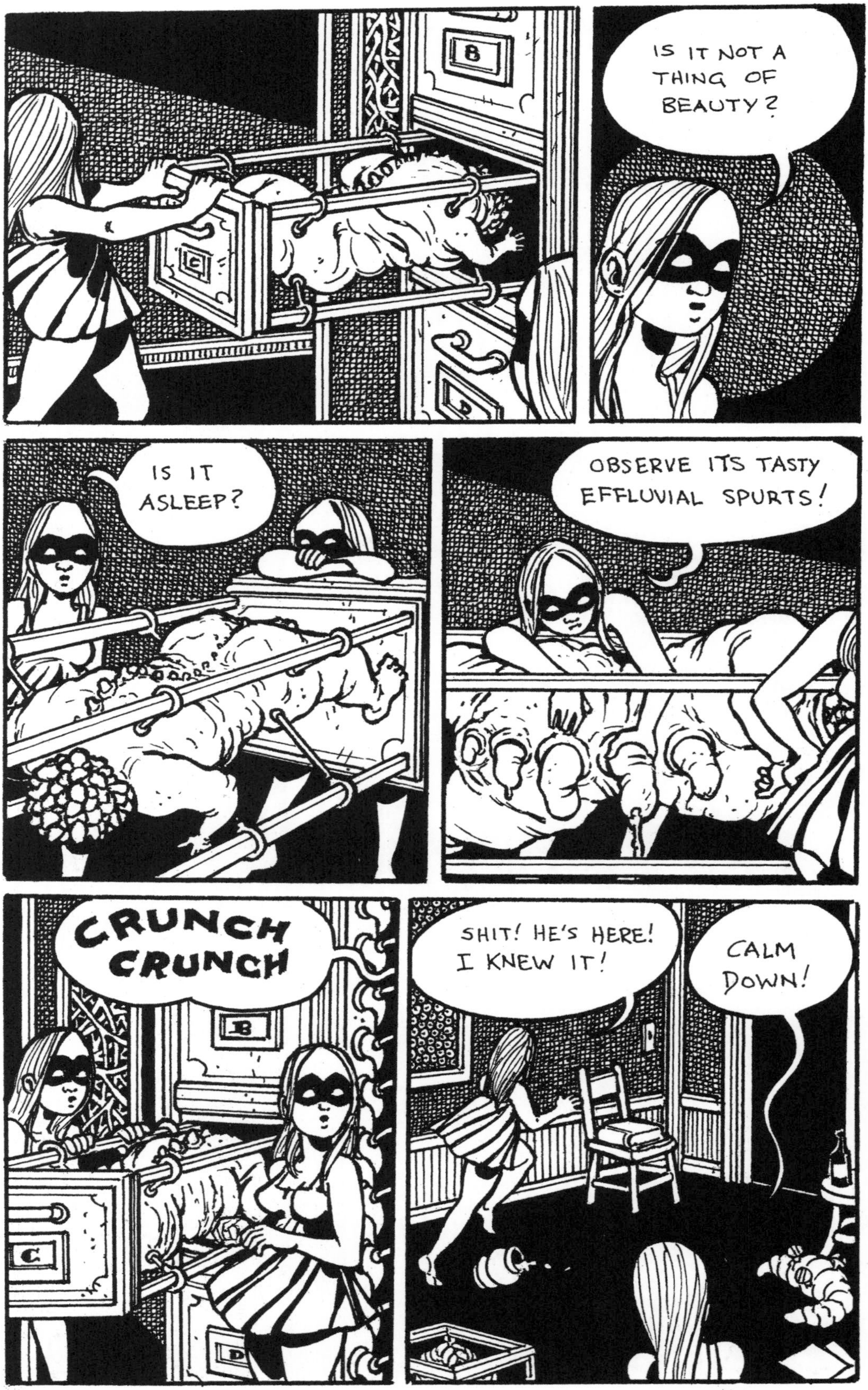
IS IT NOT A THING OF BEAUTY?
IS IT ASLEEP?
OBSERVE ITS TASTY EFFLUVIAL SPURTS!
CRUNCH CRUNCH
SHIT! HE'S HERE! I KNEW IT!
CALM DOWN!

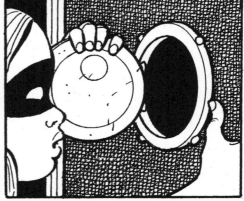

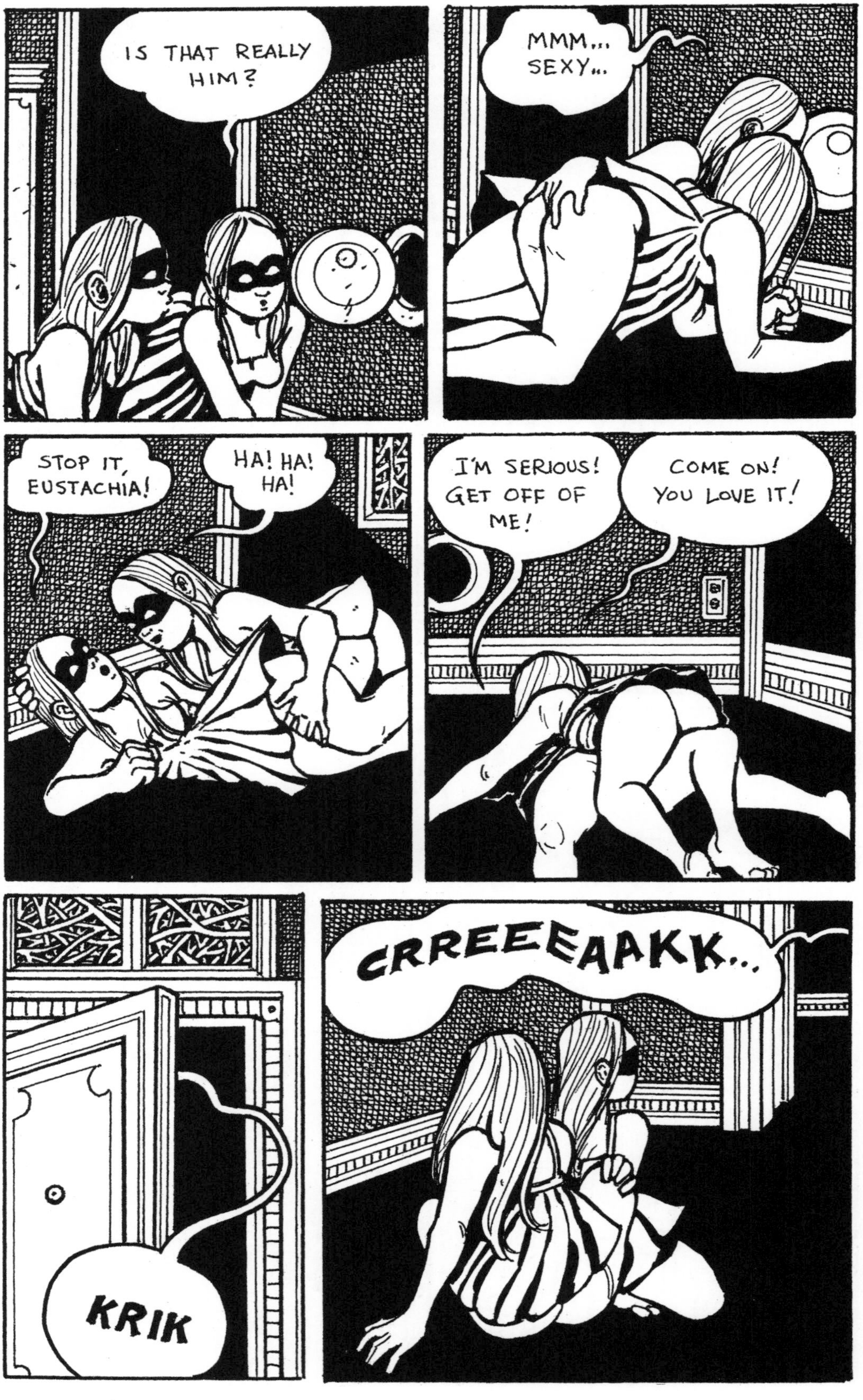
IS THAT REALLY HIM?
MMM... SEXY...
STOP IT, EUSTACHIA!
HA! HA! HA!
I'M SERIOUS! GET OFF OF ME!
COME ON! YOU LOVE IT!
KRIK
CRREEEAAKK...

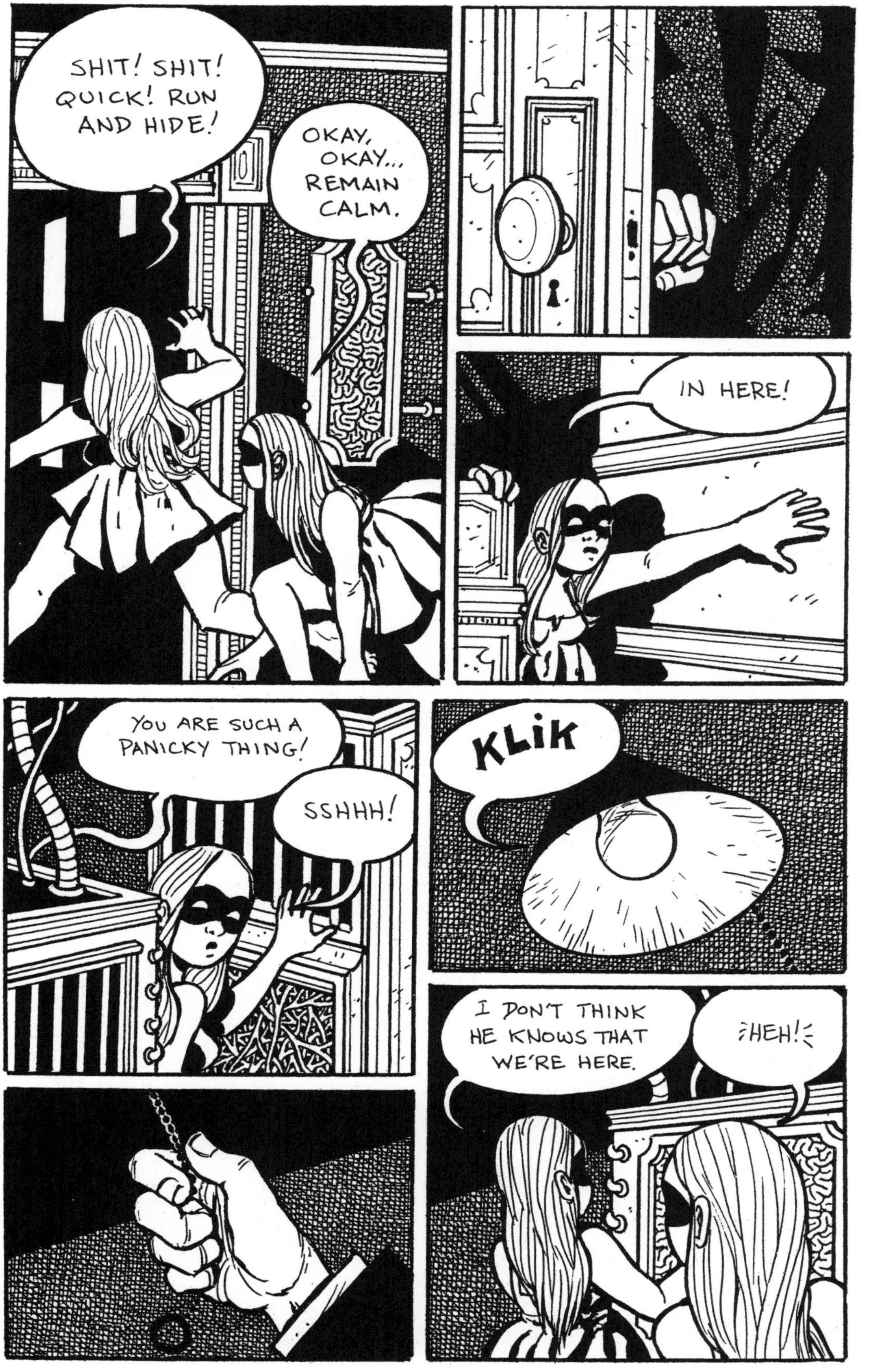
SHIT! SHIT! QUICK! RUN AND HIDE!
OKAY, OKAY... REMAIN CALM.
IN HERE!
YOU ARE SUCH A PANICKY THING!
SSHHH!
KLIK
I DON'T THINK HE KNOWS THAT WE'RE HERE.
HEH!

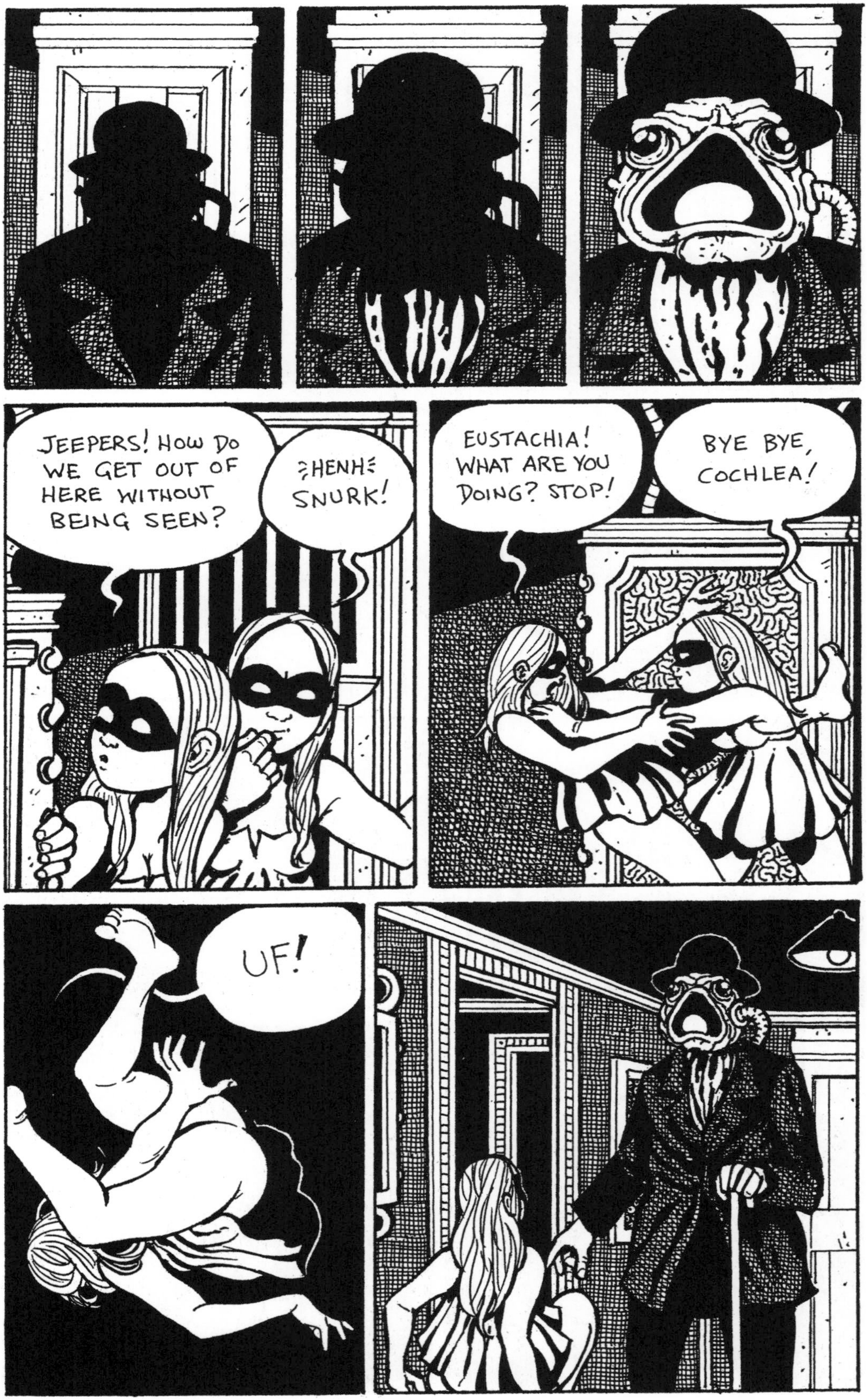
JEEPERS! HOW DO WE GET OUT OF HERE WITHOUT BEING SEEN?
HENH SNURK!
EUSTACHIA! WHAT ARE YOU DOING? STOP!
BYE BYE, COCHLEA!
UF!

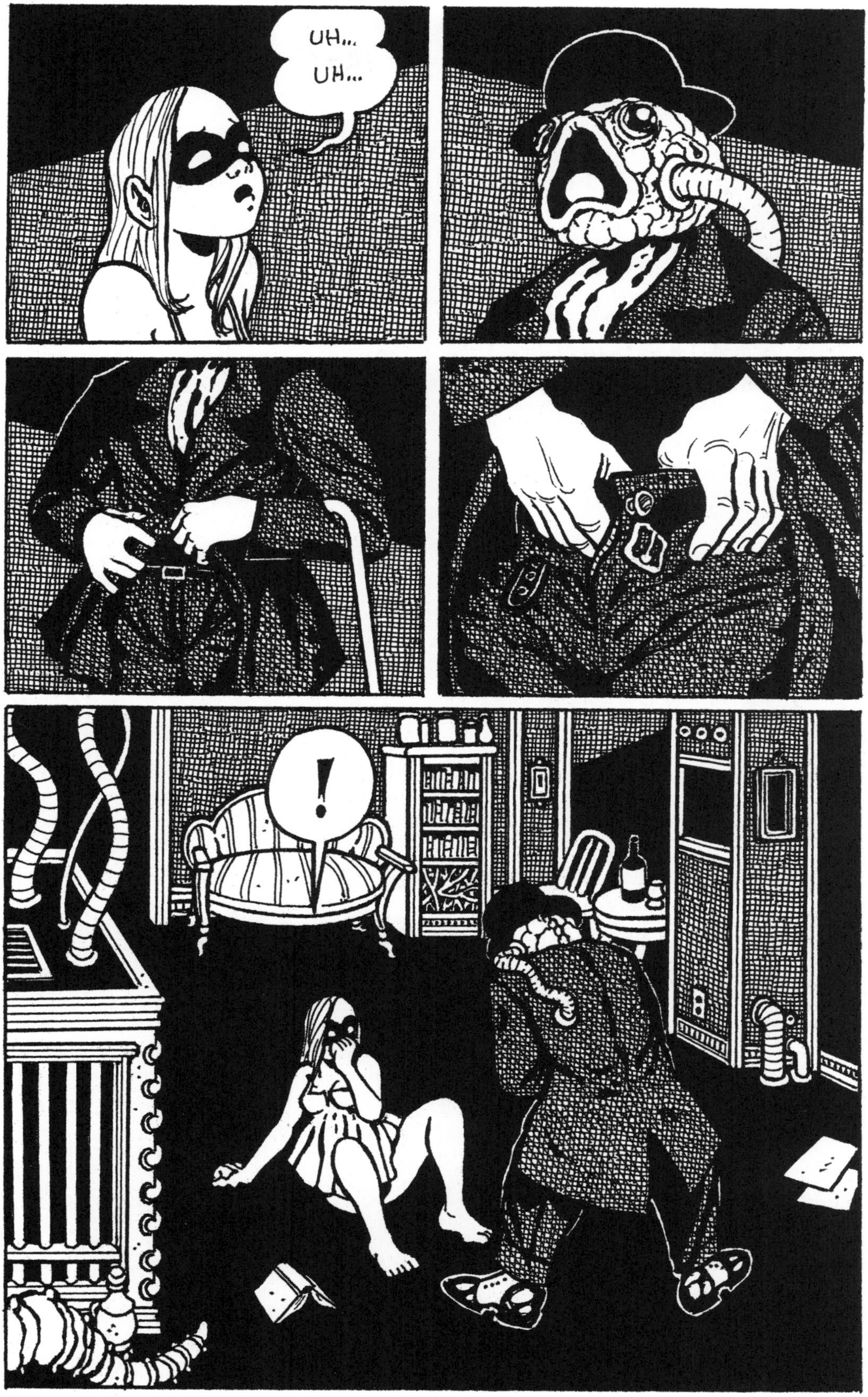
UH... UH...
!

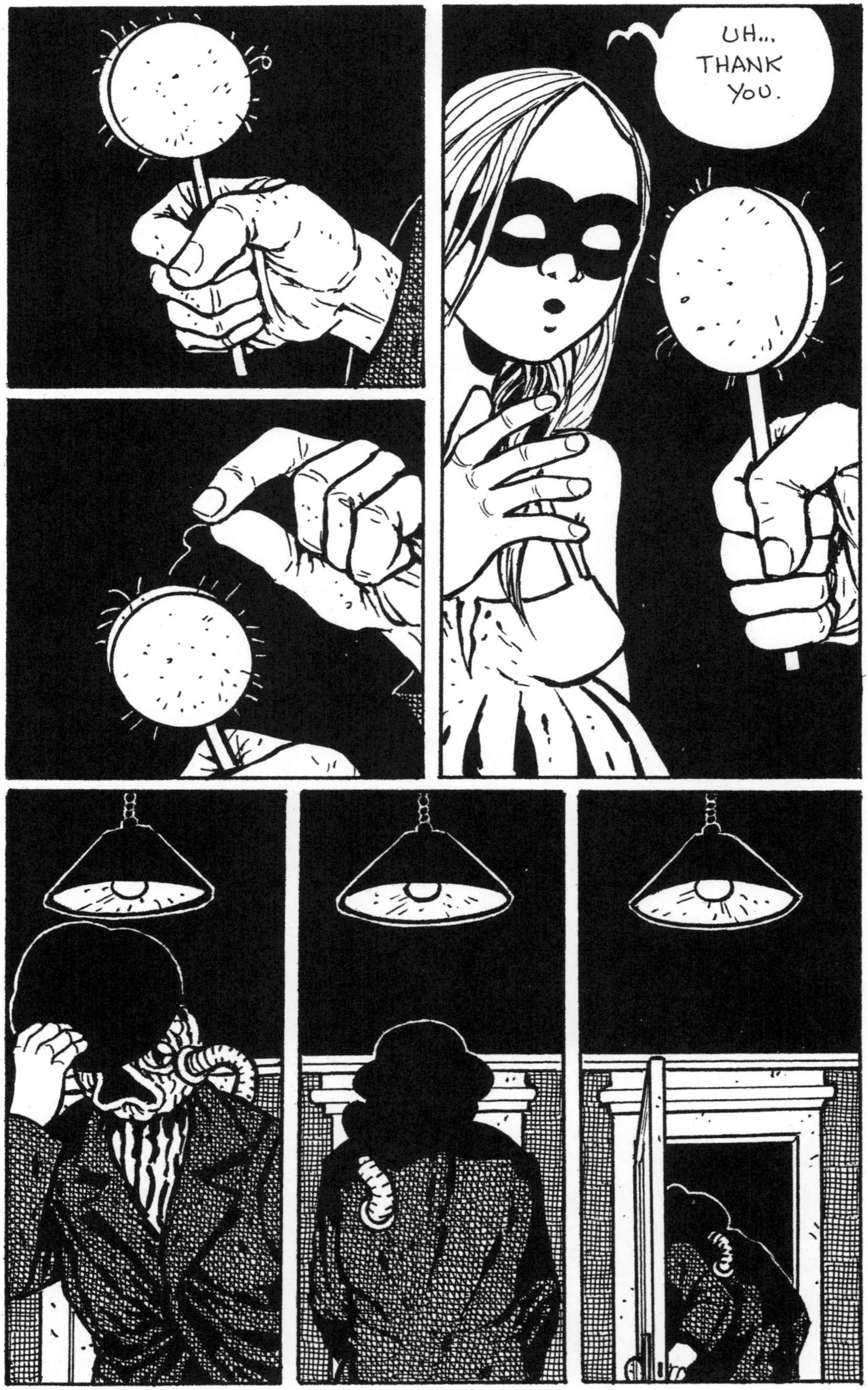
UH... THANK YOU.

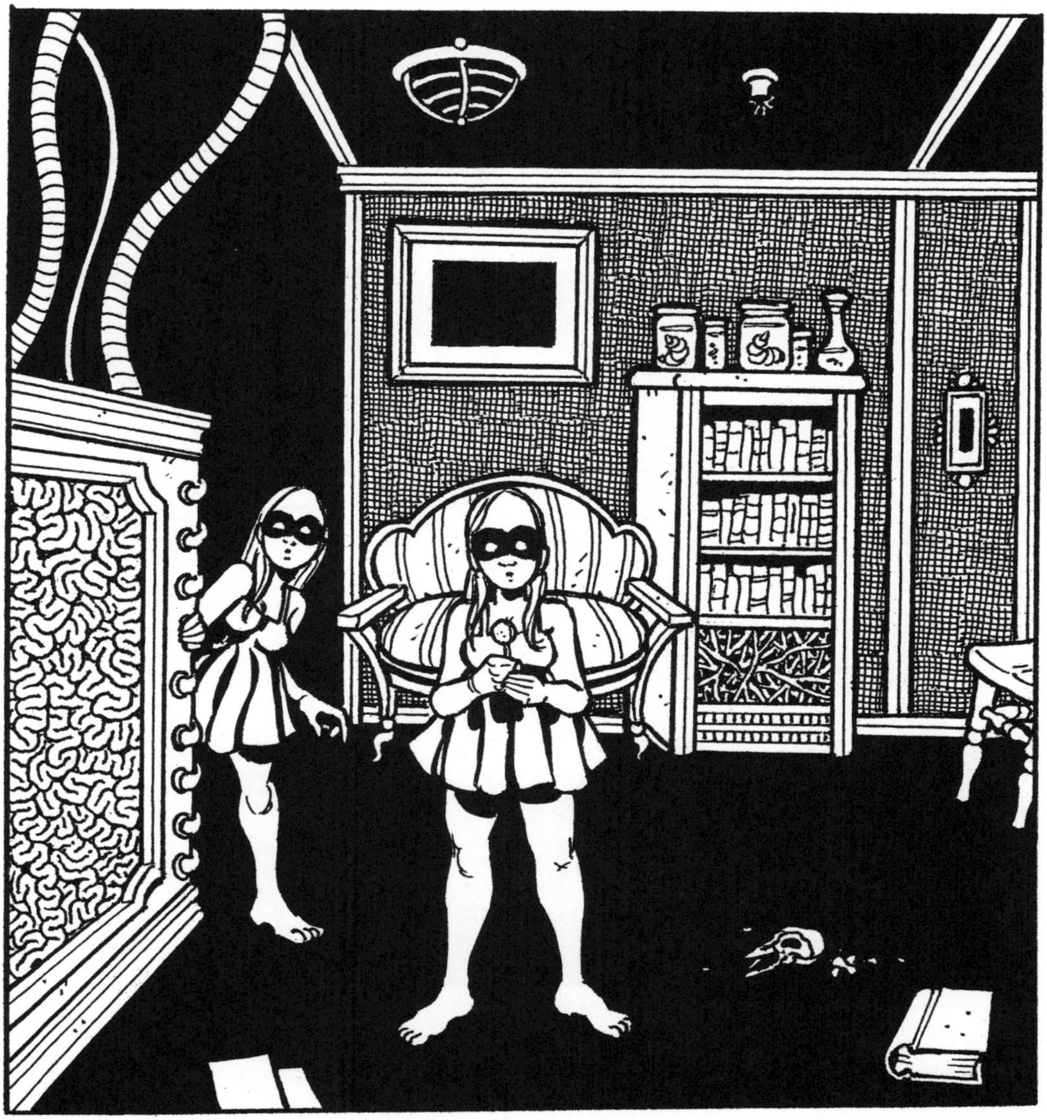

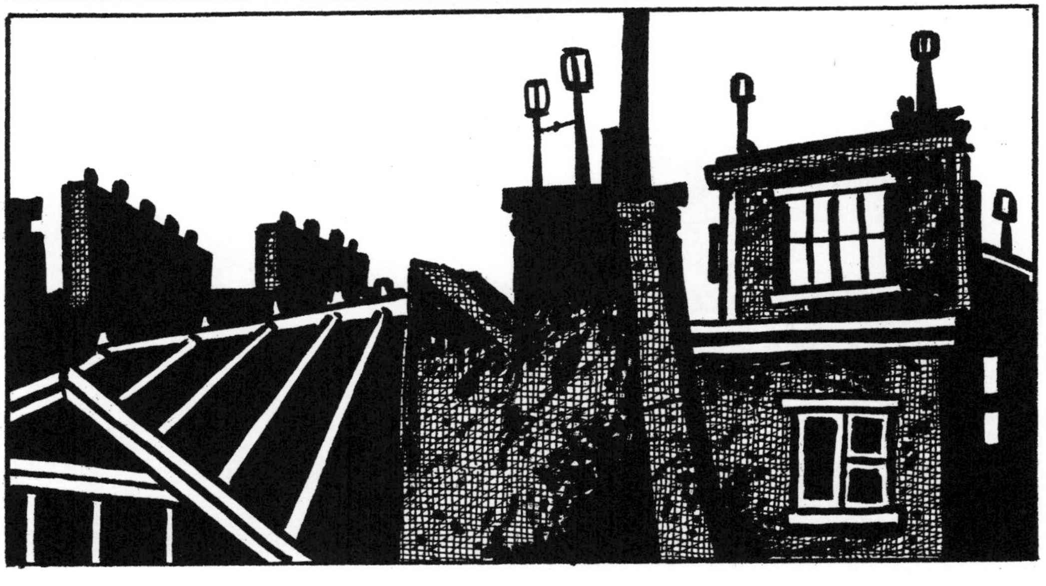

FOLLY.

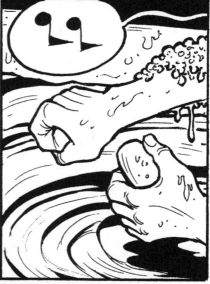

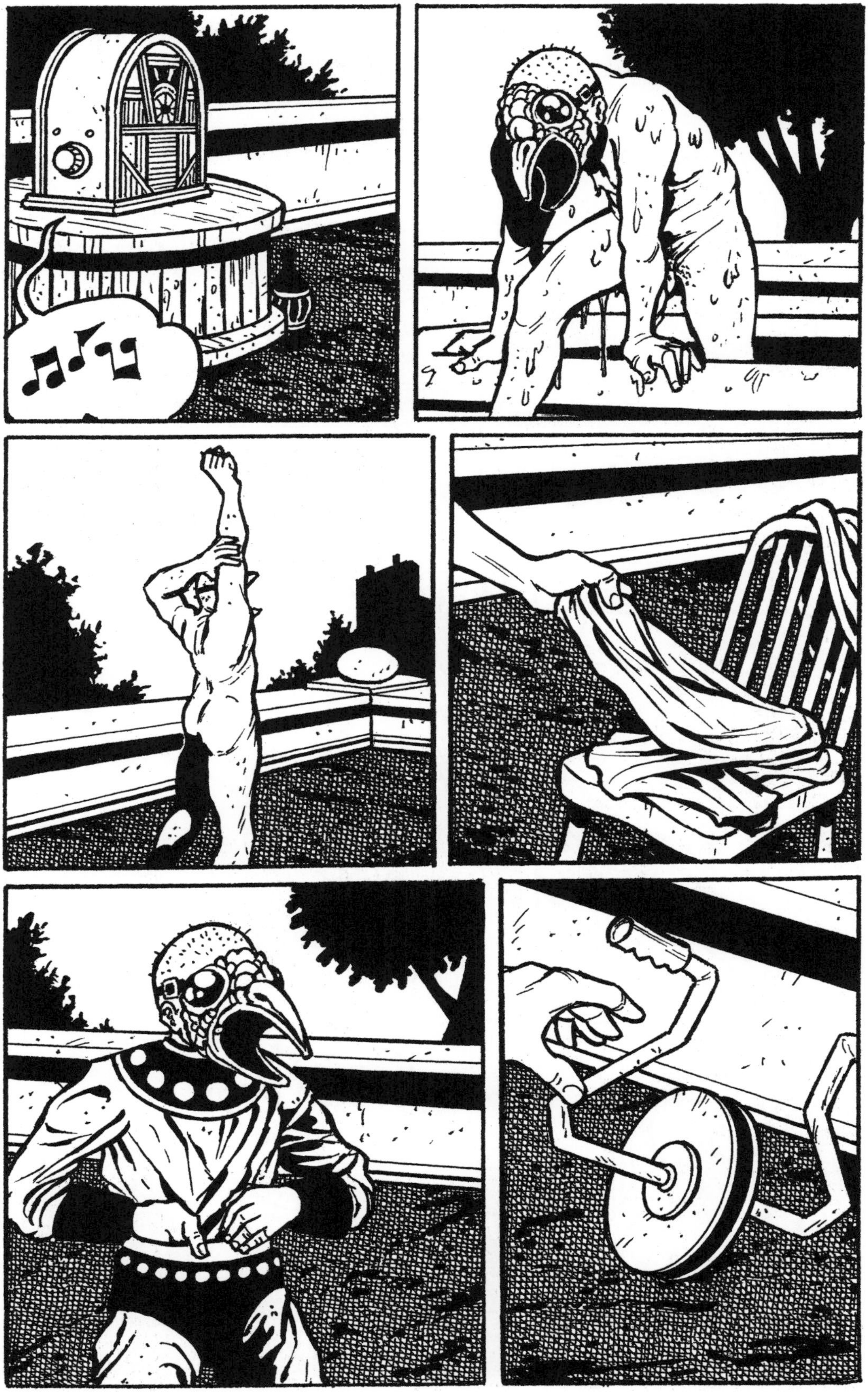

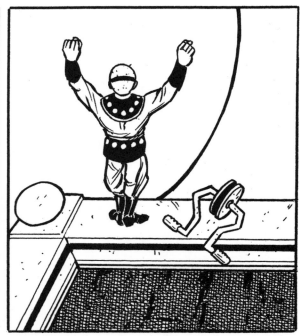
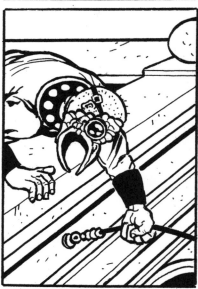

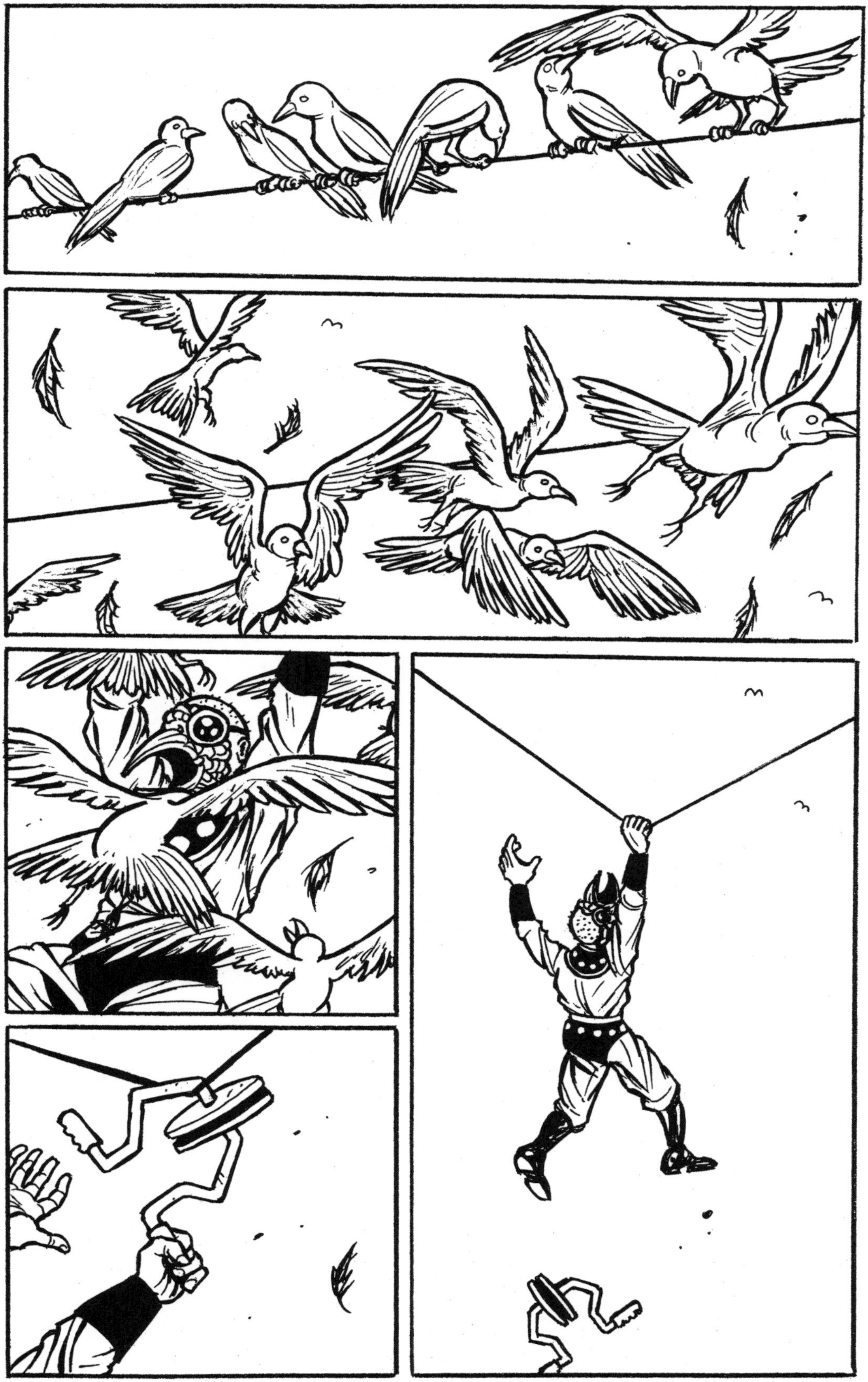

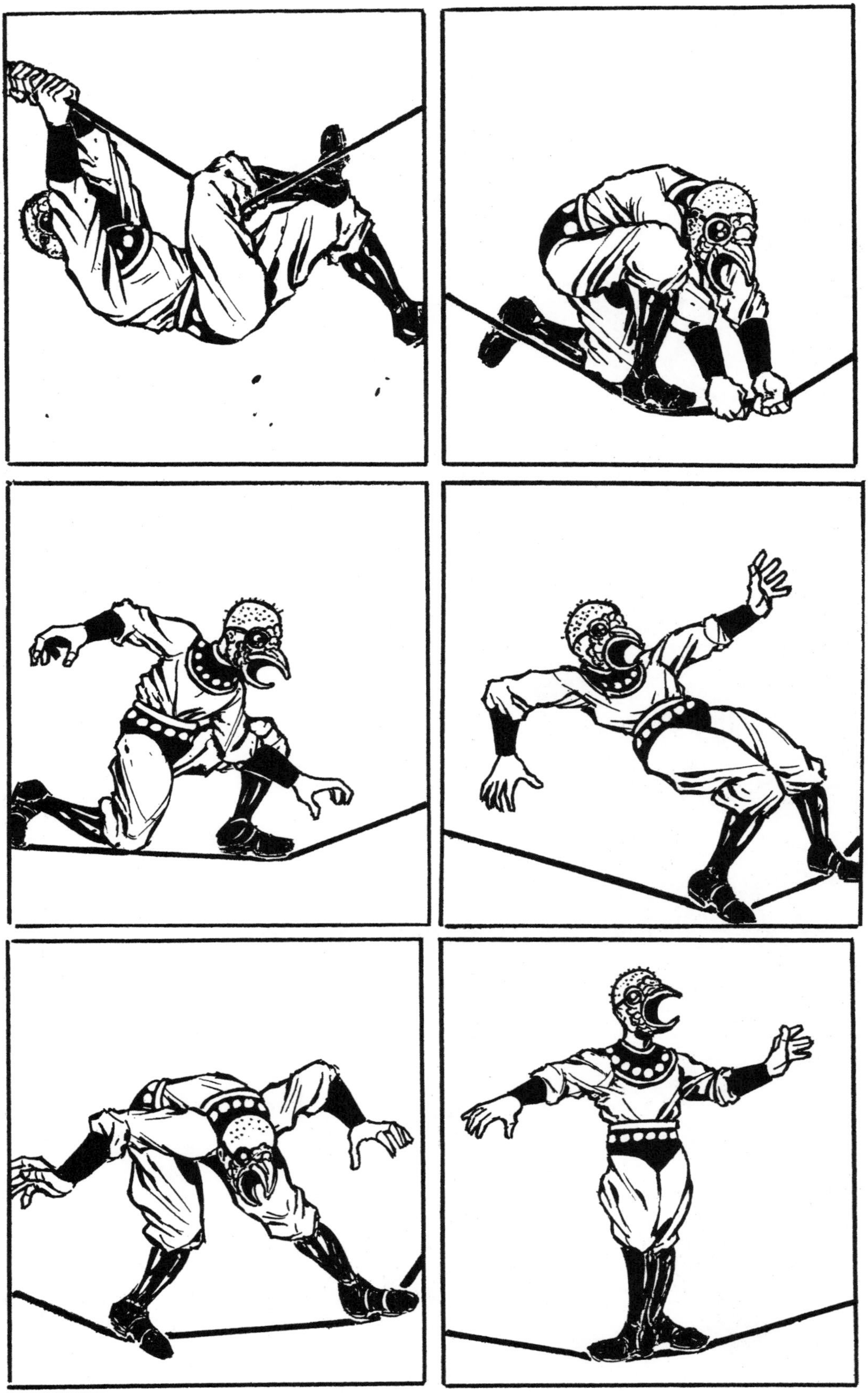

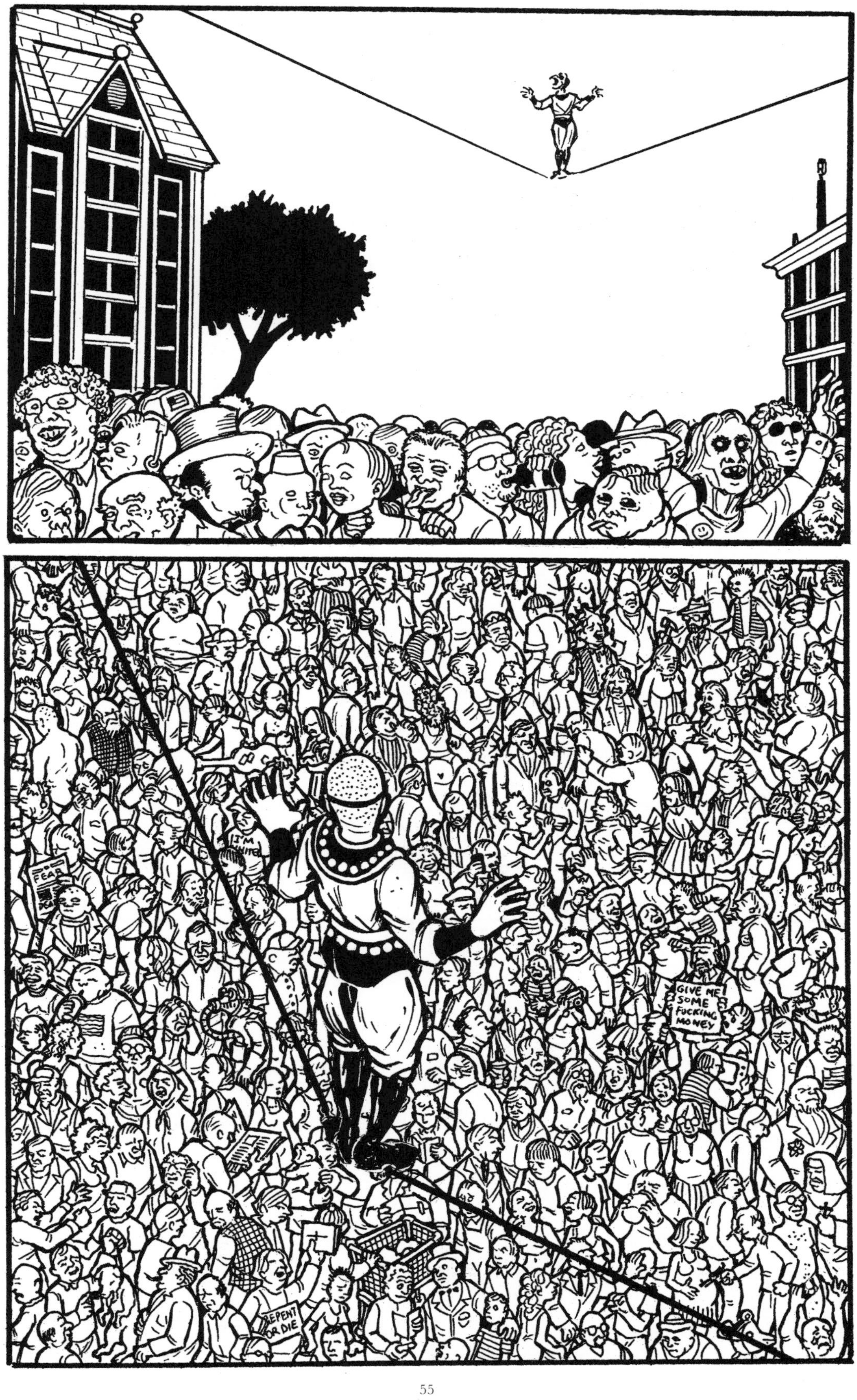
FEAR
GIVE ME SOME FUCKING MONEY
REPENT OR DIE

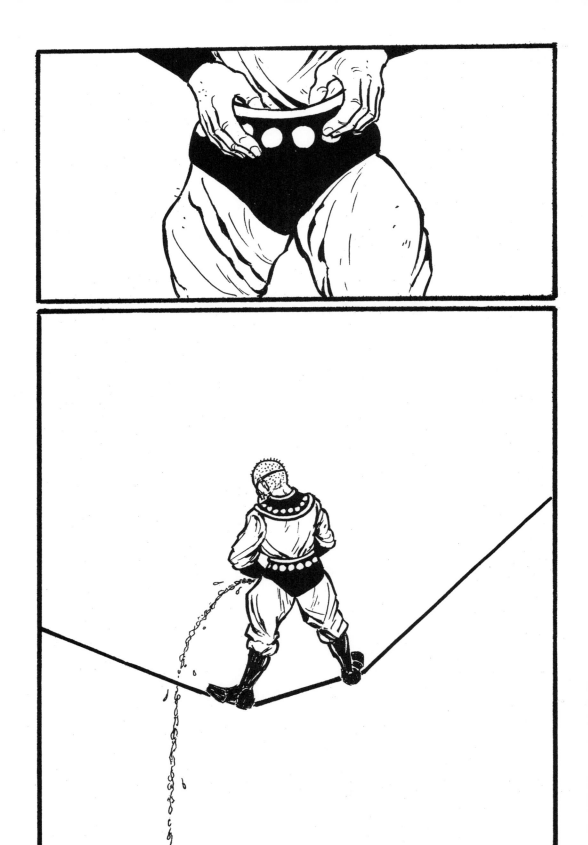

NOW IT'S YOUR TURN.

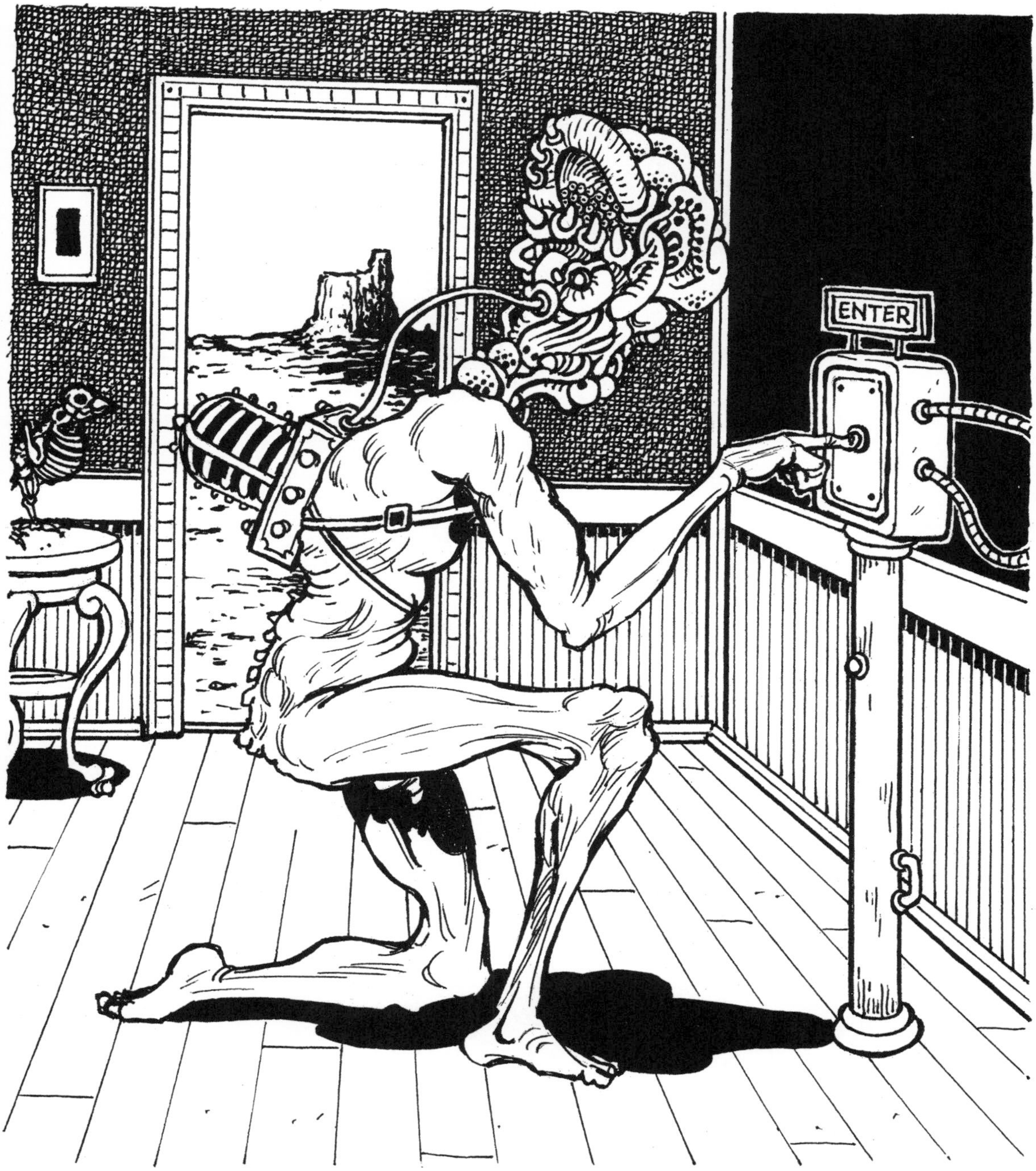
ENTER

3

CAUT

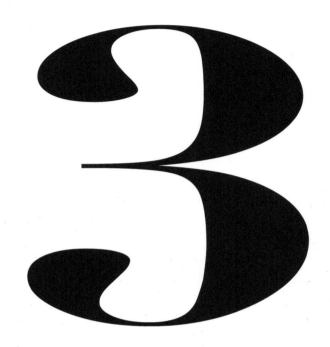

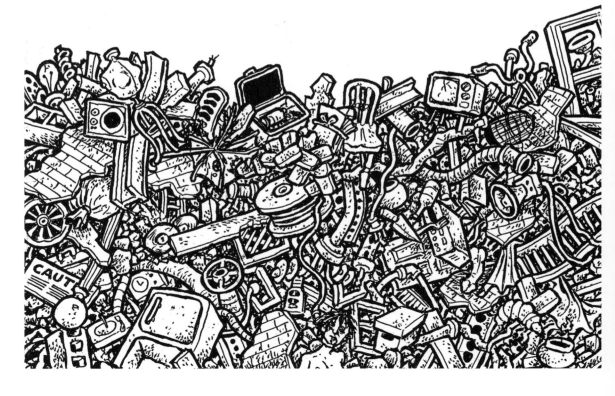

MADAM MOLLUSK

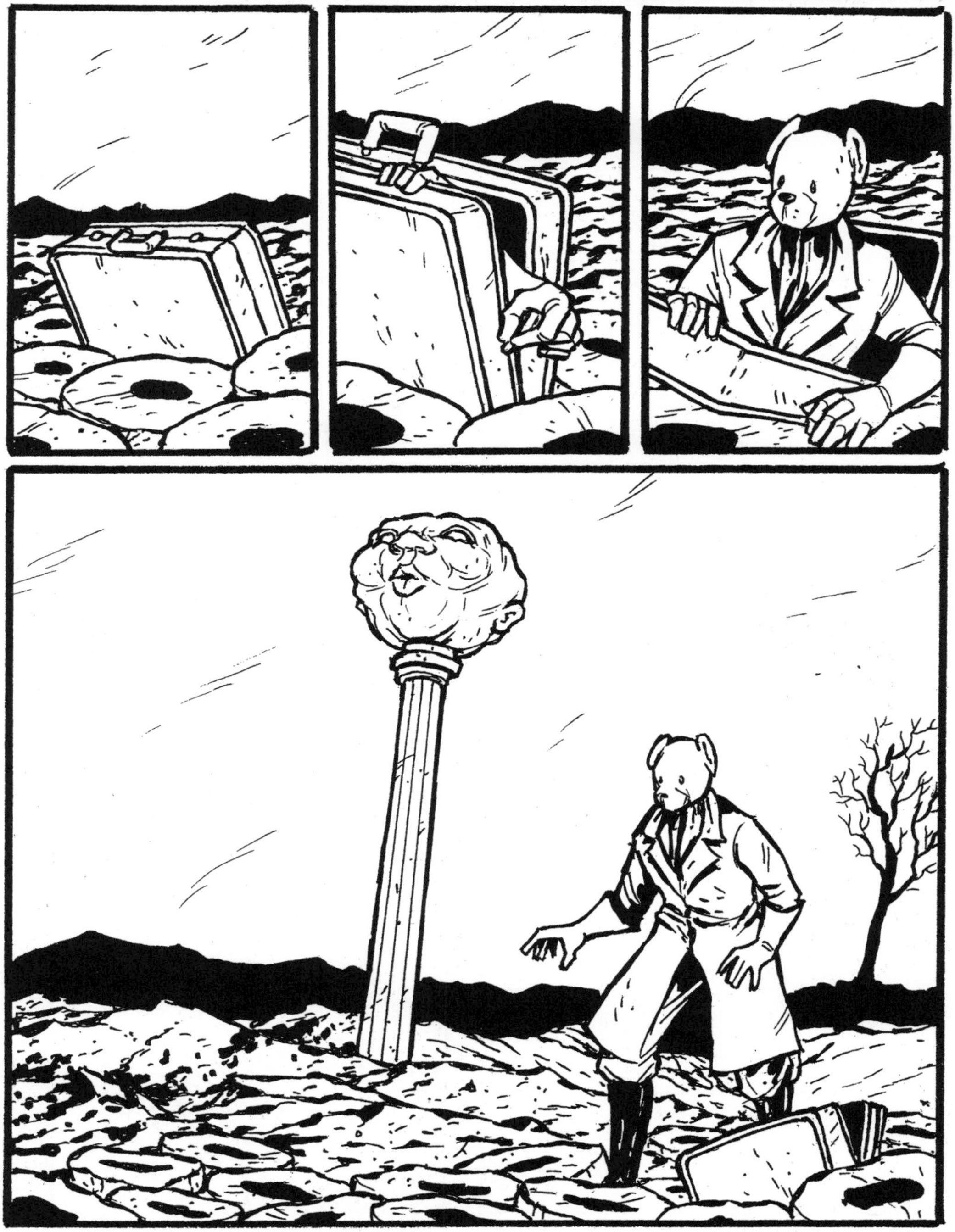

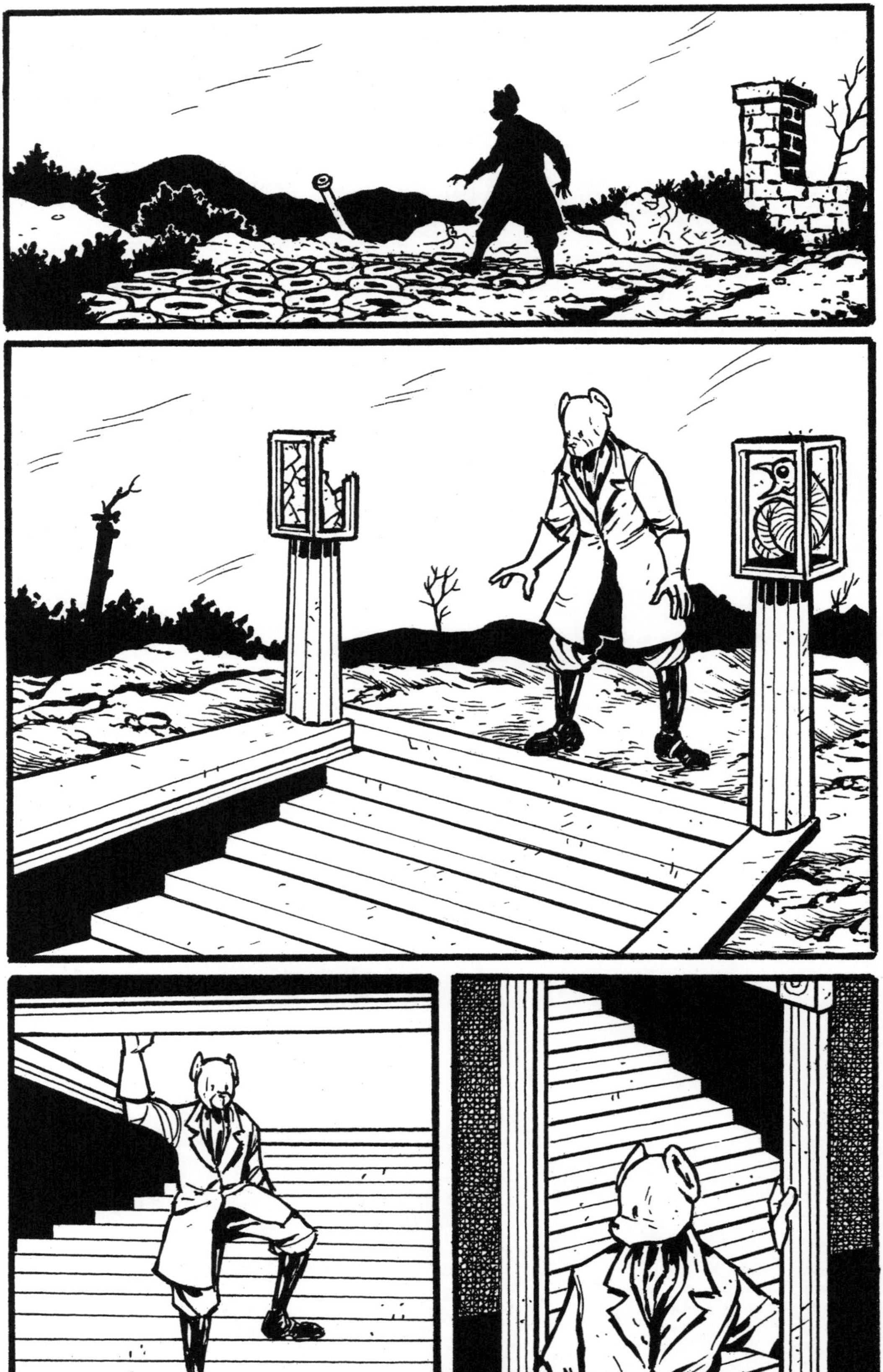

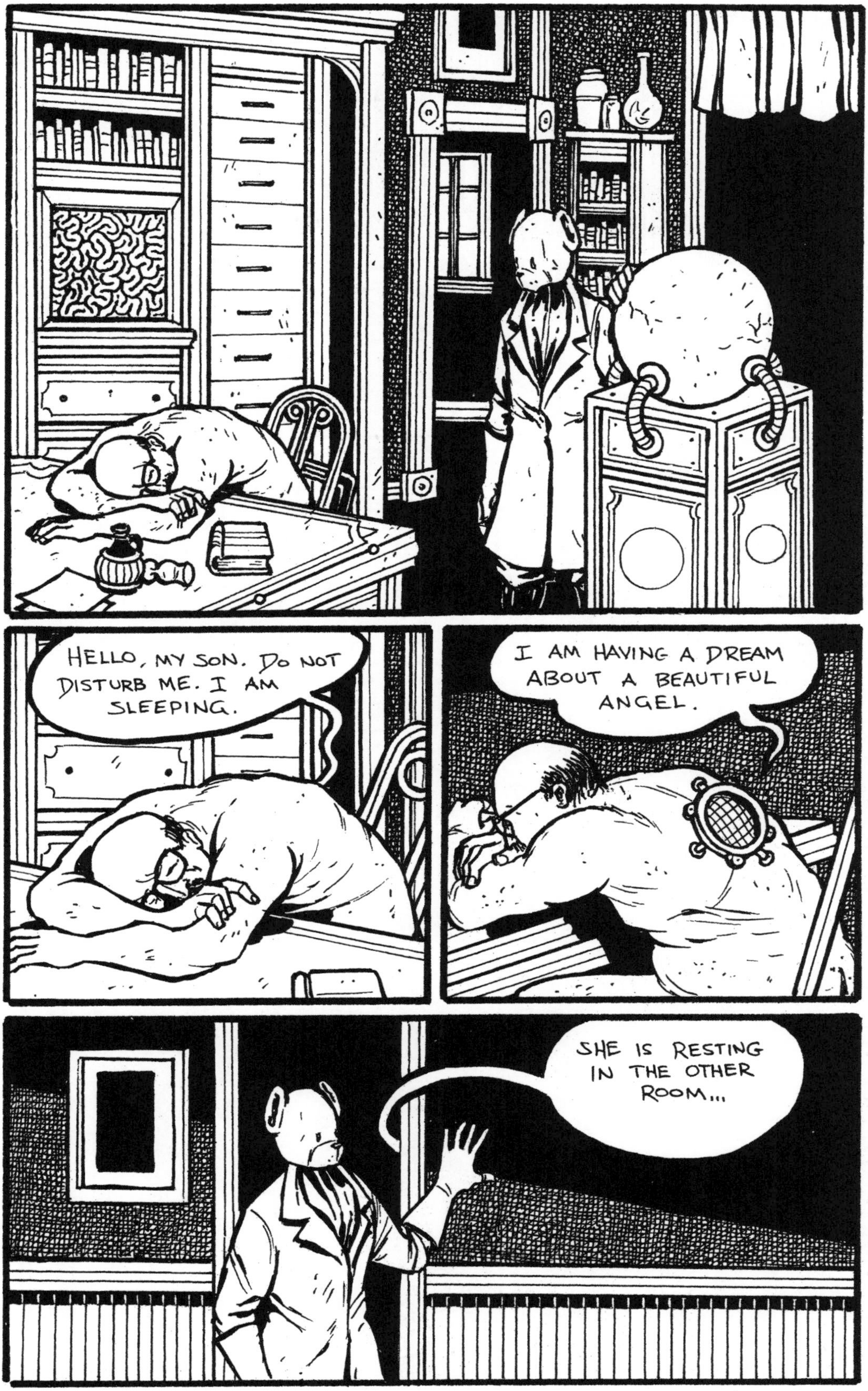
HELLO, MY SON. DO NOT DISTURB ME. I AM SLEEPING.
I AM HAVING A DREAM ABOUT A BEAUTIFUL ANGEL.
SHE IS RESTING IN THE OTHER ROOM...

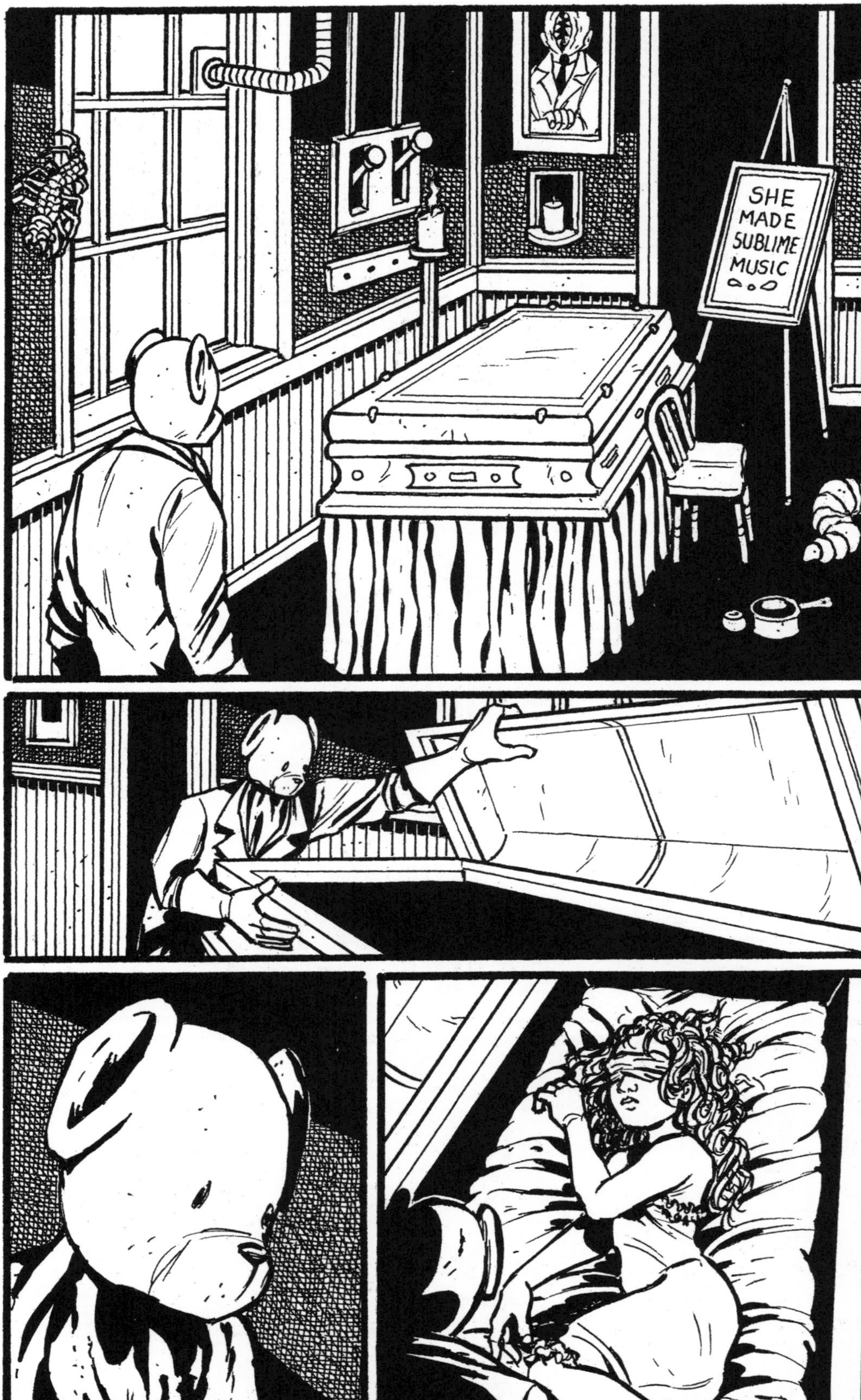
SHE MADE SUBLIME MUSIC

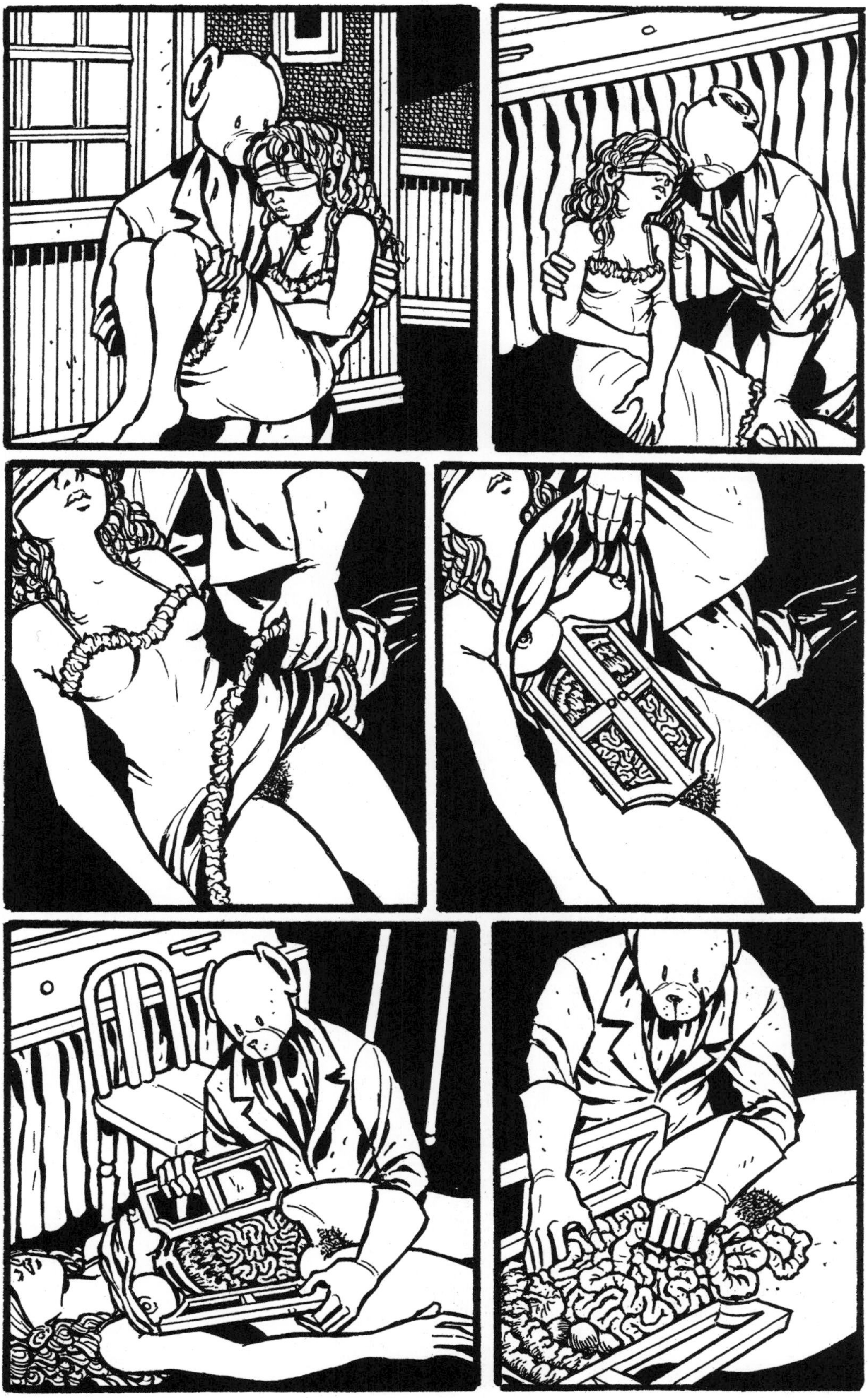

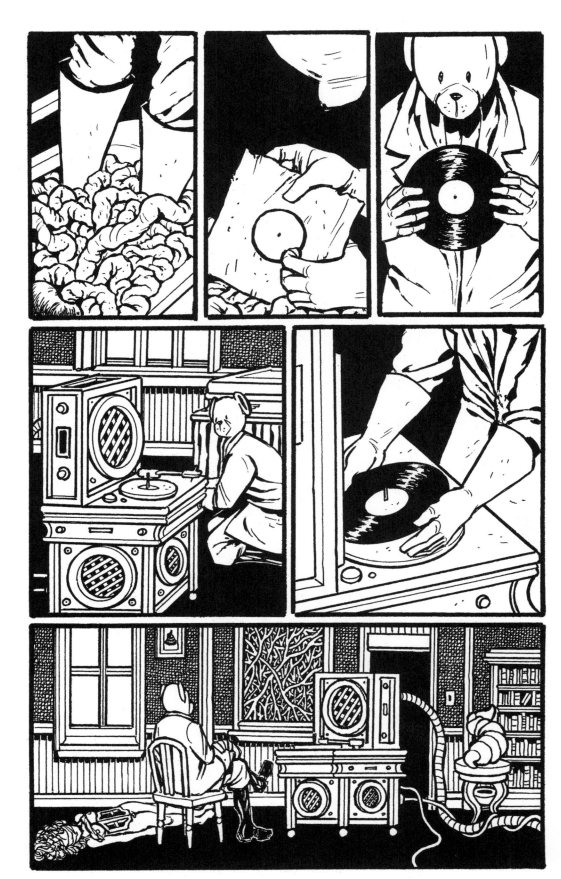

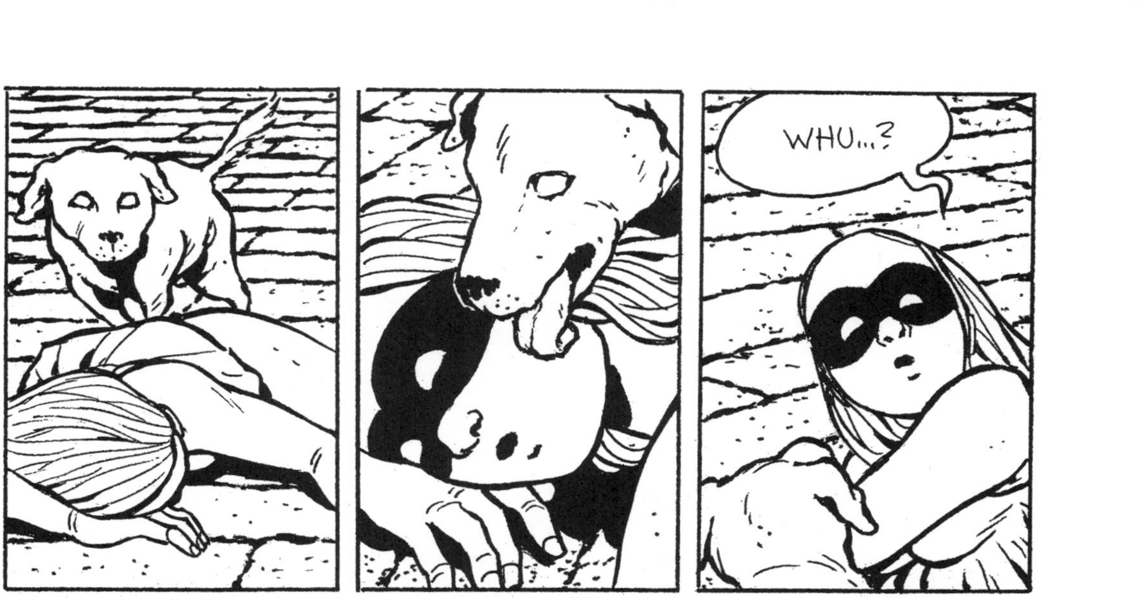
WHU...?

COCHLEA AND EUSTACHIA

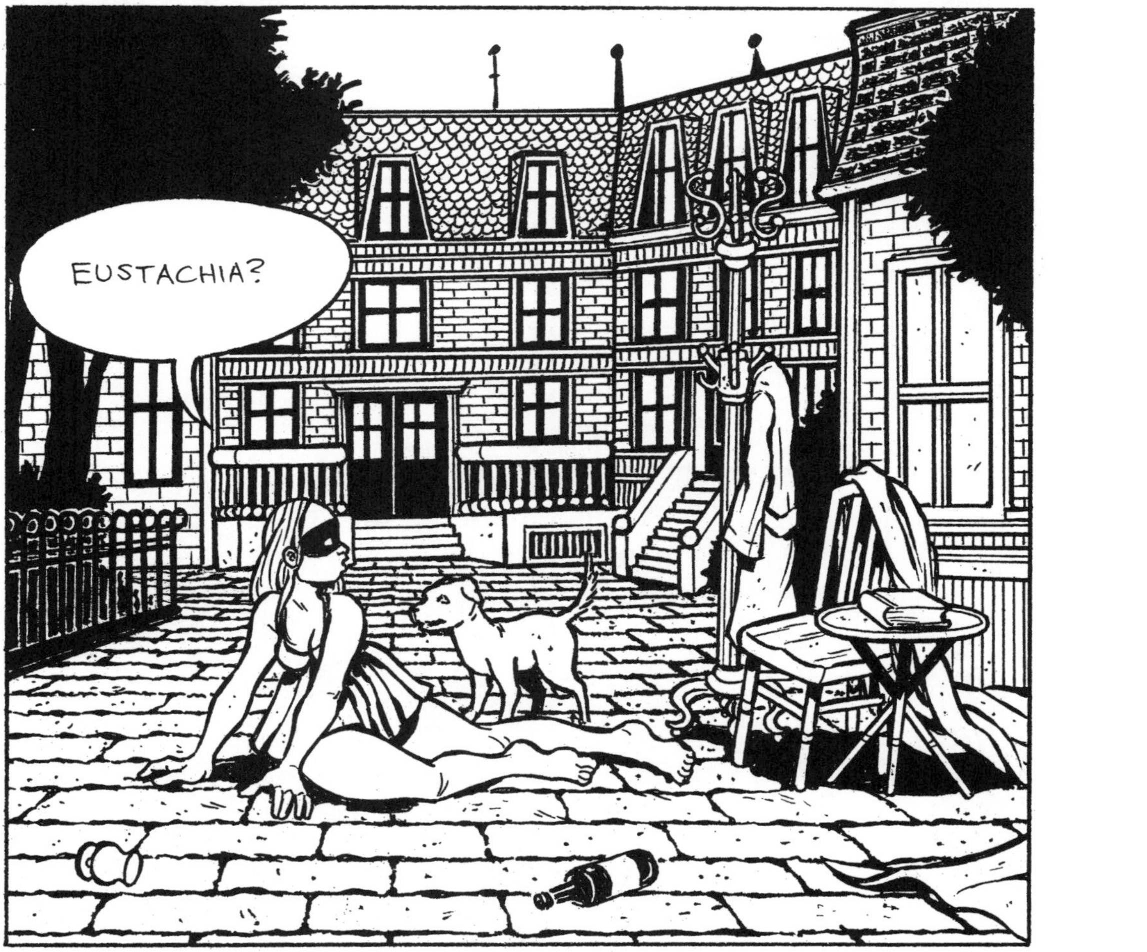
EUSTACHIA?

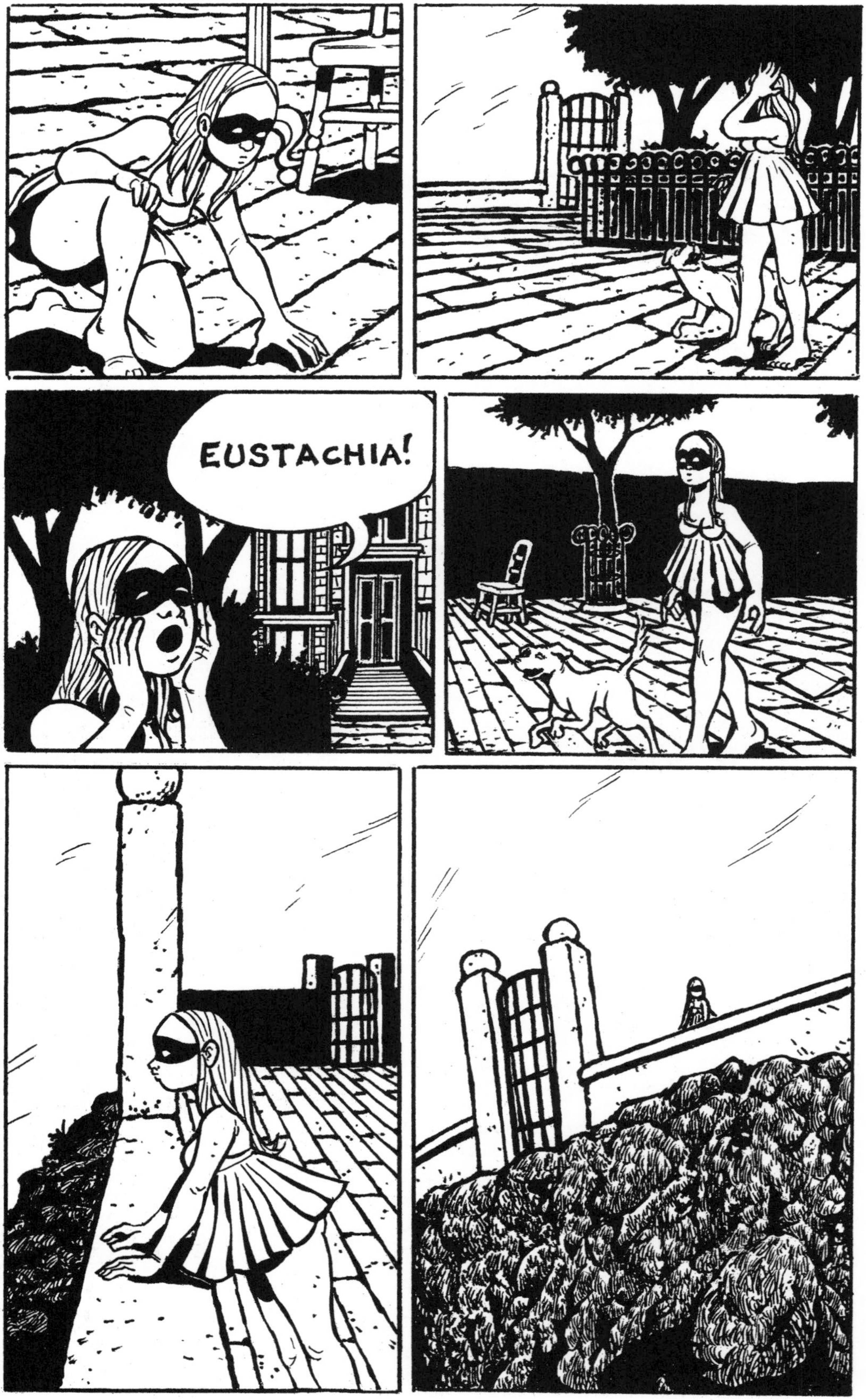
EUSTACHIA!

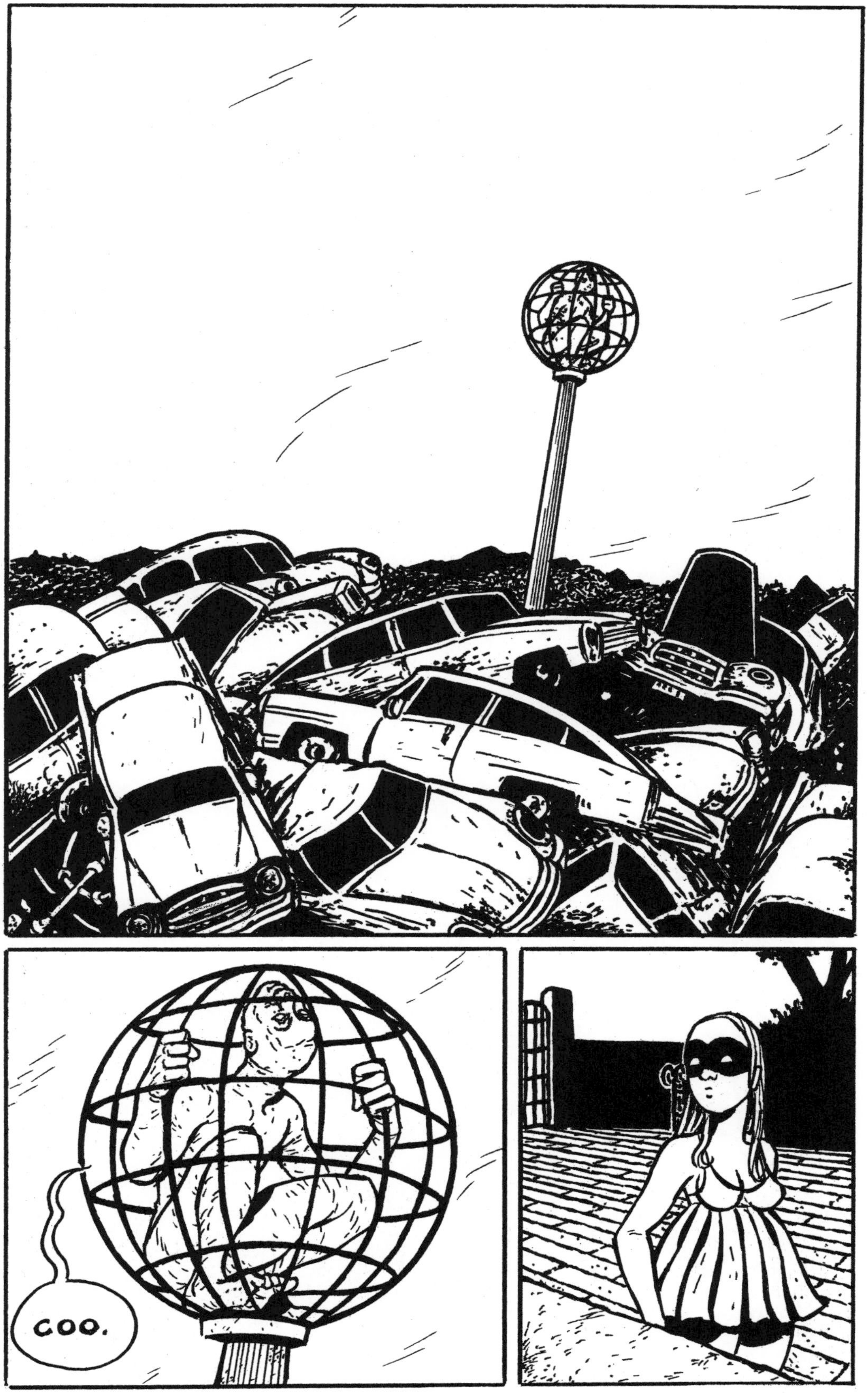
COO.

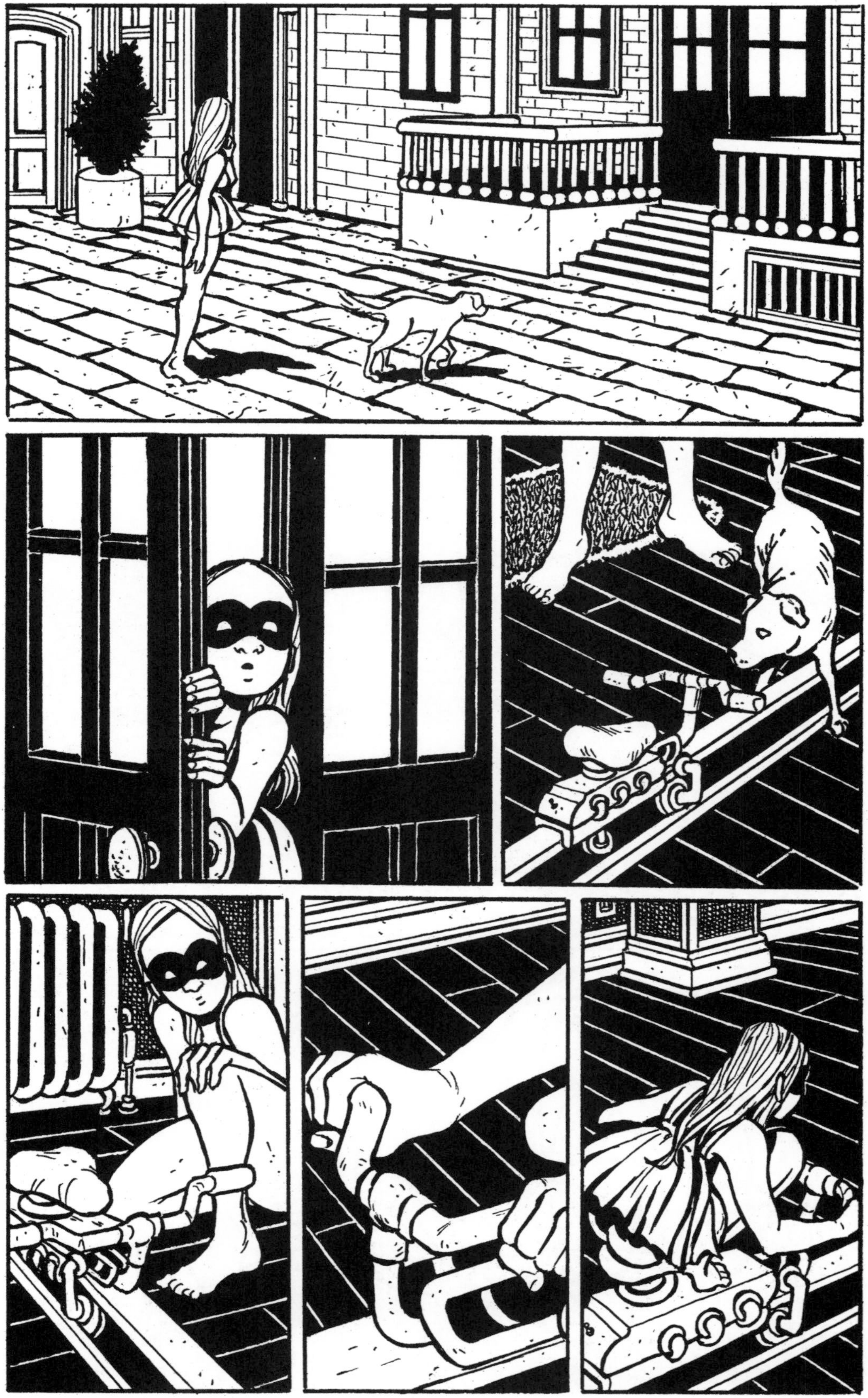

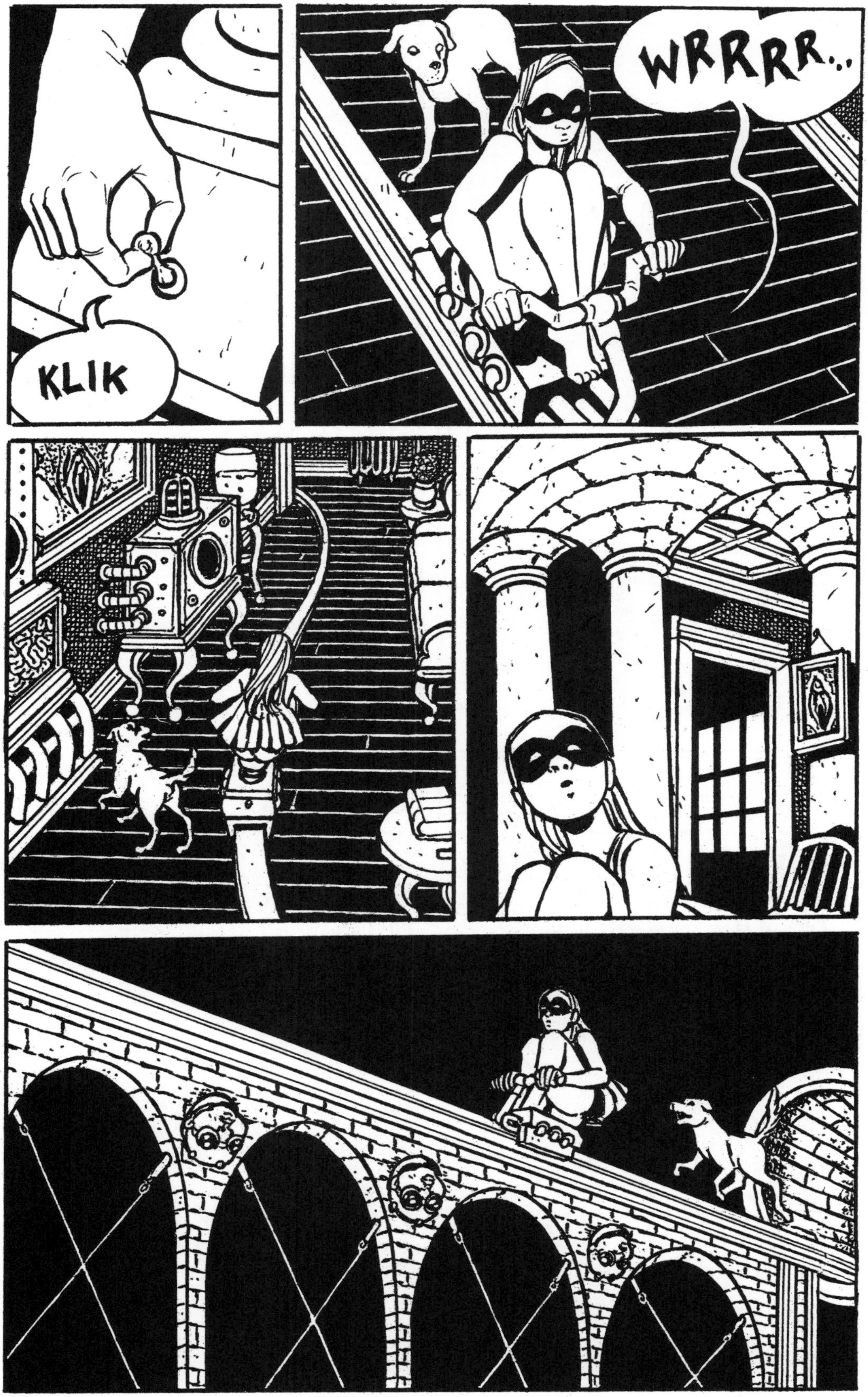
KLIK
WRRRR...

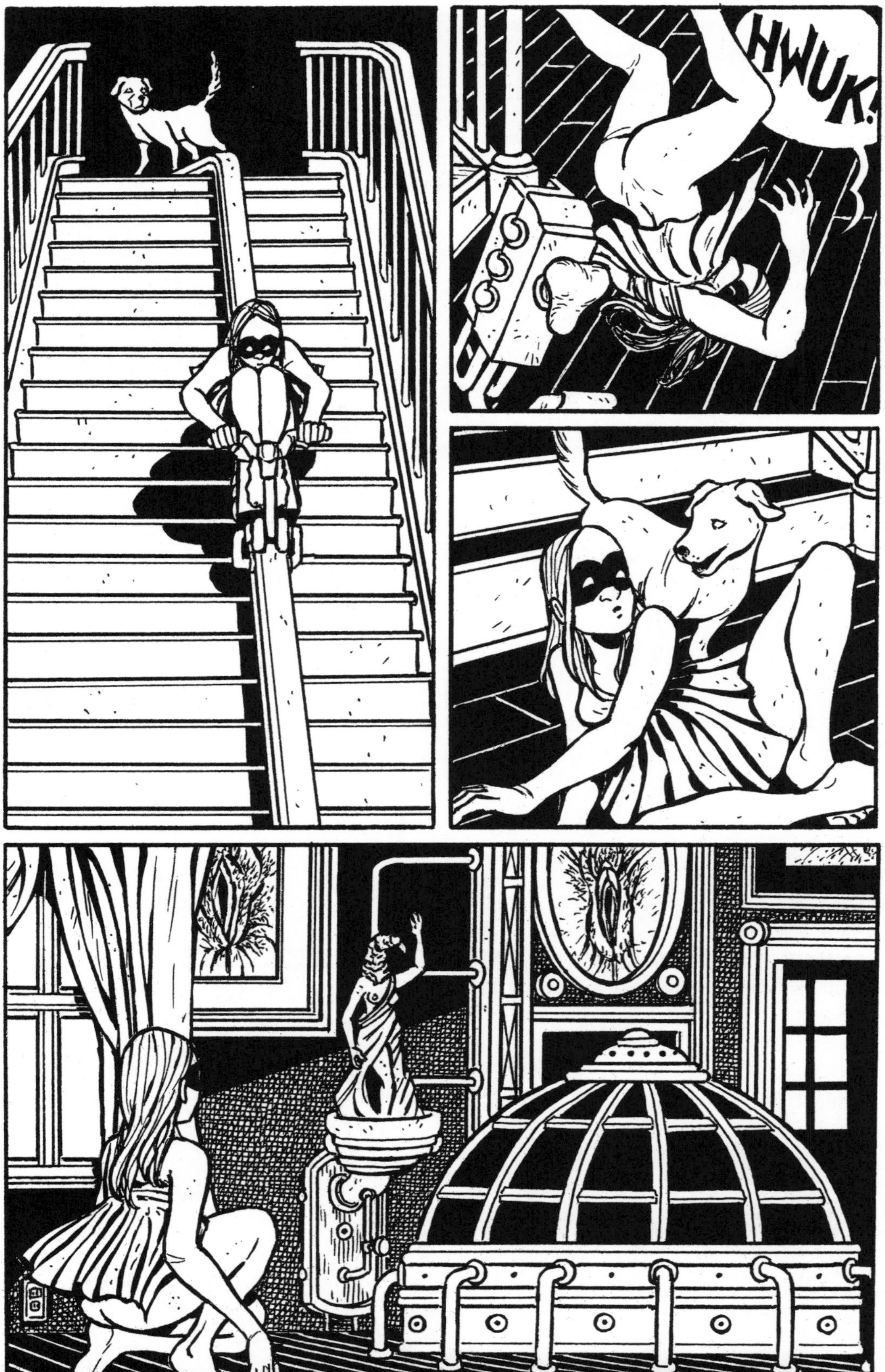
HWUK!

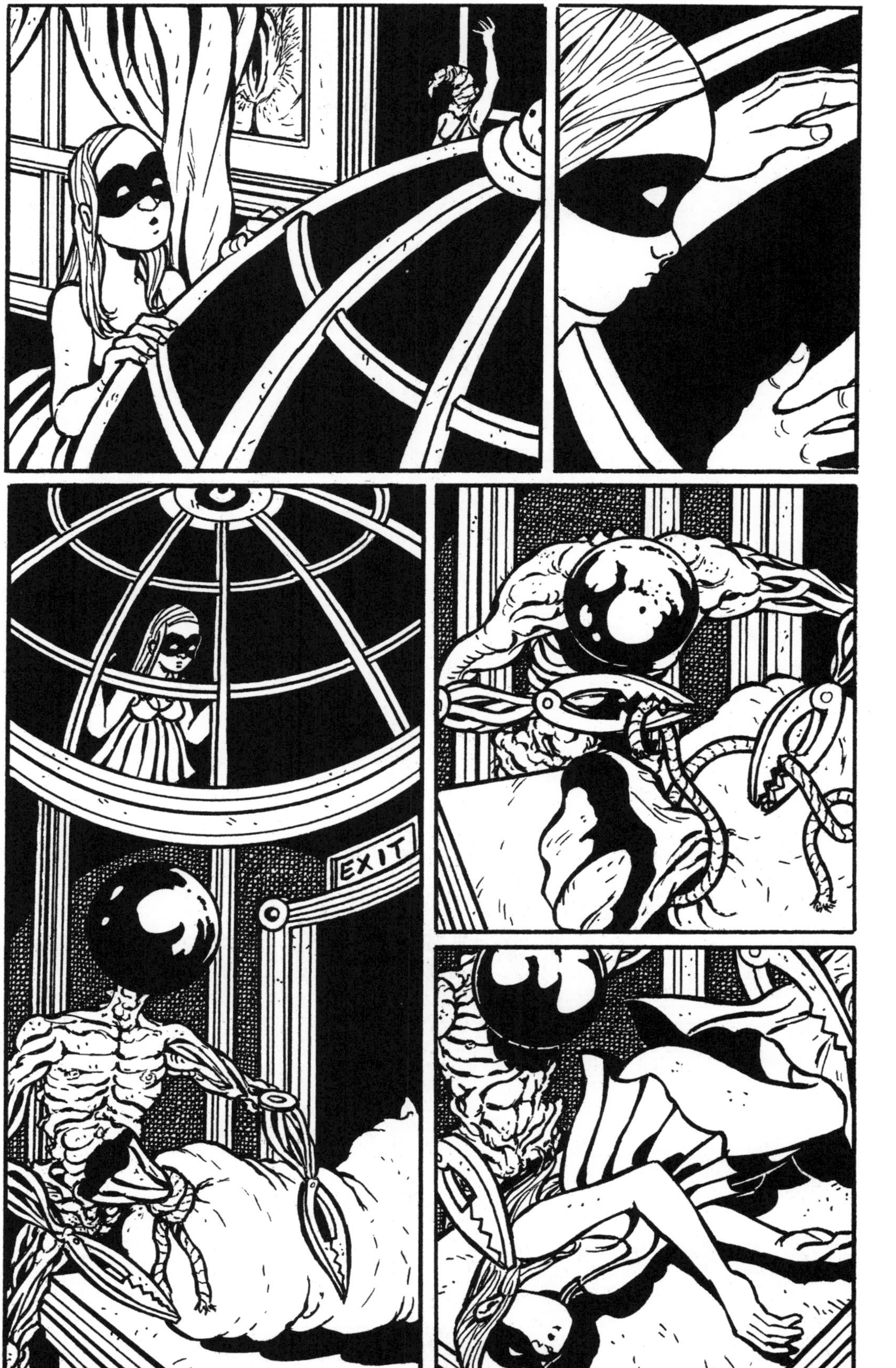
EXIT

EUSTACHIA!

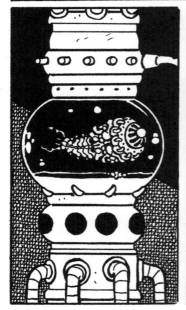

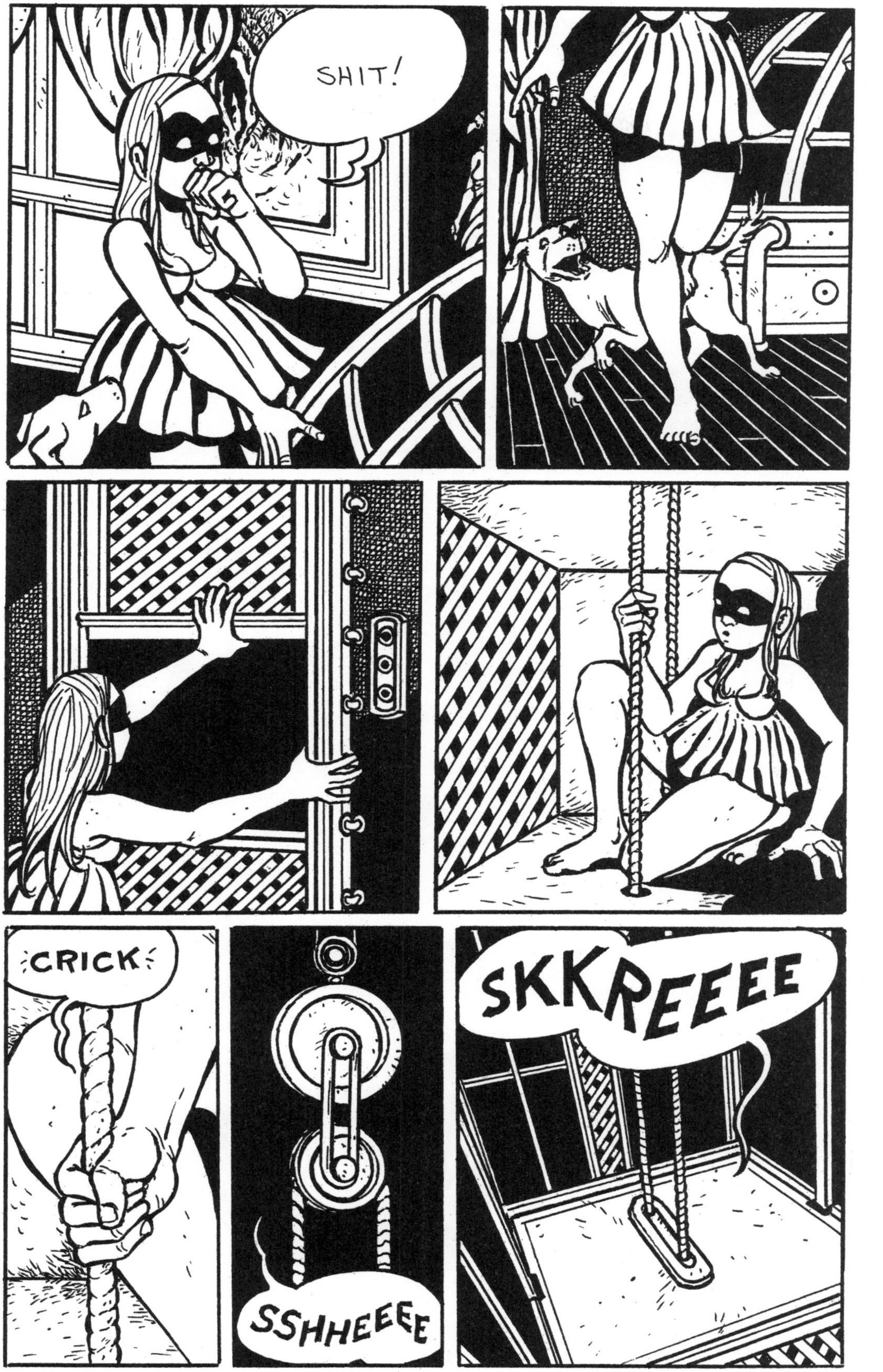
SHIT!
CRICK
SSHHEEEE
SKKREEEE

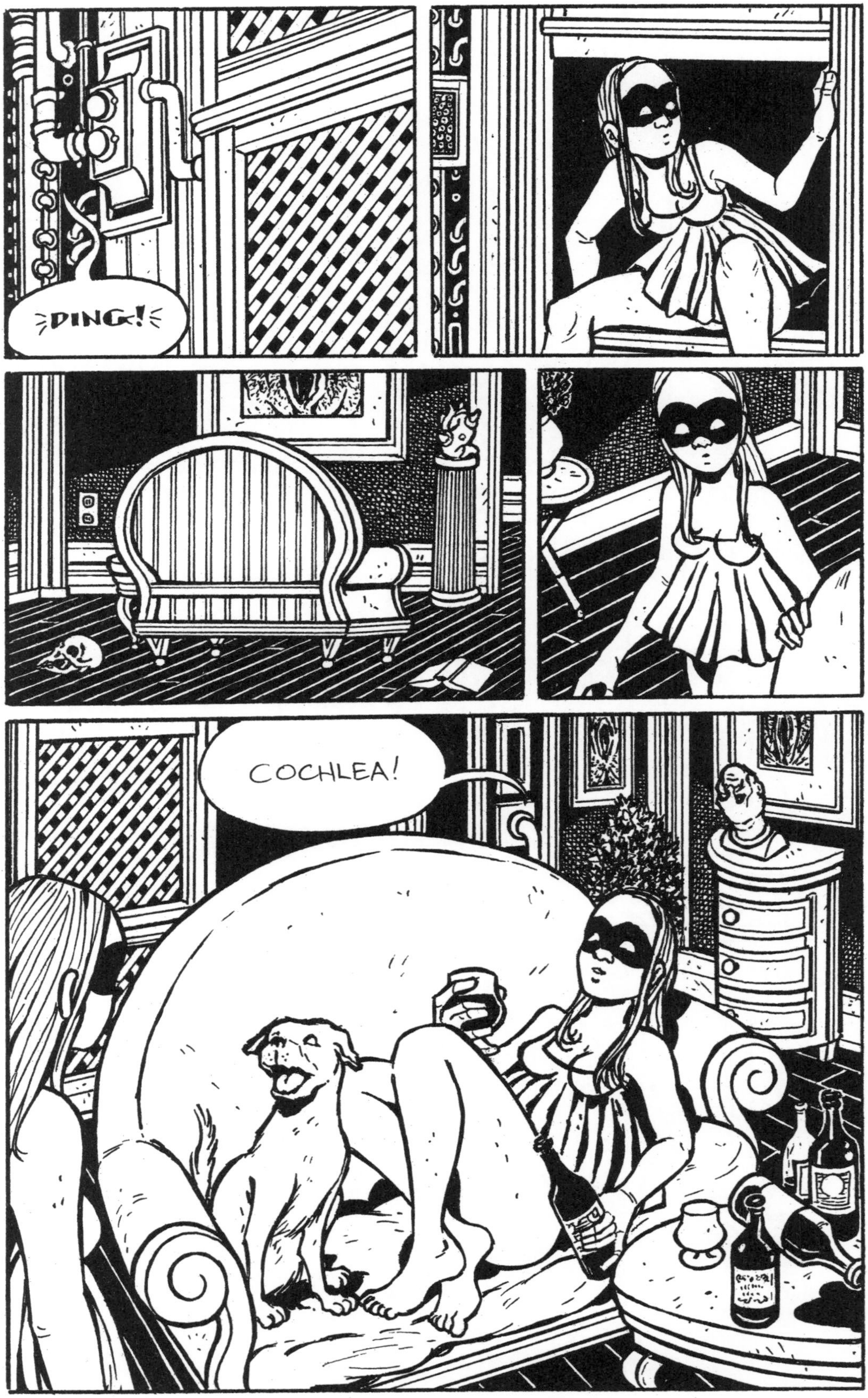
DING!
COCHLEA!

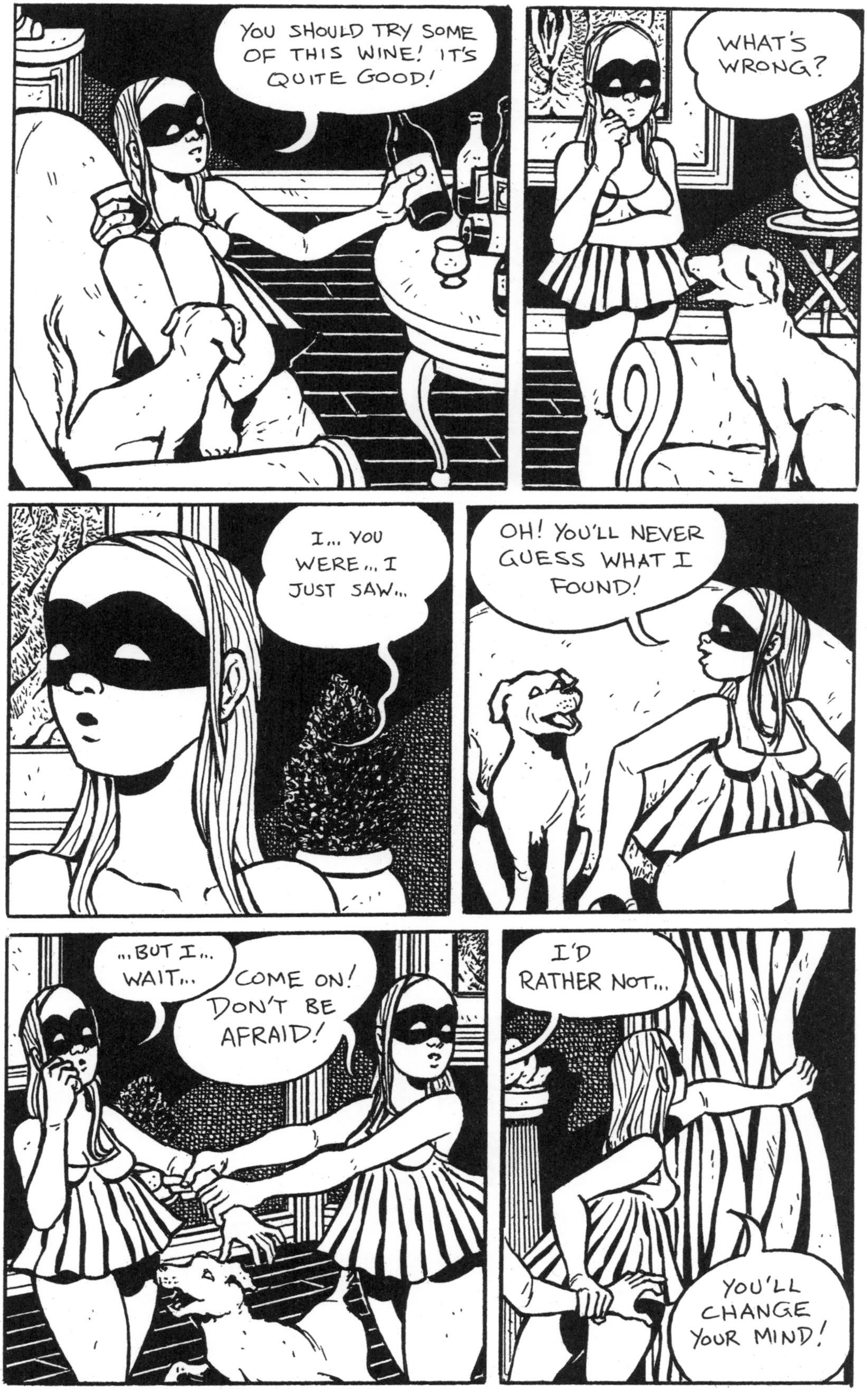
YOU SHOULD TRY SOME OF THIS WINE! IT'S QUITE GOOD!
WHAT'S WRONG?
I... YOU WERE... I JUST SAW...
OH! YOU'LL NEVER GUESS WHAT I FOUND!
...BUT I... WAIT...
COME ON! DON'T BE AFRAID!
I'D RATHER NOT...
YOU'LL CHANGE YOUR MIND!

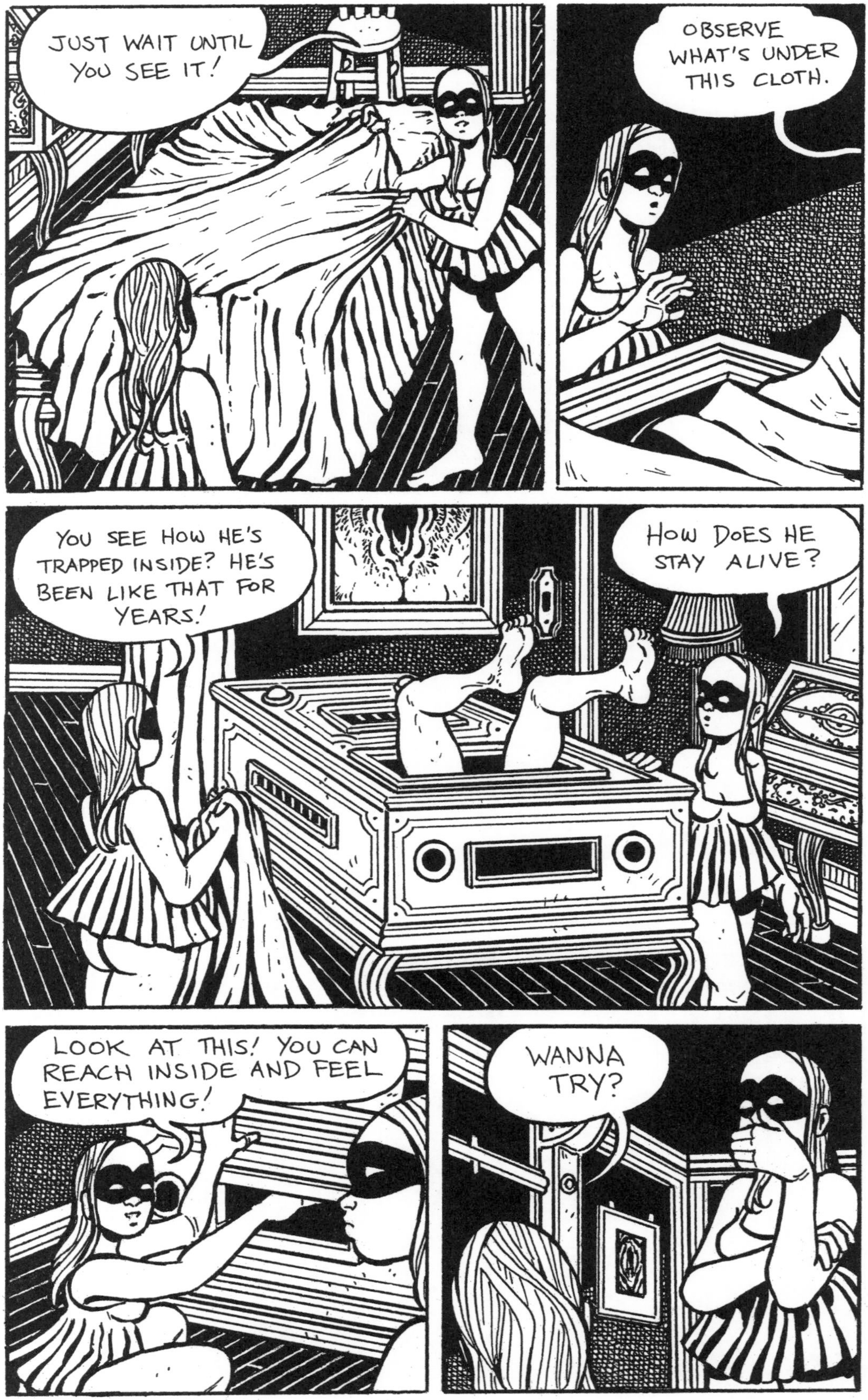
JUST WAIT UNTIL YOU SEE IT!
OBSERVE WHAT'S UNDER THIS CLOTH.
YOU SEE HOW HE'S TRAPPED INSIDE? HE'S BEEN LIKE THAT FOR YEARS!
HOW DOES HE STAY ALIVE?
LOOK AT THIS! YOU CAN REACH INSIDE AND FEEL EVERYTHING!
WANNA TRY?

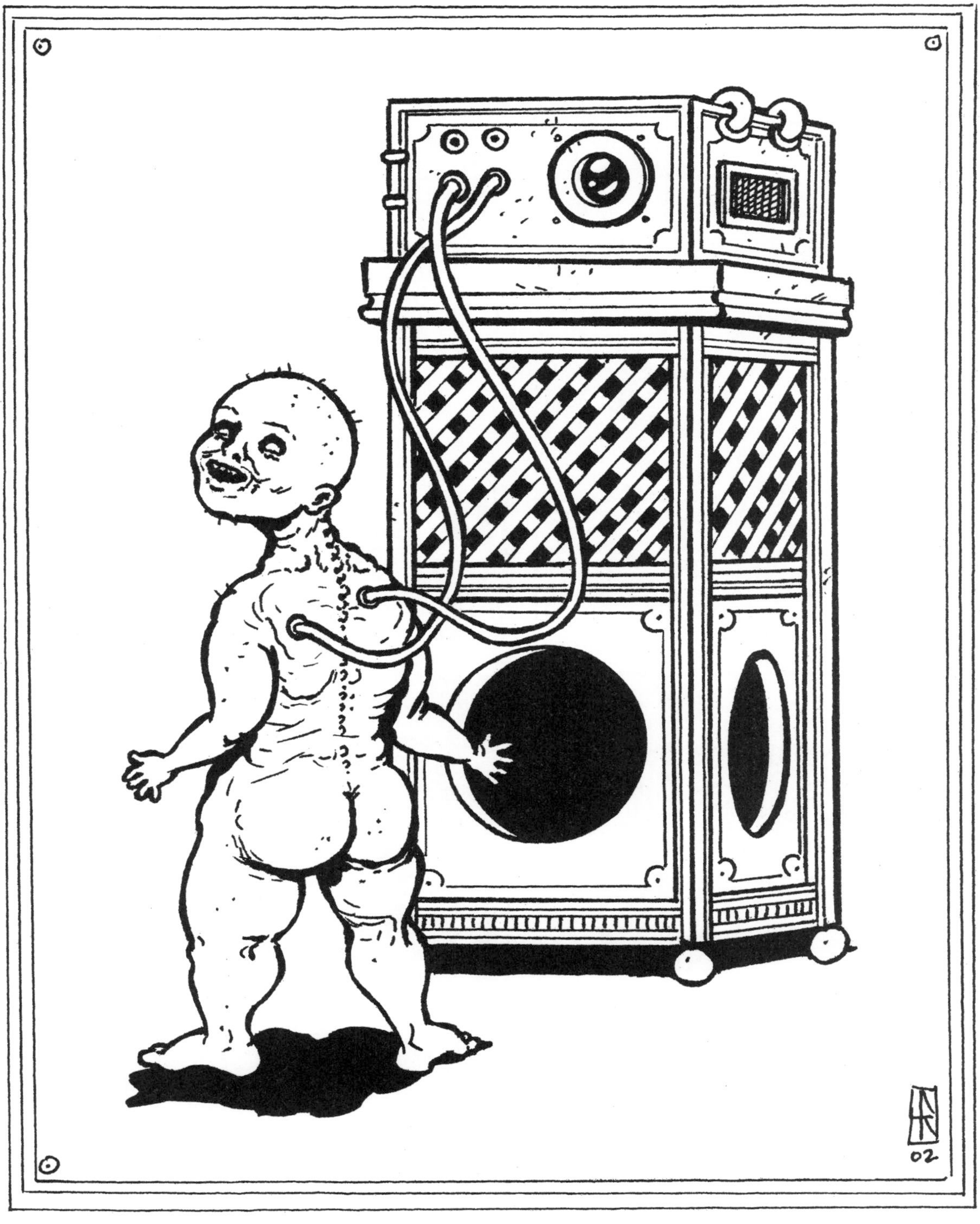

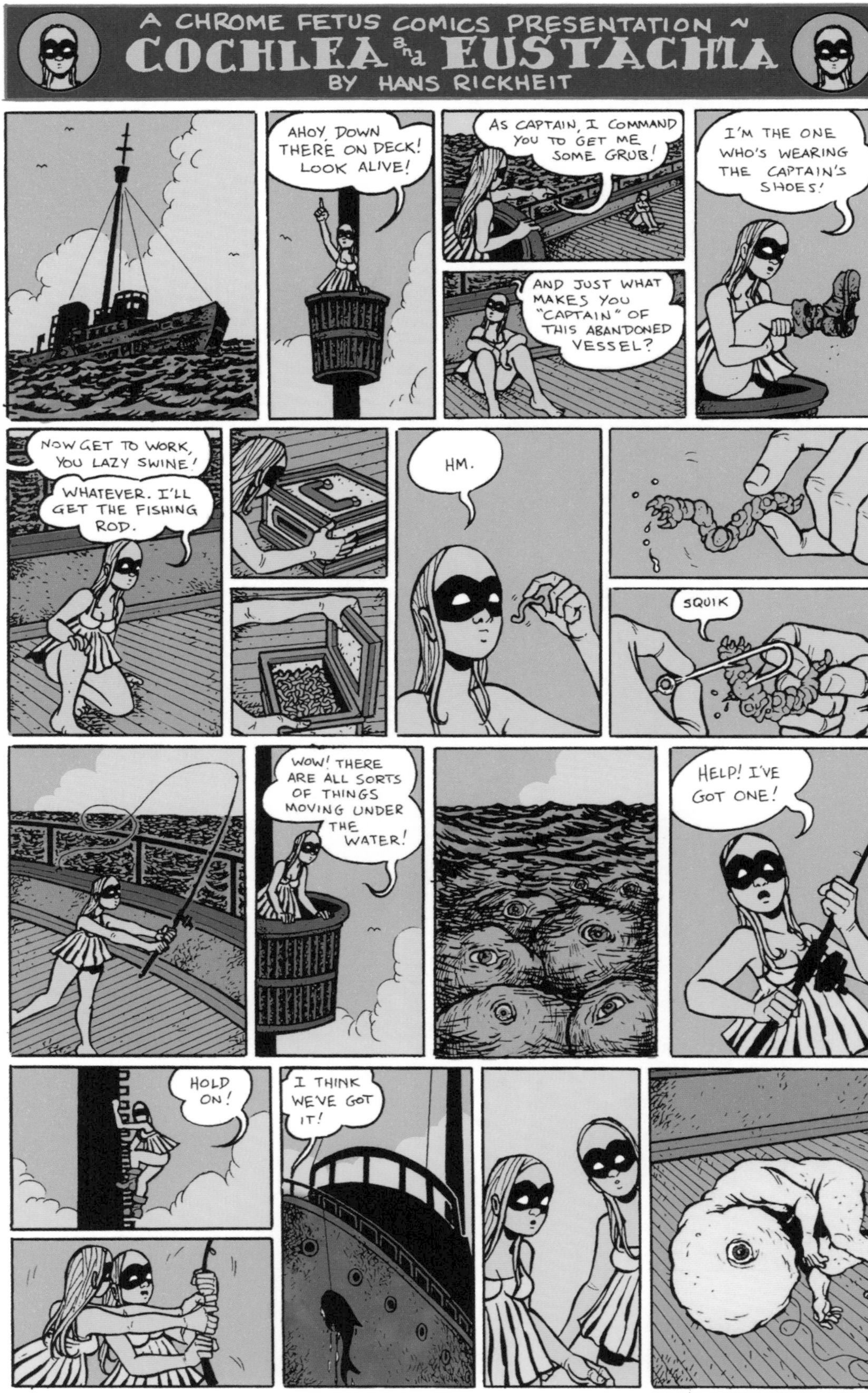
A CHROME FETUS COMICS PRESENTATION ~
COCHLEA and EUSTACHIA
BY HANS RICKHEIT
AHOY, DOWN THERE ON DECK! LOOK ALIVE!
AS CAPTAIN, I COMMAND YOU TO GET ME SOME GRUB!
AND JUST WHAT MAKES YOU "CAPTAIN" OF THIS ABANDONED VESSEL?
I'M THE ONE WHO'S WEARING THE CAPTAIN'S SHOES!
NOW GET TO WORK, YOU LAZY SWINE!
WHATEVER. I'LL GET THE FISHING ROD.
HM.
SQUIK
WOW! THERE ARE ALL SORTS OF THINGS MOVING UNDER THE WATER!
HELP! I'VE GOT ONE!
HOLD ON!
I THINK WE'VE GOT IT!

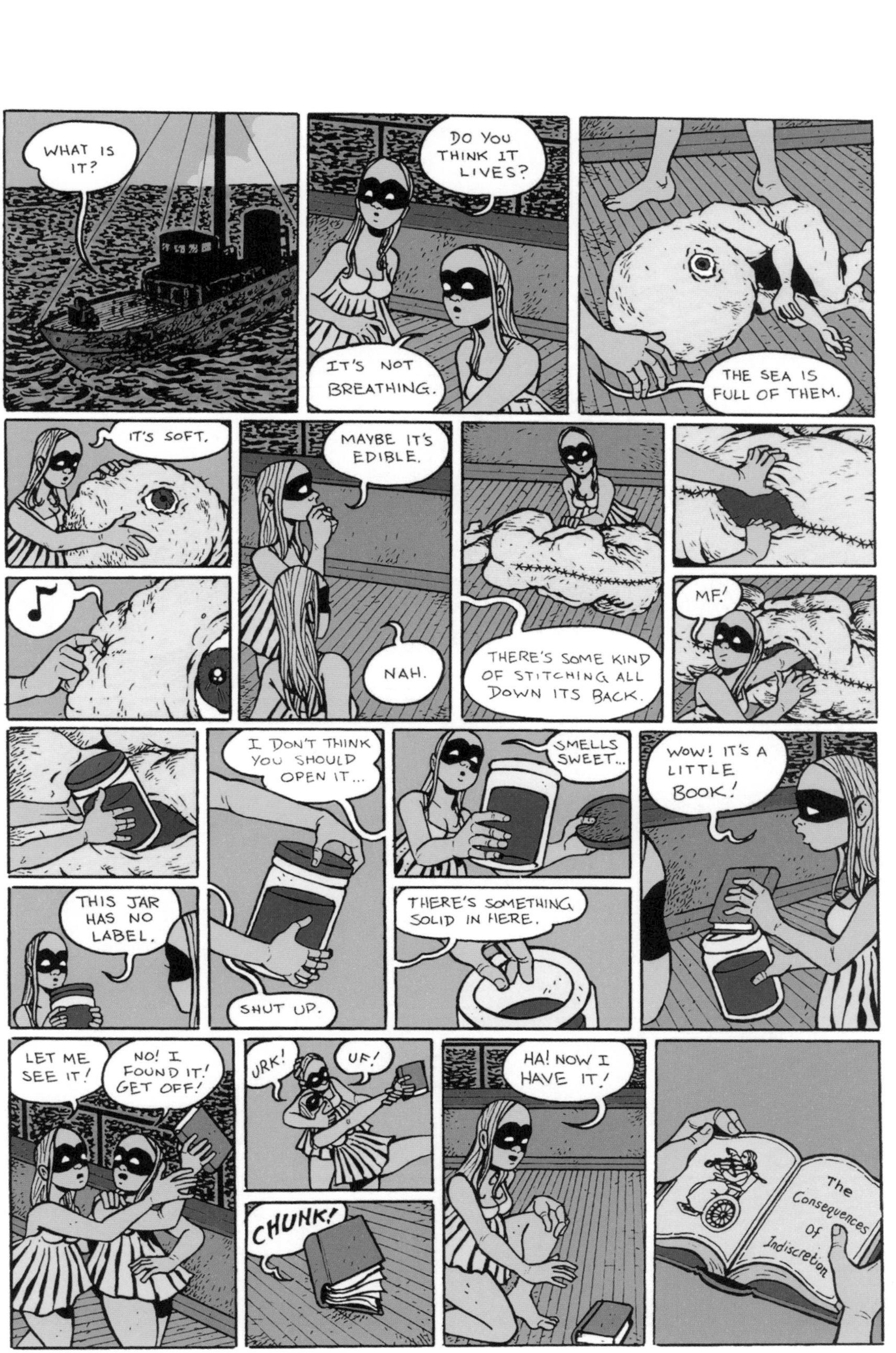
WHAT IS IT?
DO YOU THINK IT LIVES?
IT'S NOT BREATHING.
THE SEA IS FULL OF THEM.
IT'S SOFT.
MAYBE IT'S EDIBLE.
NAH.
THERE'S SOME KIND OF STITCHING ALL DOWN ITS BACK.
MF!
I DON'T THINK YOU SHOULD OPEN IT...
SHUT UP.
SMELLS SWEET...
WOW! IT'S A LITTLE BOOK!
THIS JAR HAS NO LABEL.
THERE'S SOMETHING SOLID IN HERE.
LET ME SEE IT!
NO! I FOUND IT! GET OFF!
URK!
UF!
CHUNK!
HA! NOW I HAVE IT!
The Consequences Of Indiscretion

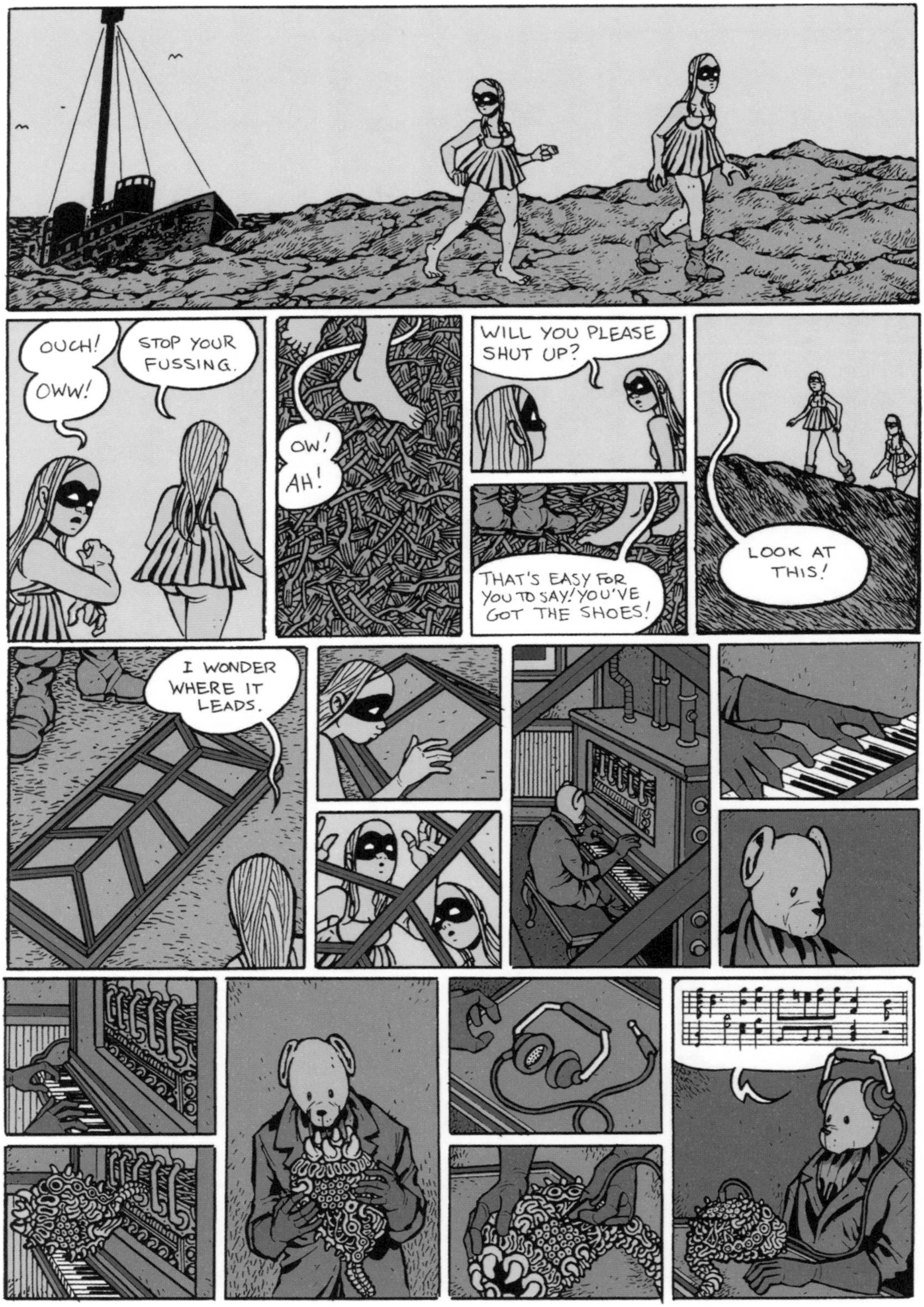
OUCH!
OWW!
STOP YOUR FUSSING.
OW!
AH!
WILL YOU PLEASE SHUT UP?
THAT'S EASY FOR YOU TO SAY! YOU'VE GOT THE SHOES!
LOOK AT THIS!
I WONDER WHERE IT LEADS.

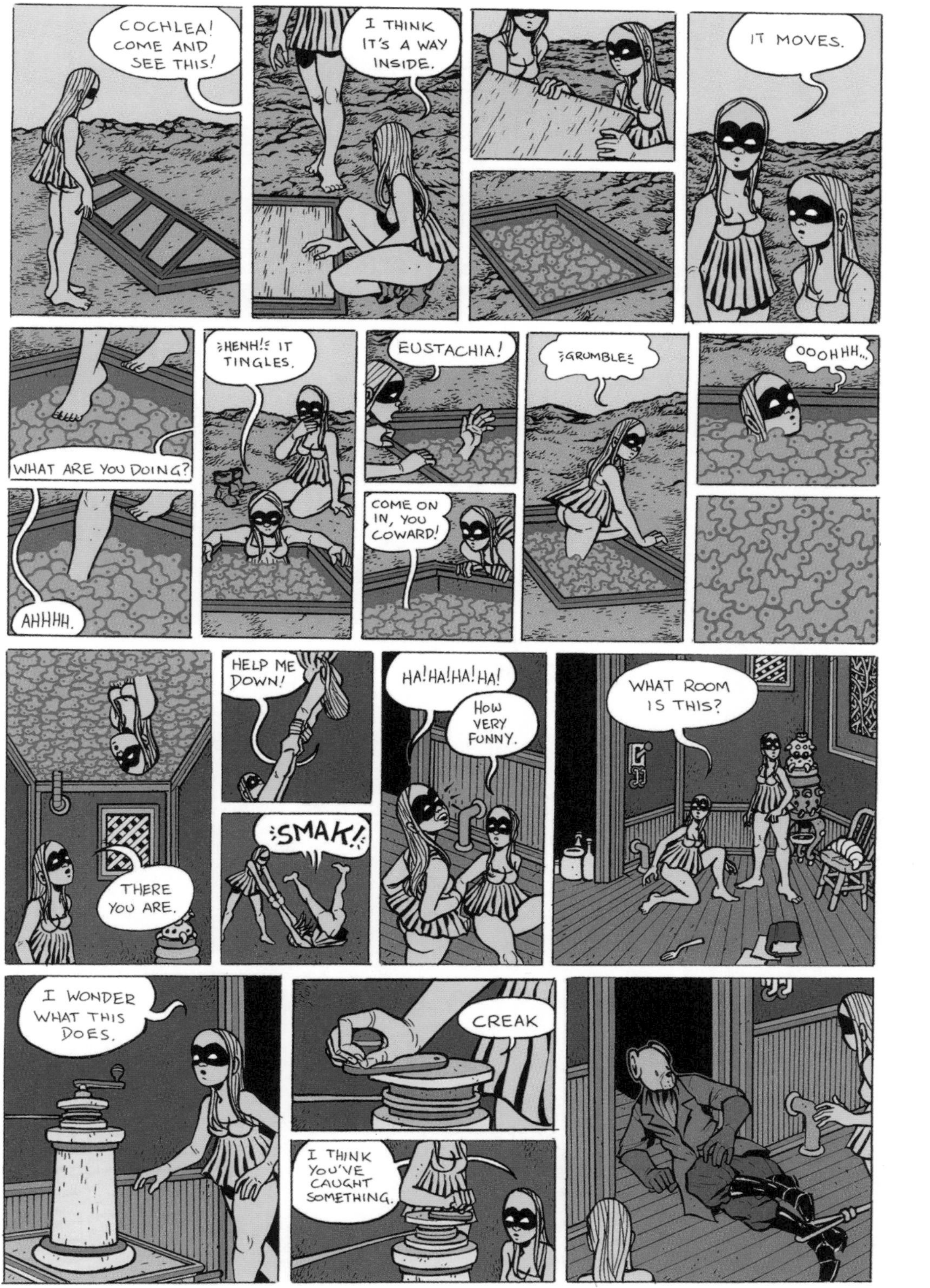

COCHLEA! COME AND SEE THIS!
I THINK IT'S A WAY INSIDE.
IT MOVES.
WHAT ARE YOU DOING?
AHHHH.
HENH! IT TINGLES.
EUSTACHIA!
COME ON IN, YOU COWARD!
GRUMBLE
OOOHHH...
HELP ME DOWN!
THERE YOU ARE.
SMAK!
HA! HA! HA! HA!
HOW VERY FUNNY.
WHAT ROOM IS THIS?
I WONDER WHAT THIS DOES.
CREAK
I THINK YOU'VE CAUGHT SOMETHING.

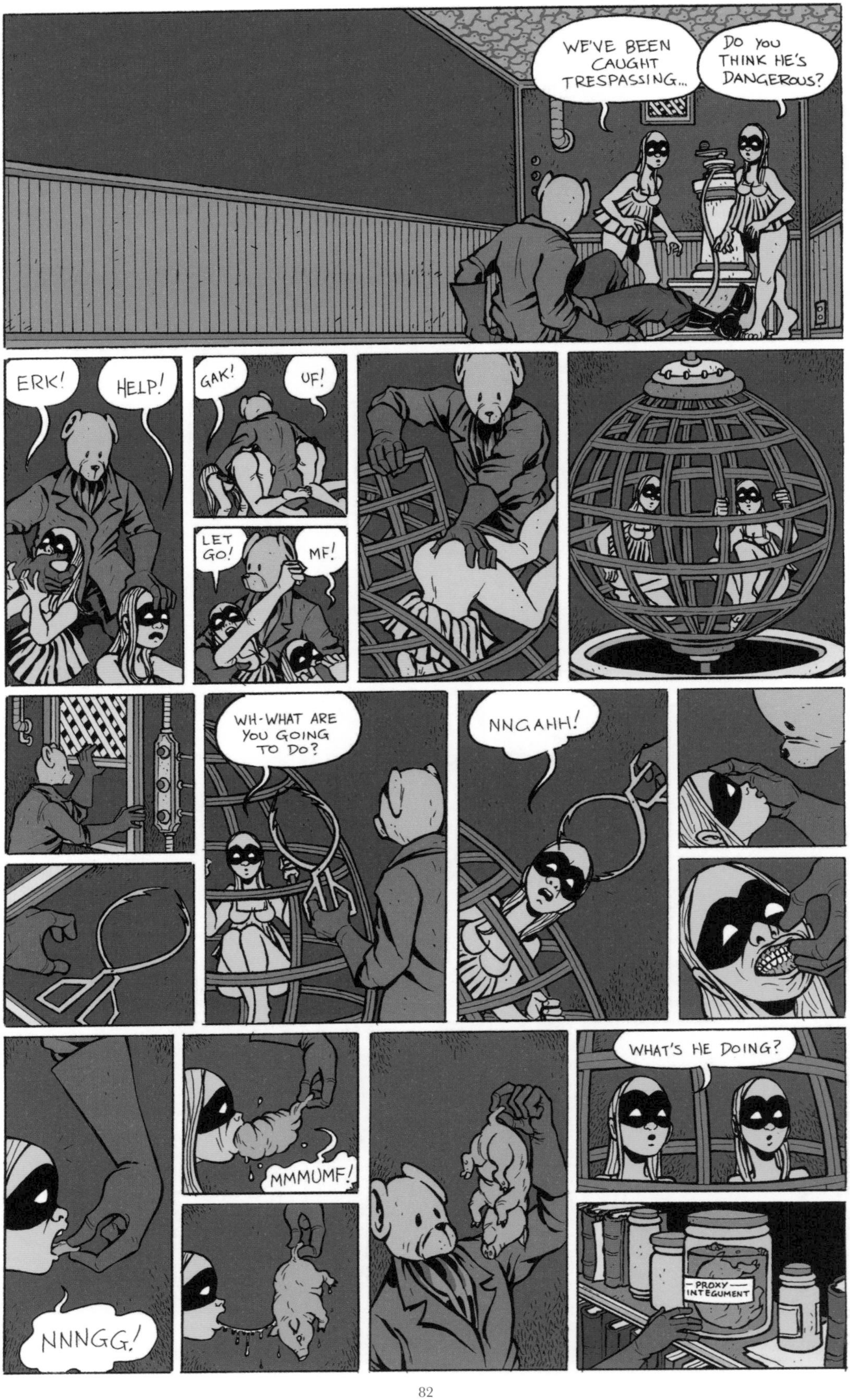
WE'VE BEEN CAUGHT TRESPASSING...
DO YOU THINK HE'S DANGEROUS?
ERK!
HELP!
GAK!
UF!
LET GO!
MF!
WH-WHAT ARE YOU GOING TO DO?
NNGAHH!
MMMUMF!
NNNGG!
WHAT'S HE DOING?
PROXY INTEGUMENT

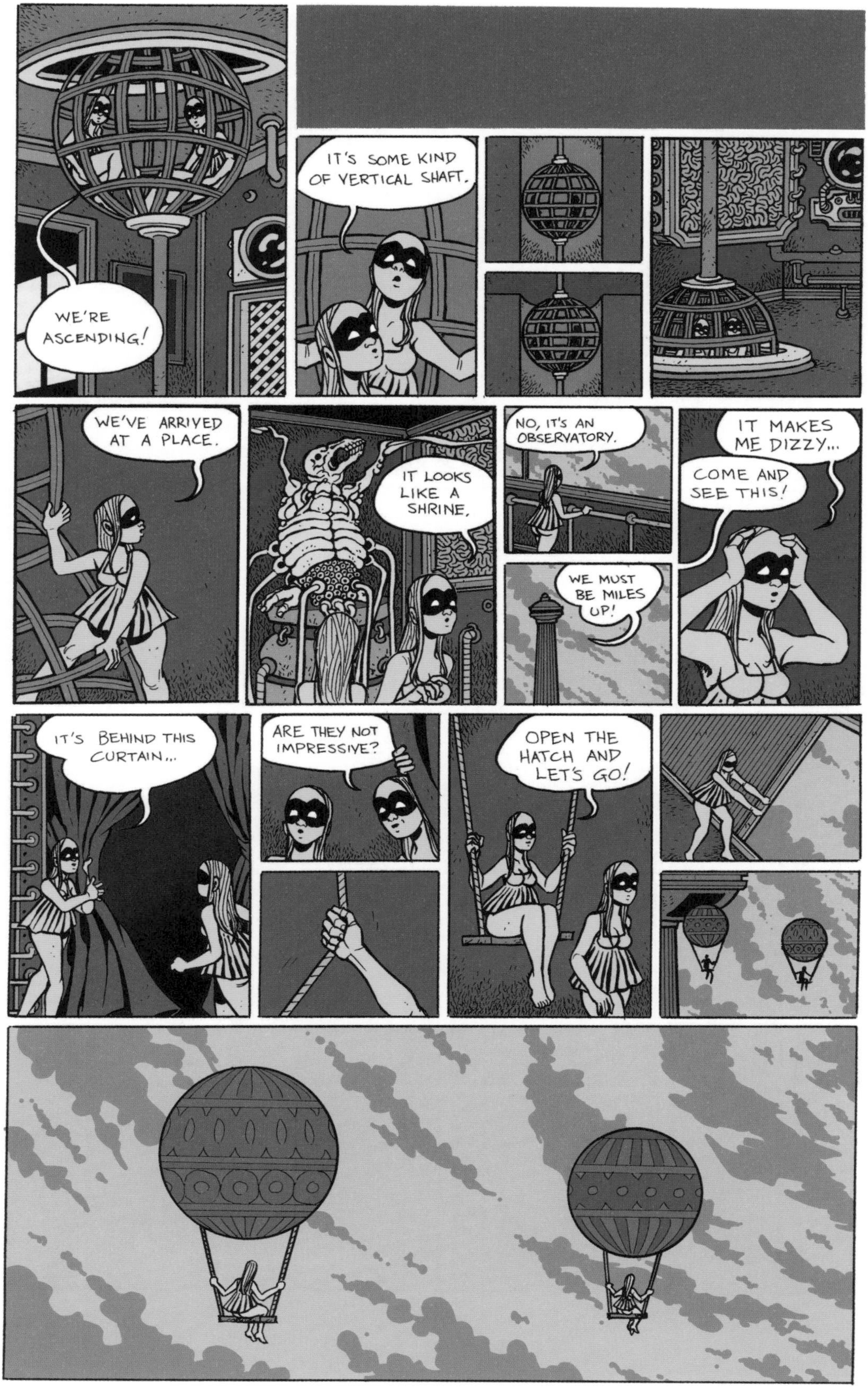
WE'RE ASCENDING!
IT'S SOME KIND OF VERTICAL SHAFT.
WE'VE ARRIVED AT A PLACE.
IT LOOKS LIKE A SHRINE.
NO, IT'S AN OBSERVATORY.
WE MUST BE MILES UP!
IT MAKES ME DIZZY...
COME AND SEE THIS!
IT'S BEHIND THIS CURTAIN...
ARE THEY NOT IMPRESSIVE?
OPEN THE HATCH AND LET'S GO!

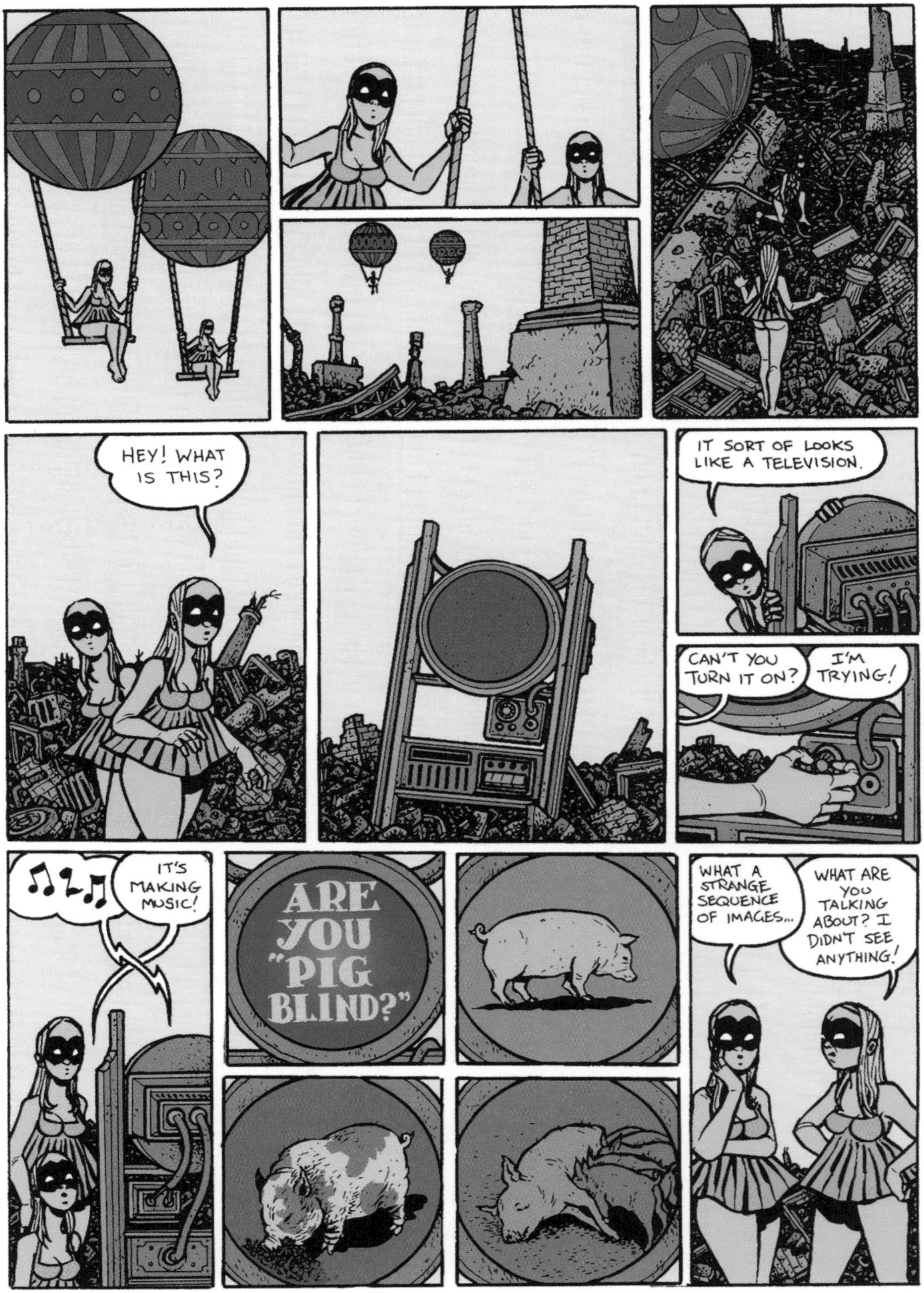
HEY! WHAT IS THIS?
IT SORT OF LOOKS LIKE A TELEVISION.
CAN'T YOU TURN IT ON?
I'M TRYING!
IT'S MAKING MUSIC!
ARE YOU "PIG BLIND?"
WHAT A STRANGE SEQUENCE OF IMAGES...
WHAT ARE YOU TALKING ABOUT? I DIDN'T SEE ANYTHING!

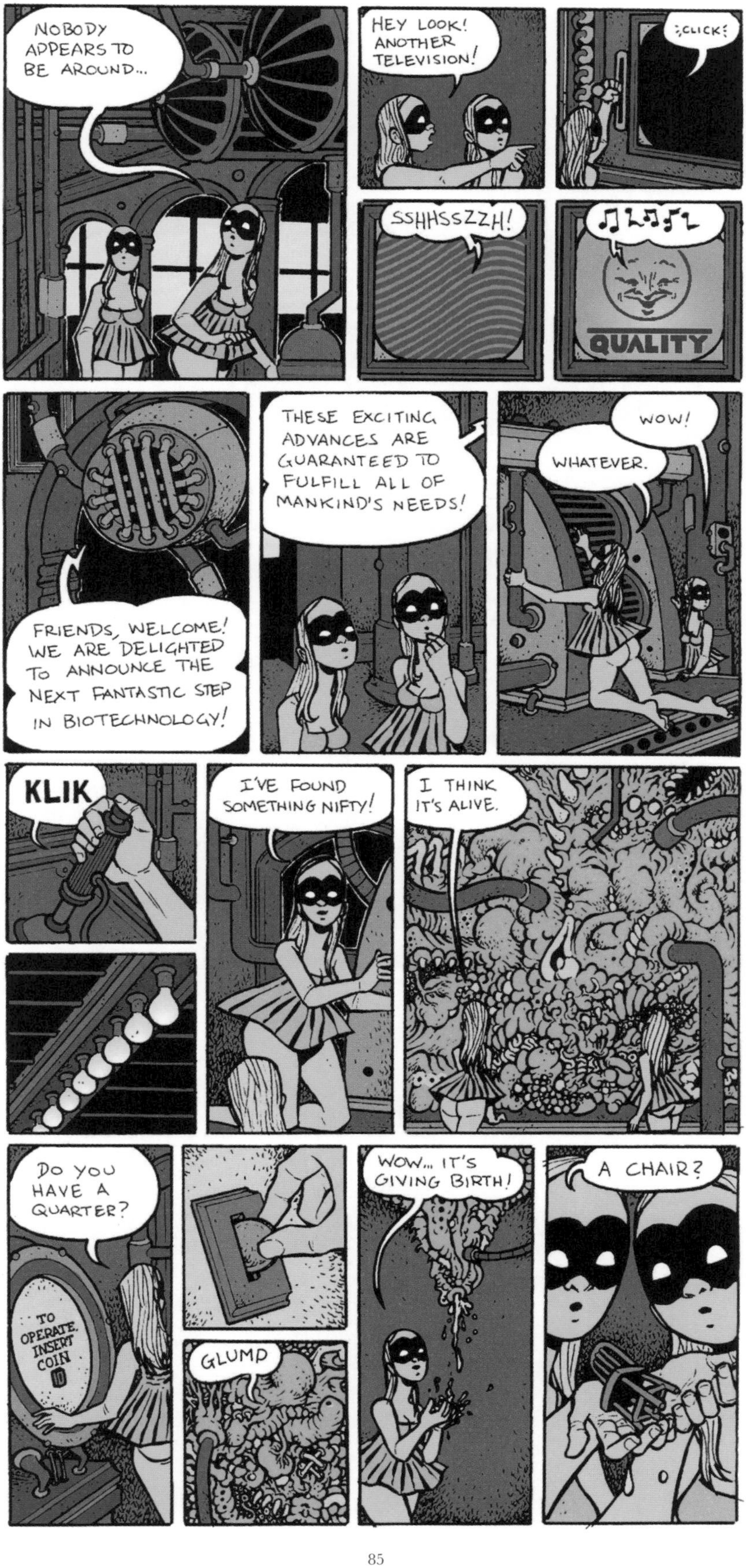
NOBODY APPEARS TO BE AROUND...
HEY LOOK! ANOTHER TELEVISION!
CLICK
SSHHSSZZH!
QUALITY
FRIENDS, WELCOME! WE ARE DELIGHTED TO ANNOUNCE THE NEXT FANTASTIC STEP IN BIOTECHNOLOGY!
THESE EXCITING ADVANCES ARE GUARANTEED TO FULFILL ALL OF MANKIND'S NEEDS!
WOW!
WHATEVER.
KLIK
I'VE FOUND SOMETHING NIFTY!
I THINK IT'S ALIVE.
DO YOU HAVE A QUARTER?
TO OPERATE, INSERT COIN
GLUMP
WOW... IT'S GIVING BIRTH!
A CHAIR?

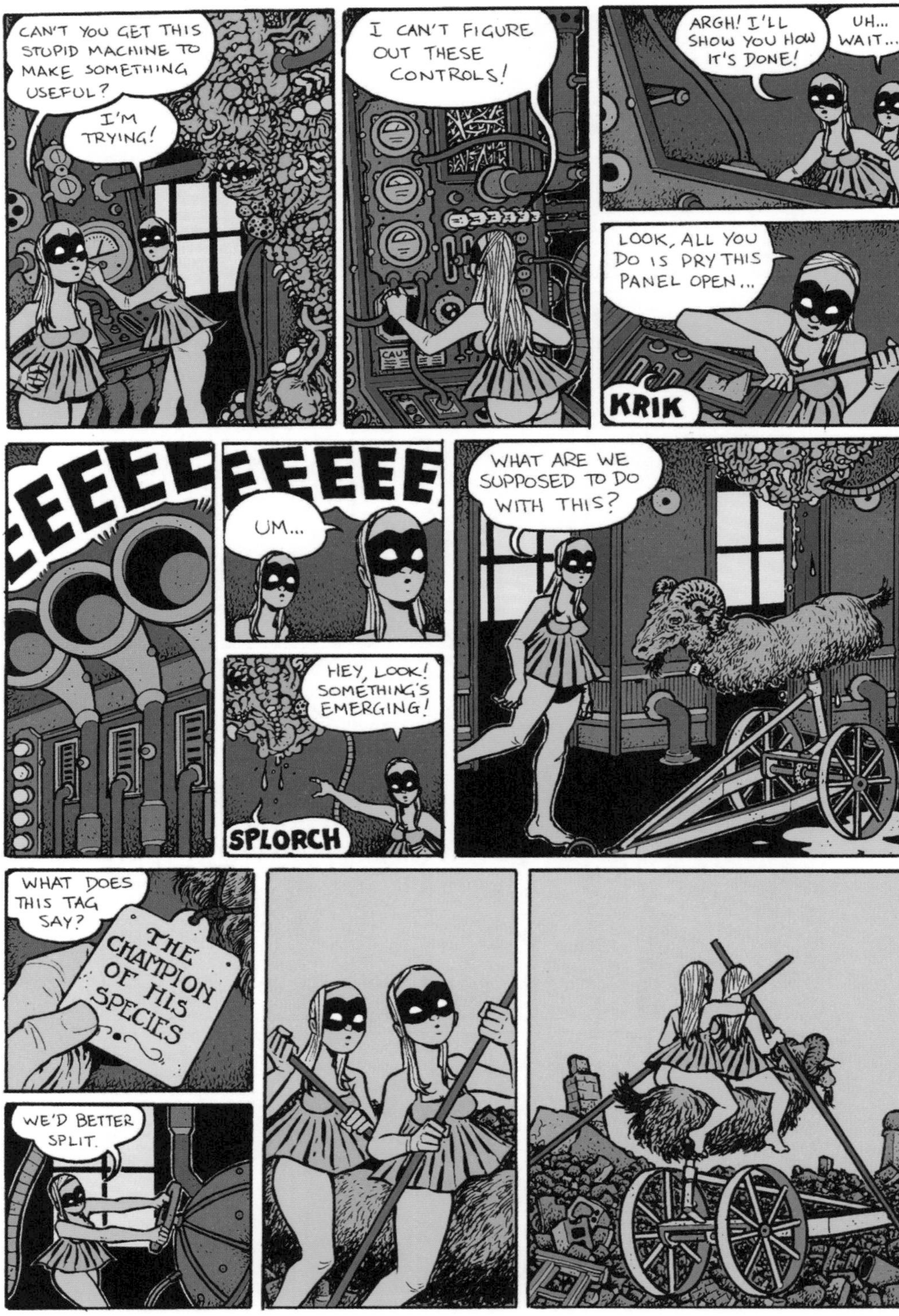
CAN'T YOU GET THIS STUPID MACHINE TO MAKE SOMETHING USEFUL?
I'M TRYING!
I CAN'T FIGURE OUT THESE CONTROLS!
ARGH! I'LL SHOW YOU HOW IT'S DONE!
UH... WAIT...
LOOK, ALL YOU DO IS PRY THIS PANEL OPEN...
KRIK
EEEEEEEEEEE
UM...
HEY, LOOK! SOMETHING'S EMERGING!
SPLORCH
WHAT ARE WE SUPPOSED TO DO WITH THIS?
WHAT DOES THIS TAG SAY?
THE CHAMPION OF HIS SPECIES
WE'D BETTER SPLIT.

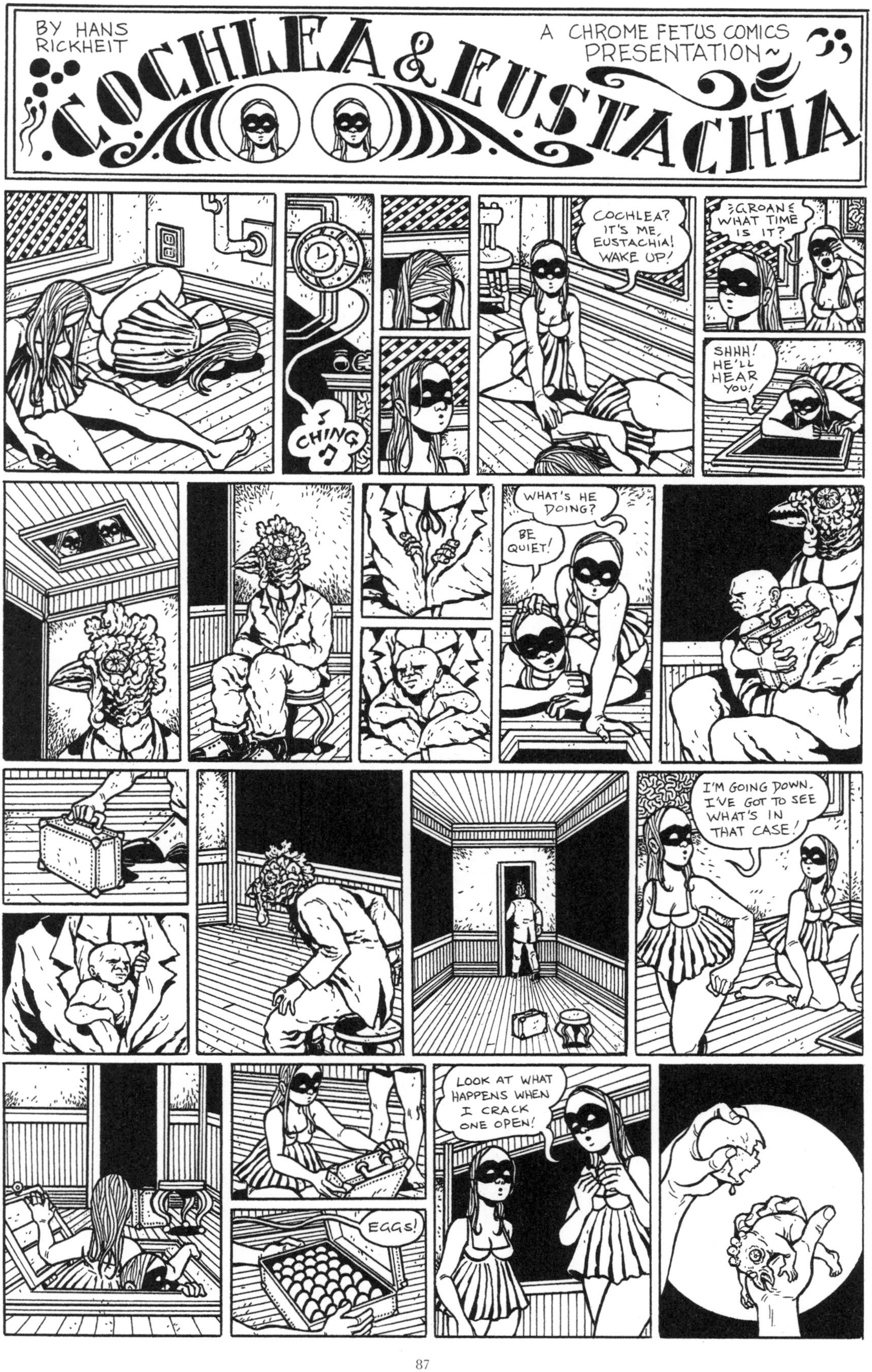
BY HANS RICKHEIT
A CHROME FETUS COMICS PRESENTATION~
COCHLEA & EUSTACHIA
CHING
COCHLEA? IT'S ME, EUSTACHIA! WAKE UP!
GROAN WHAT TIME IS IT?
SHHH! HE'LL HEAR YOU!
WHAT'S HE DOING?
BE QUIET!
I'M GOING DOWN. I'VE GOT TO SEE WHAT'S IN THAT CASE!
LOOK AT WHAT HAPPENS WHEN I CRACK ONE OPEN!
EGGS!

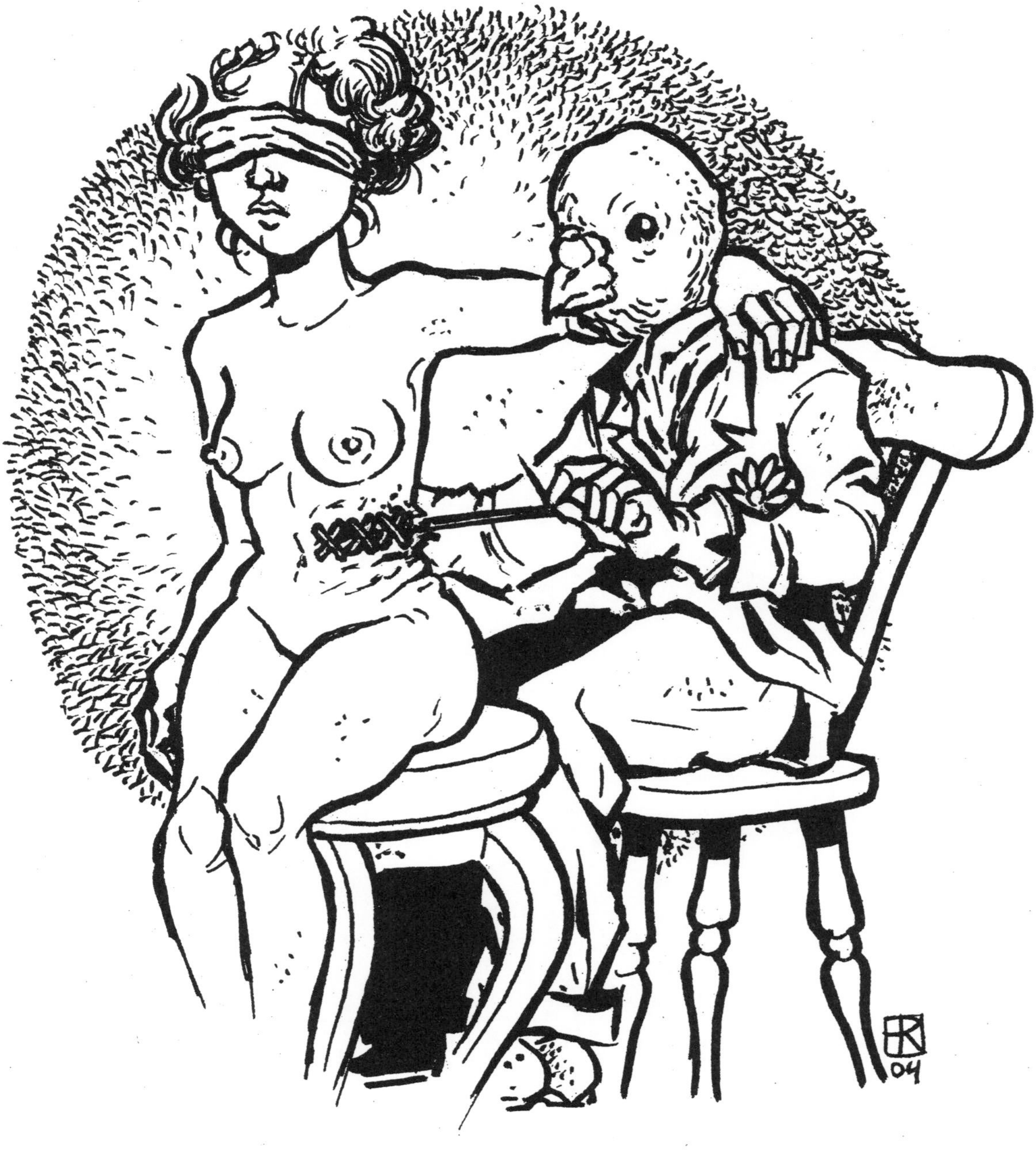

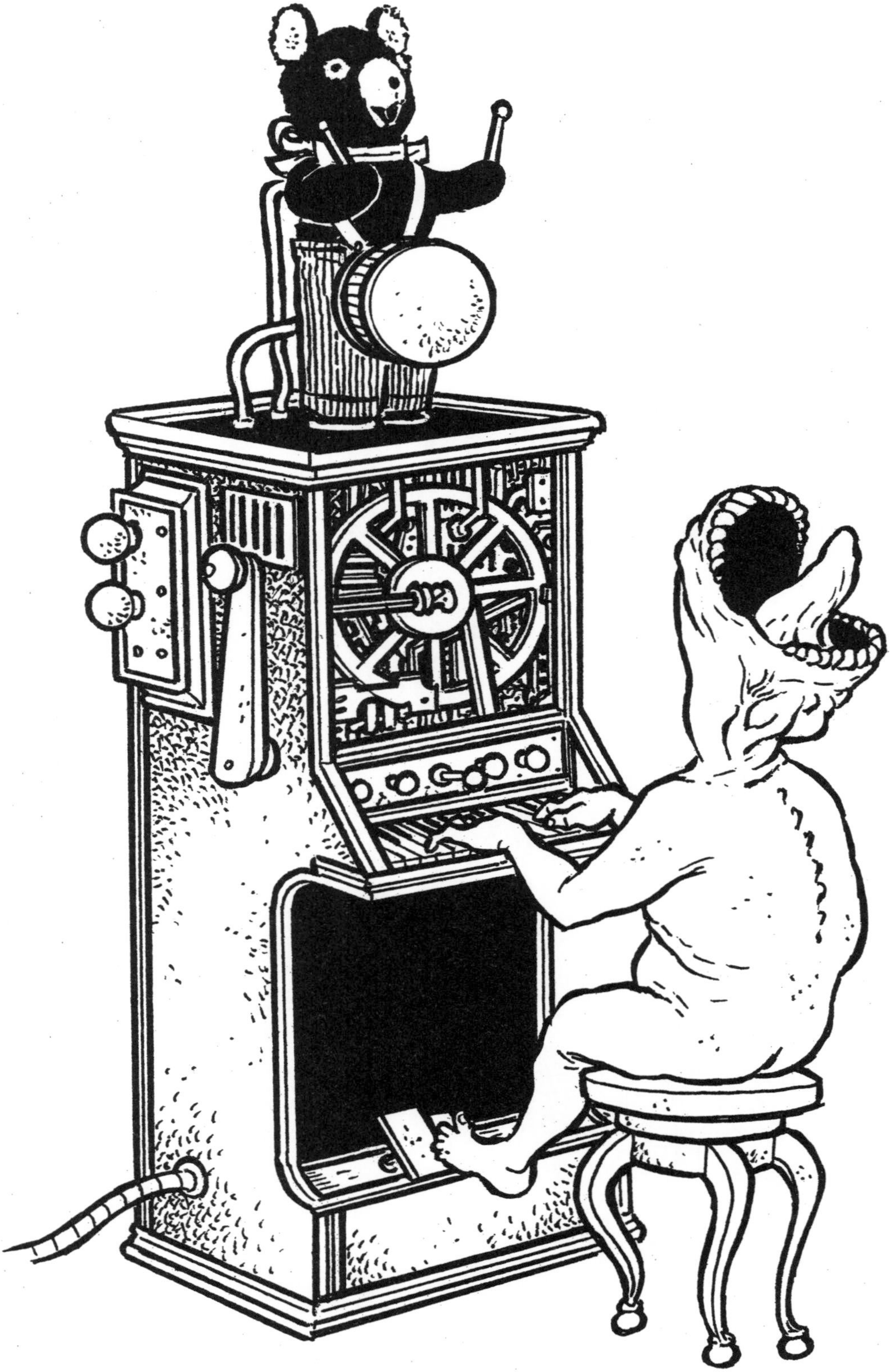

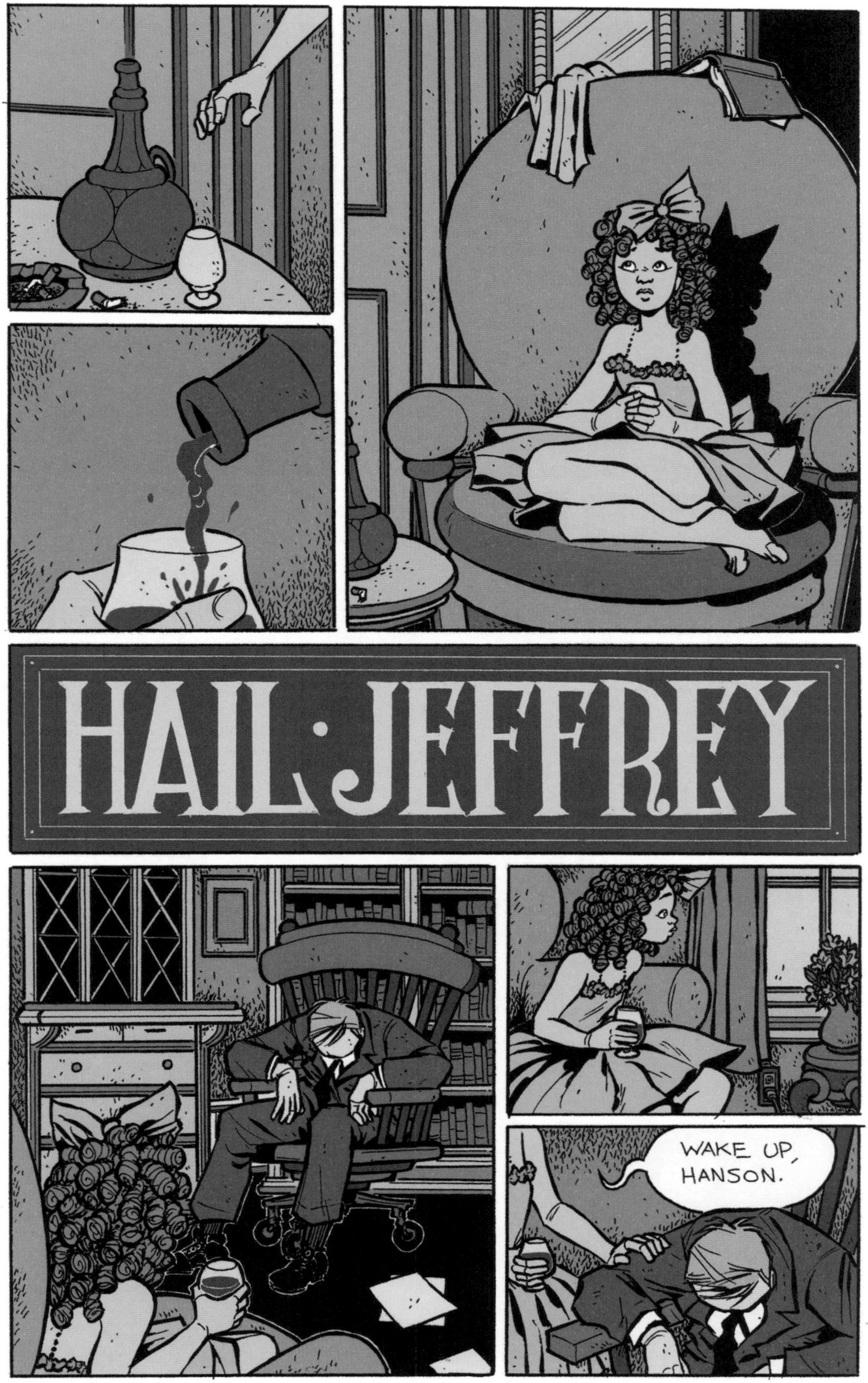
HAIL · JEFFREY
WAKE UP, HANSON.

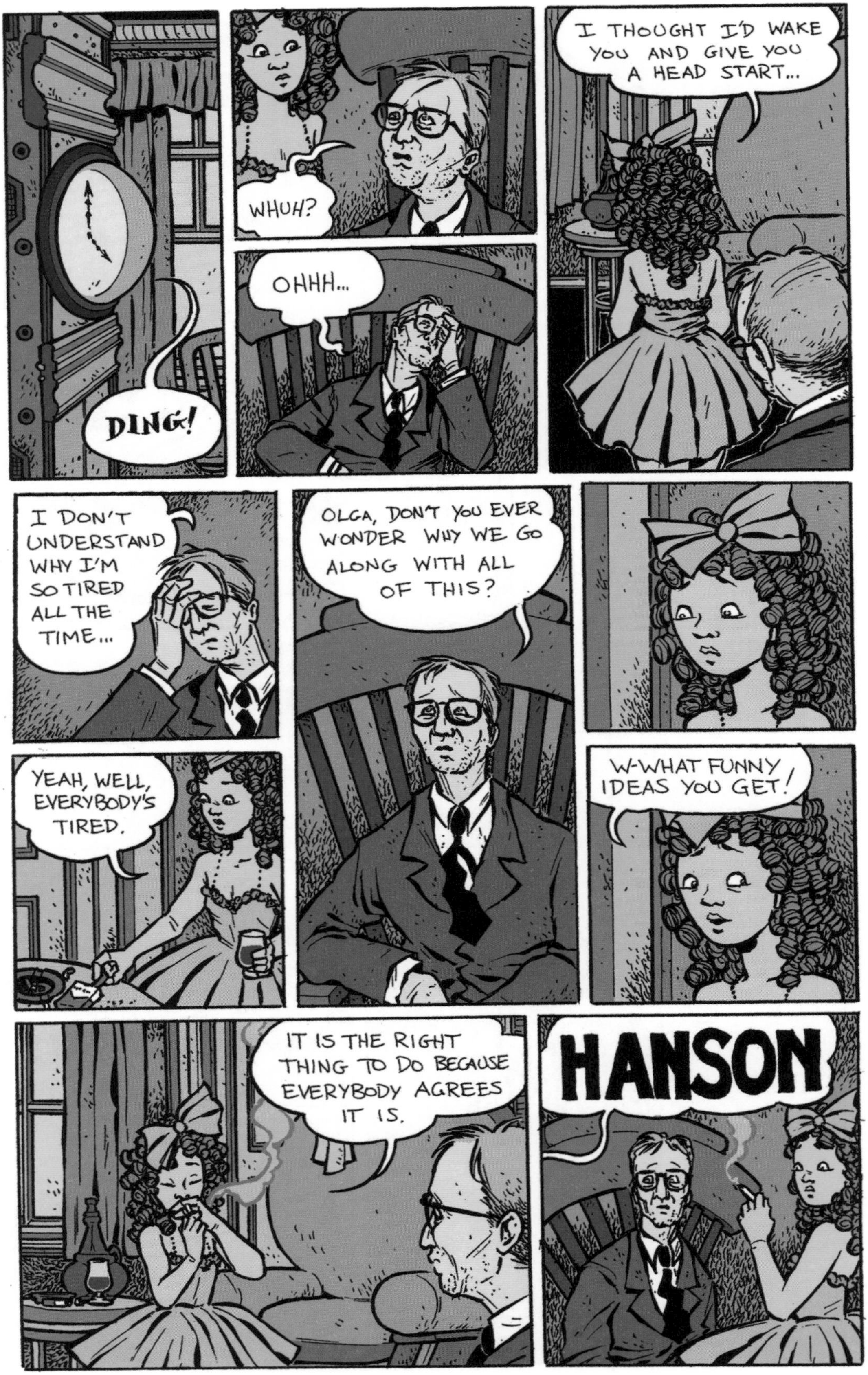
DING!
WHUH?
OHHH...
I THOUGHT I'D WAKE YOU AND GIVE YOU A HEAD START...
I DON'T UNDERSTAND WHY I'M SO TIRED ALL THE TIME...
OLGA, DON'T YOU EVER WONDER WHY WE GO ALONG WITH ALL OF THIS?
YEAH, WELL, EVERYBODY'S TIRED.
W-WHAT FUNNY IDEAS YOU GET!
IT IS THE RIGHT THING TO DO BECAUSE EVERYBODY AGREES IT IS.
HANSON

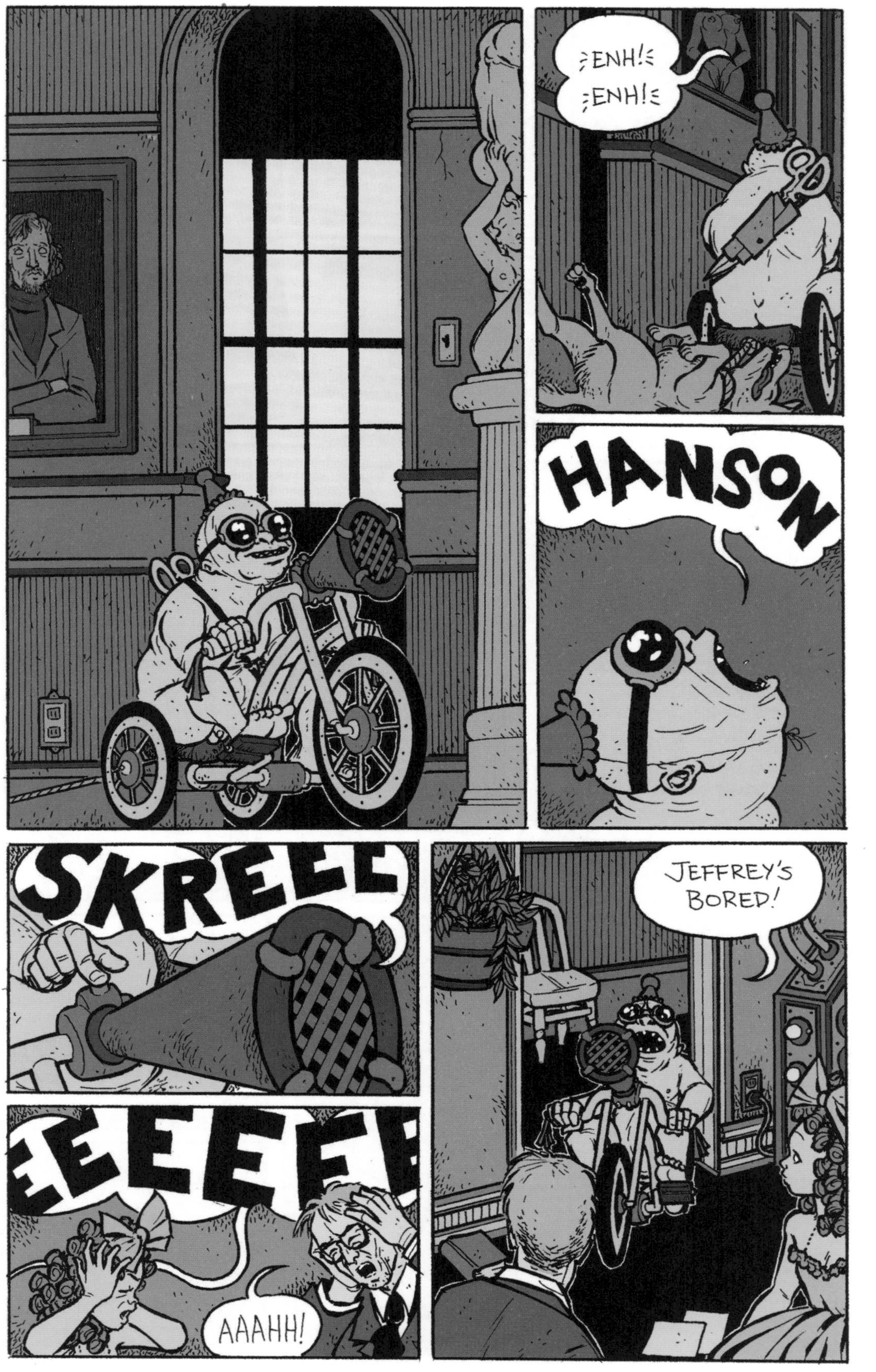
ENH! ENH!
HANSON
SKREEE
EEEEEE
AAAHH!
JEFFREY'S BORED!

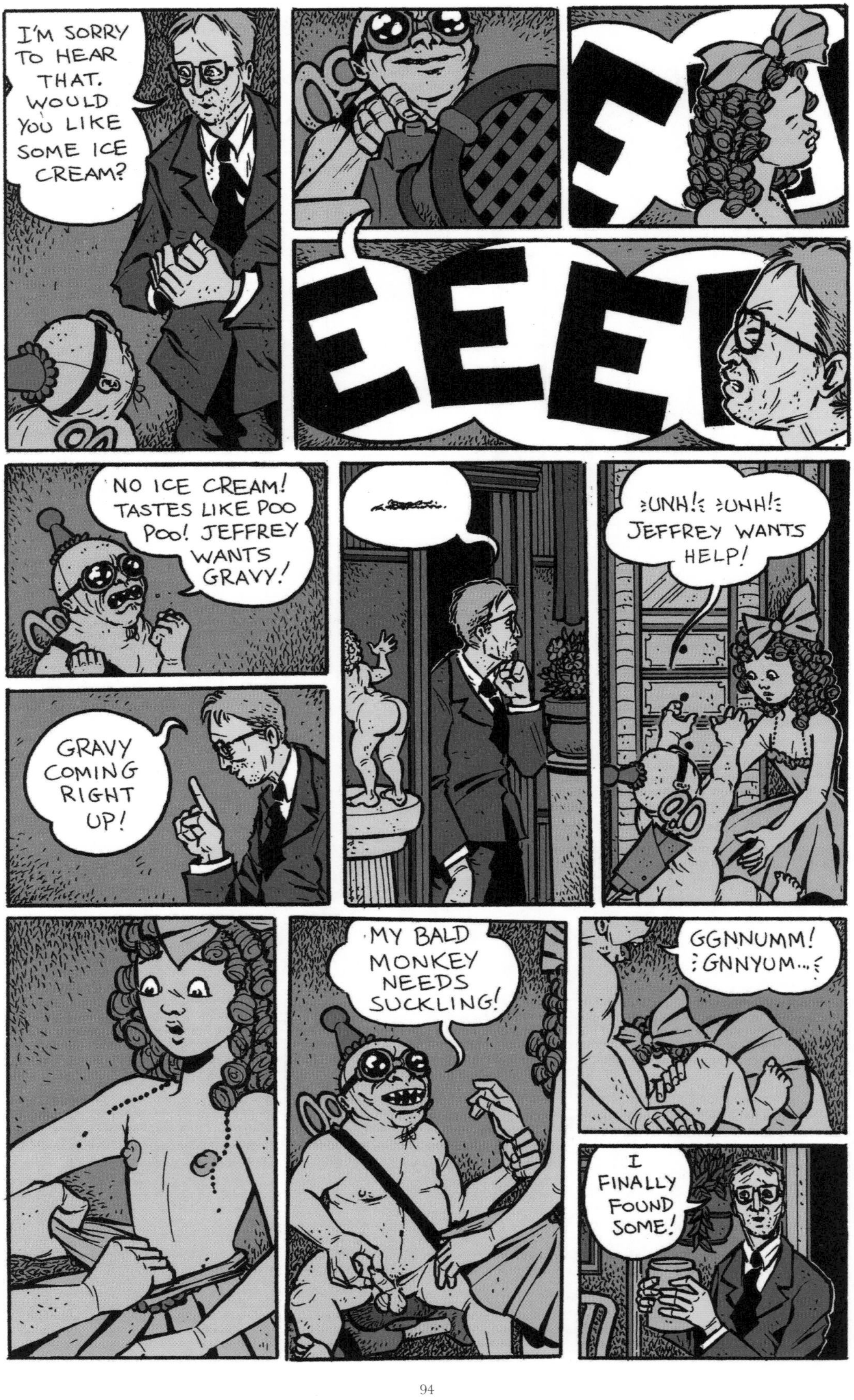
I'M SORRY TO HEAR THAT. WOULD YOU LIKE SOME ICE CREAM?
EEE
NO ICE CREAM! TASTES LIKE POO POO! JEFFREY WANTS GRAVY!
GRAVY COMING RIGHT UP!
UNH! UNH! JEFFREY WANTS HELP!
MY BALD MONKEY NEEDS SUCKLING!
GGNNUMM! GNNYUM...
I FINALLY FOUND SOME!

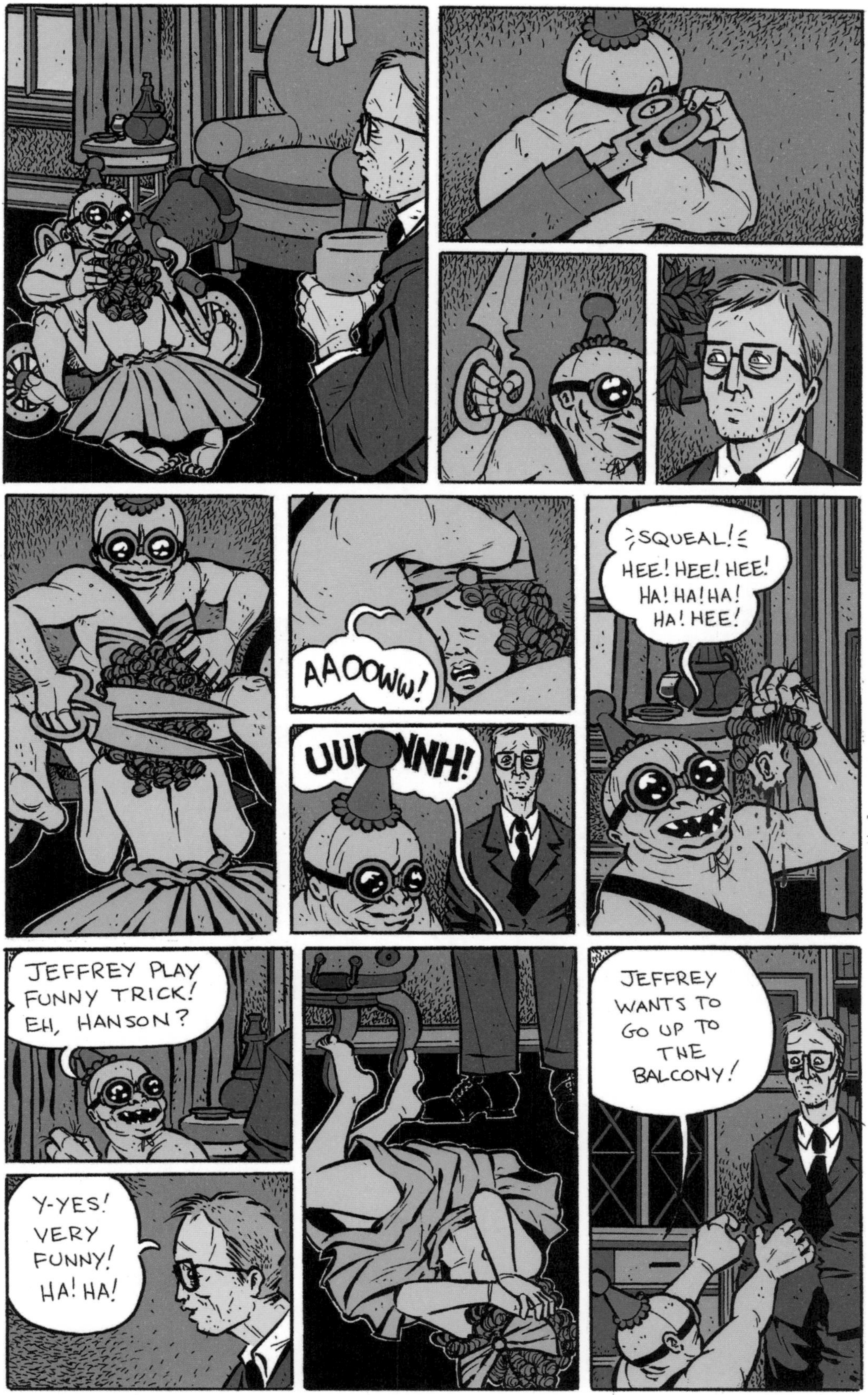
SQUEAL!
HEE! HEE! HEE! HA! HA! HA! HA! HEE!
AAOOWW!
UU NNH!
JEFFREY PLAY FUNNY TRICK! EH, HANSON?
Y-YES! VERY FUNNY! HA! HA!
JEFFREY WANTS TO GO UP TO THE BALCONY!

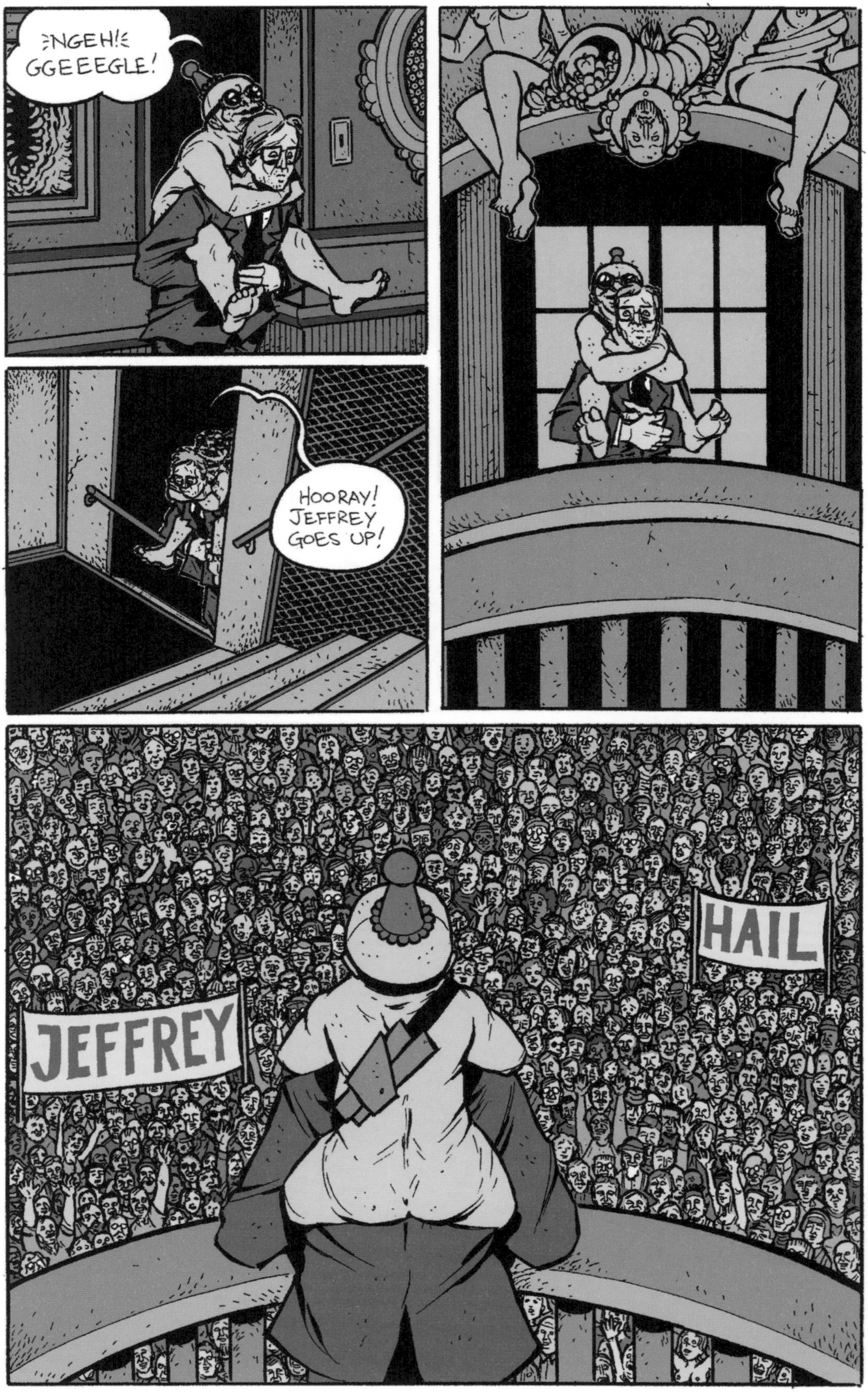

NGEH! GGEEEGLE!
HOORAY! JEFFREY GOES UP!
HAIL
JEFFREY

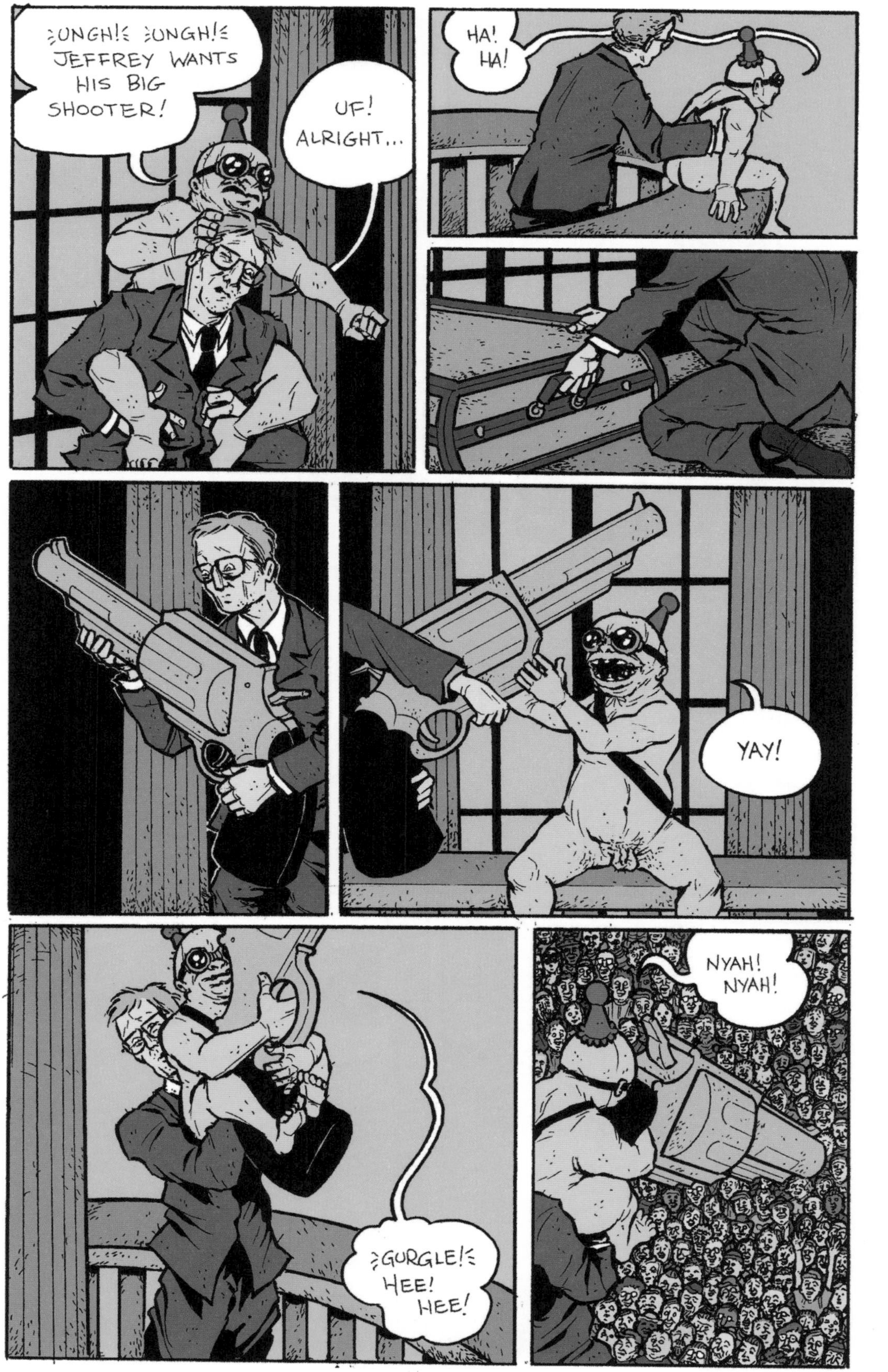

UNGH! UNGH! JEFFREY WANTS HIS BIG SHOOTER!
UF! ALRIGHT...
HA! HA!
YAY!
GURGLE! HEE! HEE!
NYAH! NYAH!

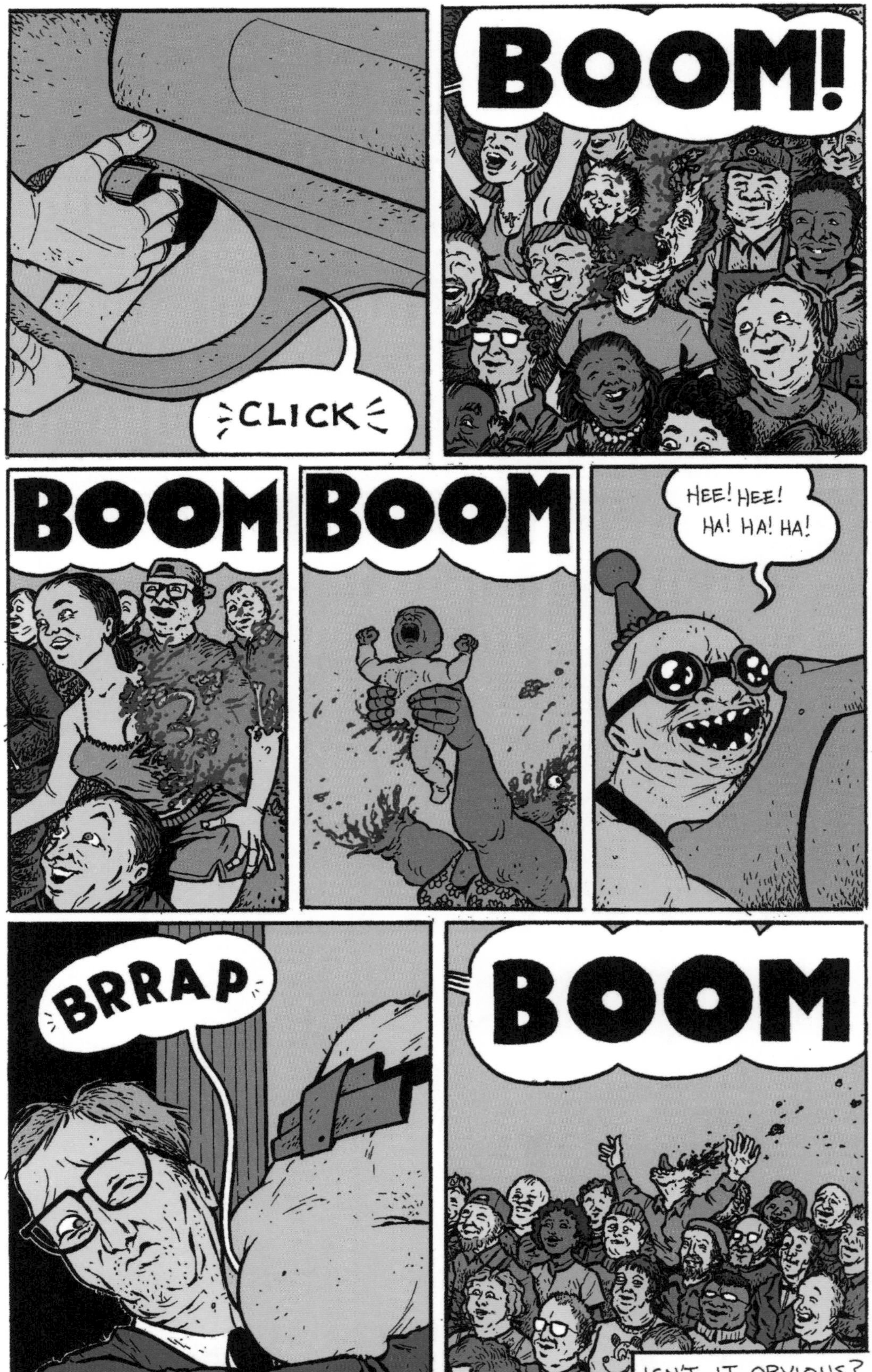
CLICK
BOOM!
BOOM
BOOM
HEE! HEE! HA! HA! HA!
BRRAP
BOOM
ISN'T IT OBVIOUS?

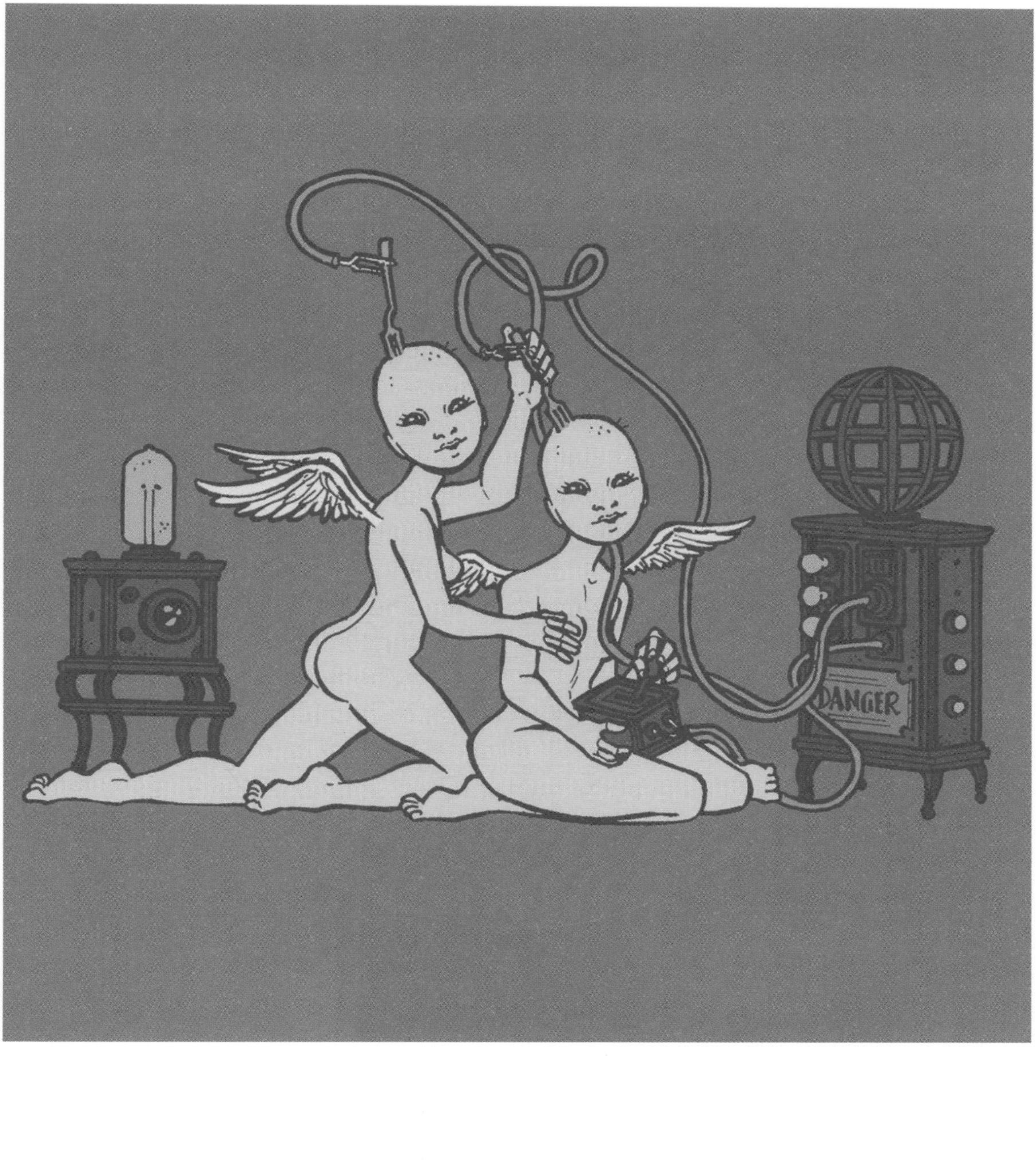
DANGER

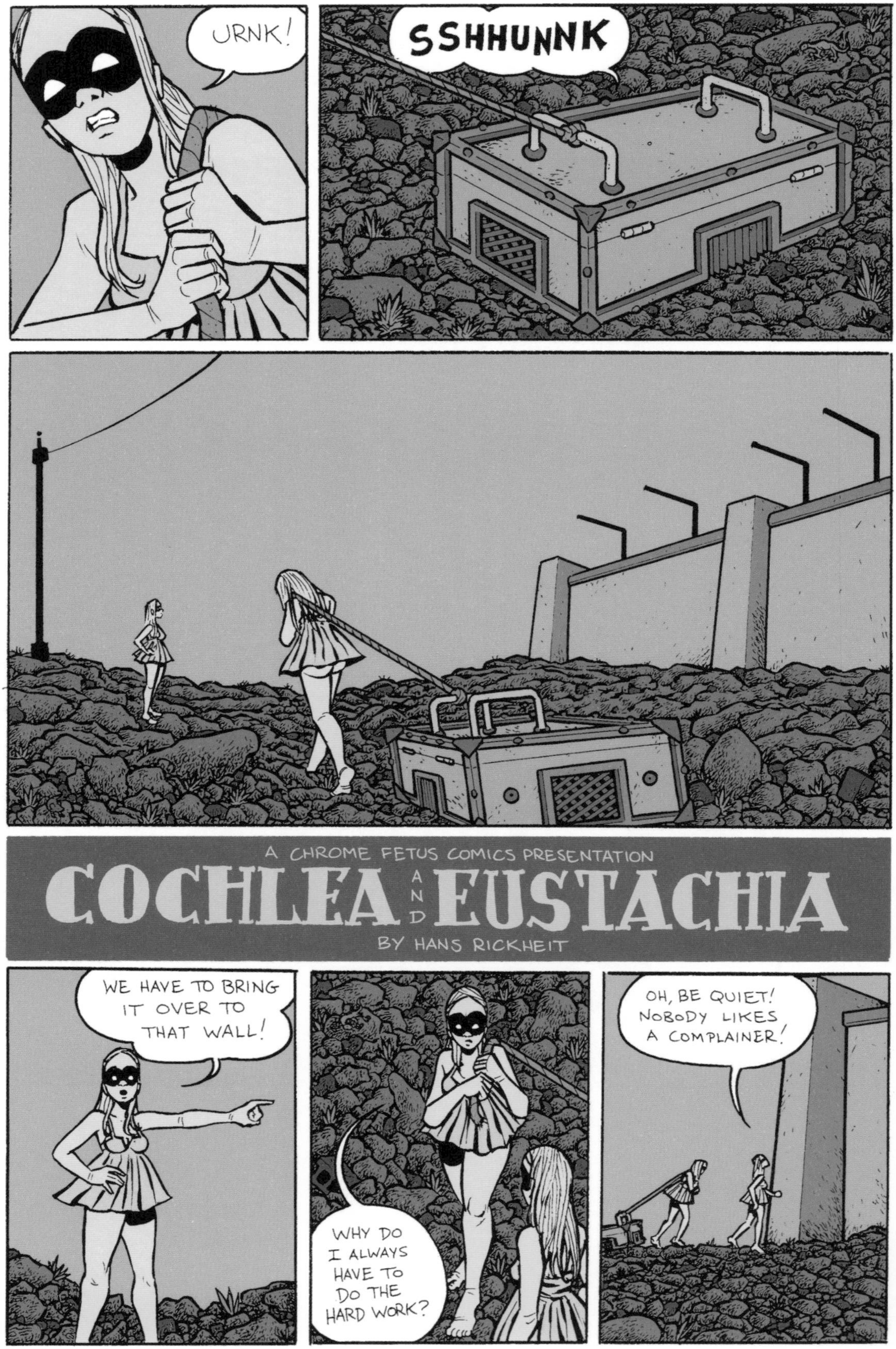
URNK!
SSHHUNNK
A CHROME FETUS COMICS PRESENTATION
COCHLEA AND EUSTACHIA
BY HANS RICKHEIT
WE HAVE TO BRING IT OVER TO THAT WALL!
WHY DO I ALWAYS HAVE TO DO THE HARD WORK?
OH, BE QUIET! NOBODY LIKES A COMPLAINER!

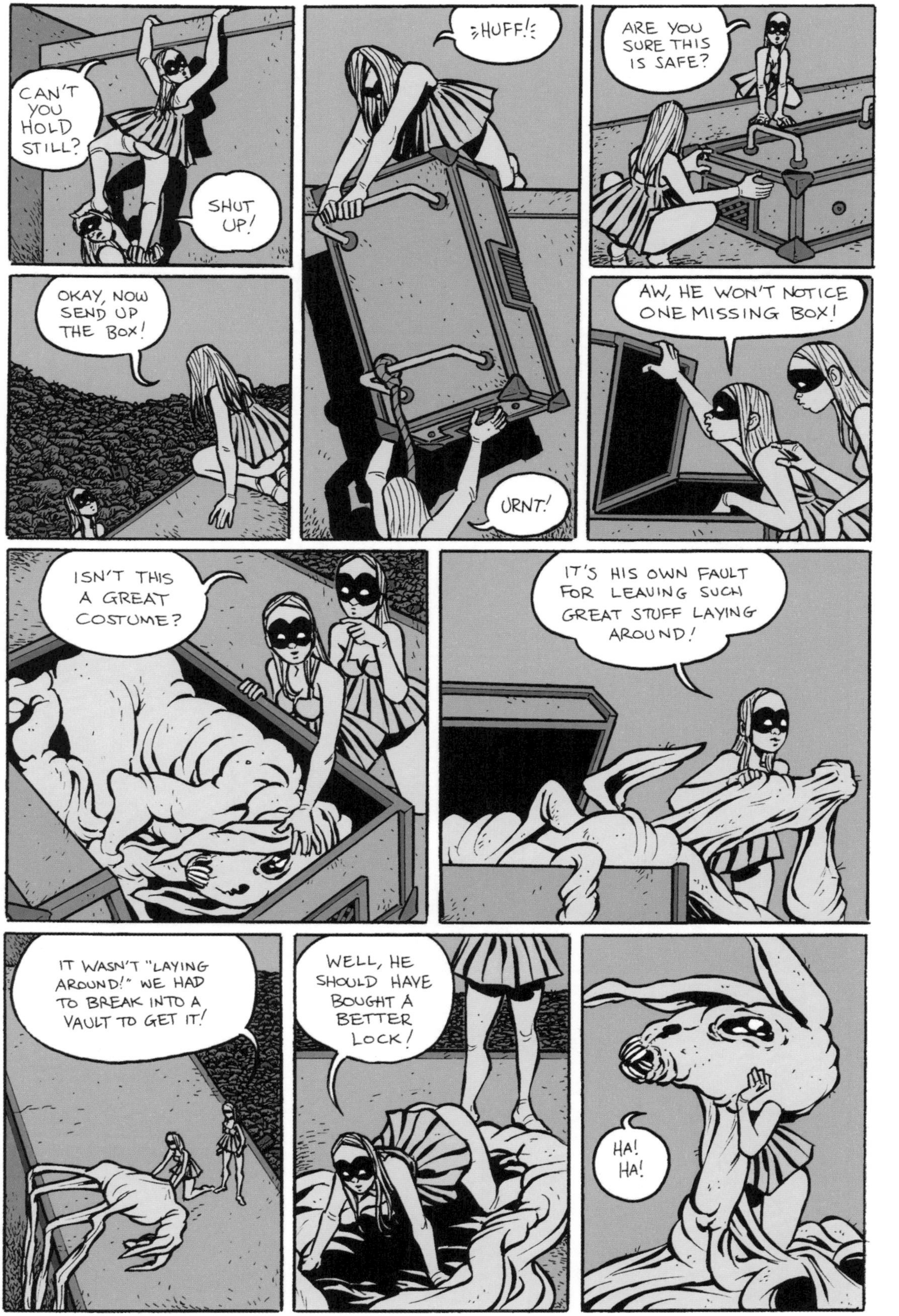
CAN'T YOU HOLD STILL?
SHUT UP!
HUFF!
ARE YOU SURE THIS IS SAFE?
OKAY, NOW SEND UP THE BOX!
URNT!
AW, HE WON'T NOTICE ONE MISSING BOX!
ISN'T THIS A GREAT COSTUME?
IT'S HIS OWN FAULT FOR LEAVING SUCH GREAT STUFF LAYING AROUND!
IT WASN'T "LAYING AROUND!" WE HAD TO BREAK INTO A VAULT TO GET IT!
WELL, HE SHOULD HAVE BOUGHT A BETTER LOCK!
HA! HA!

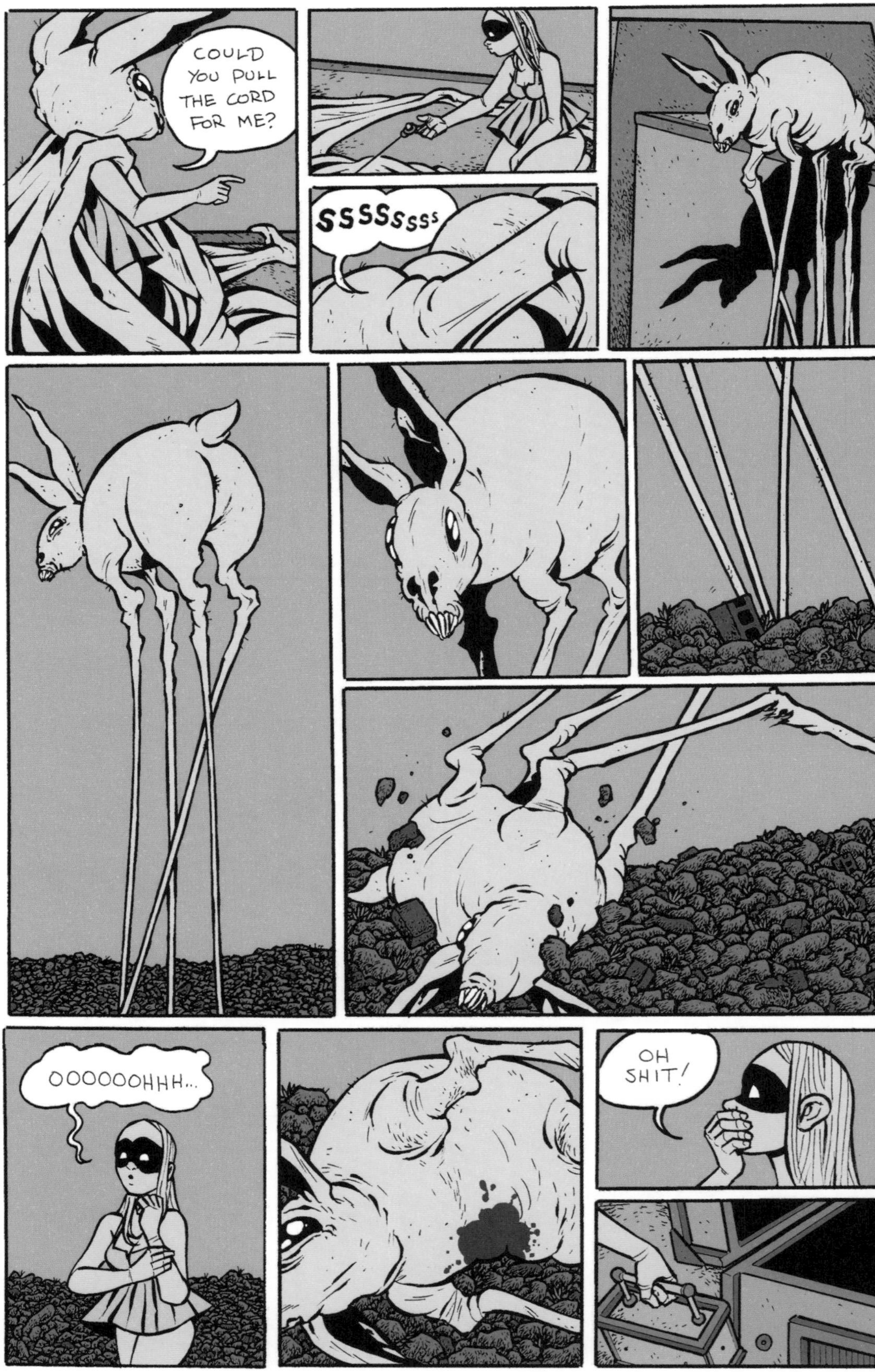
COULD YOU PULL THE CORD FOR ME?
SSSSSSSS
OOOOOOHHH...
OH SHIT!

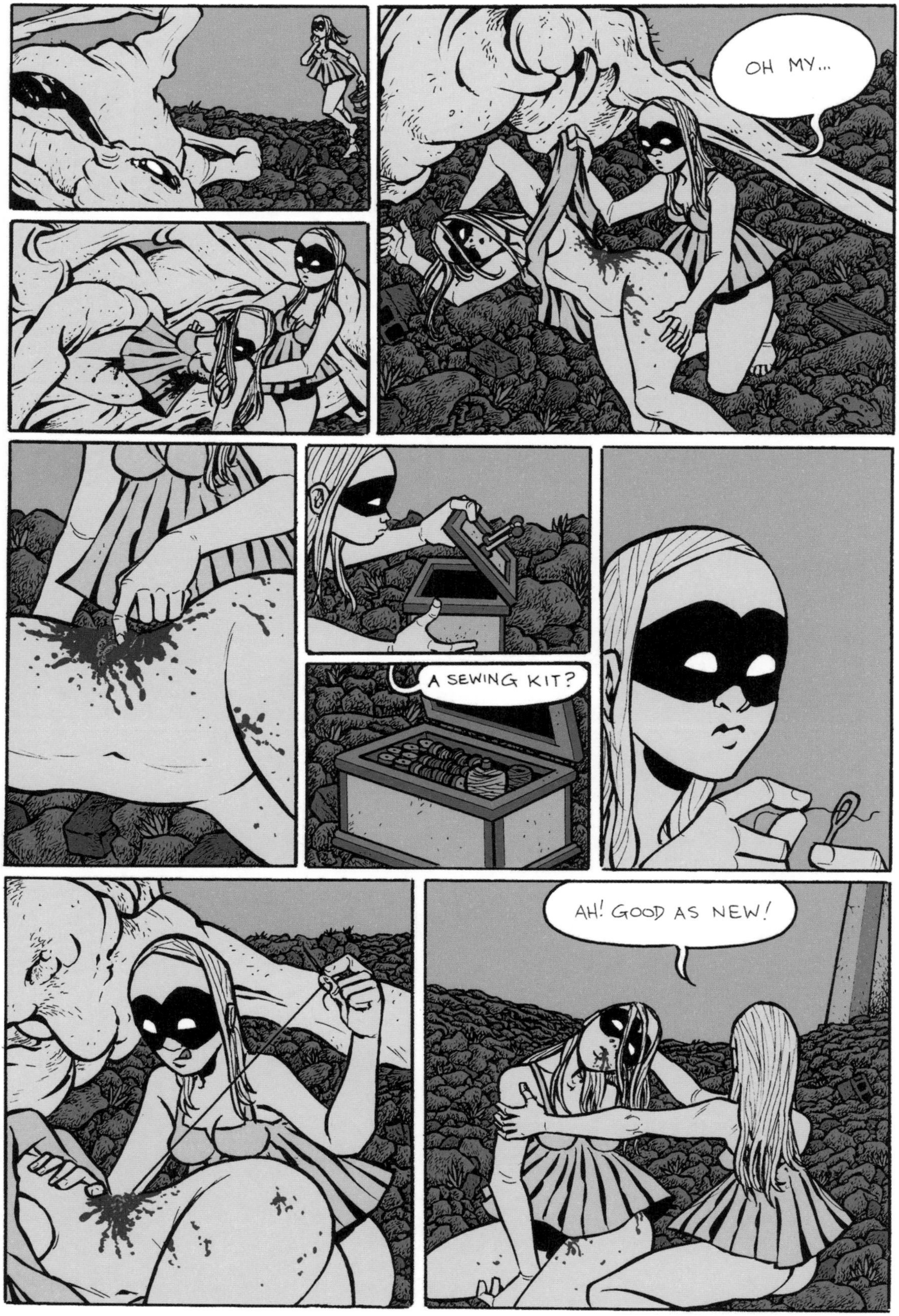
OH MY...
A SEWING KIT?
AH! GOOD AS NEW!

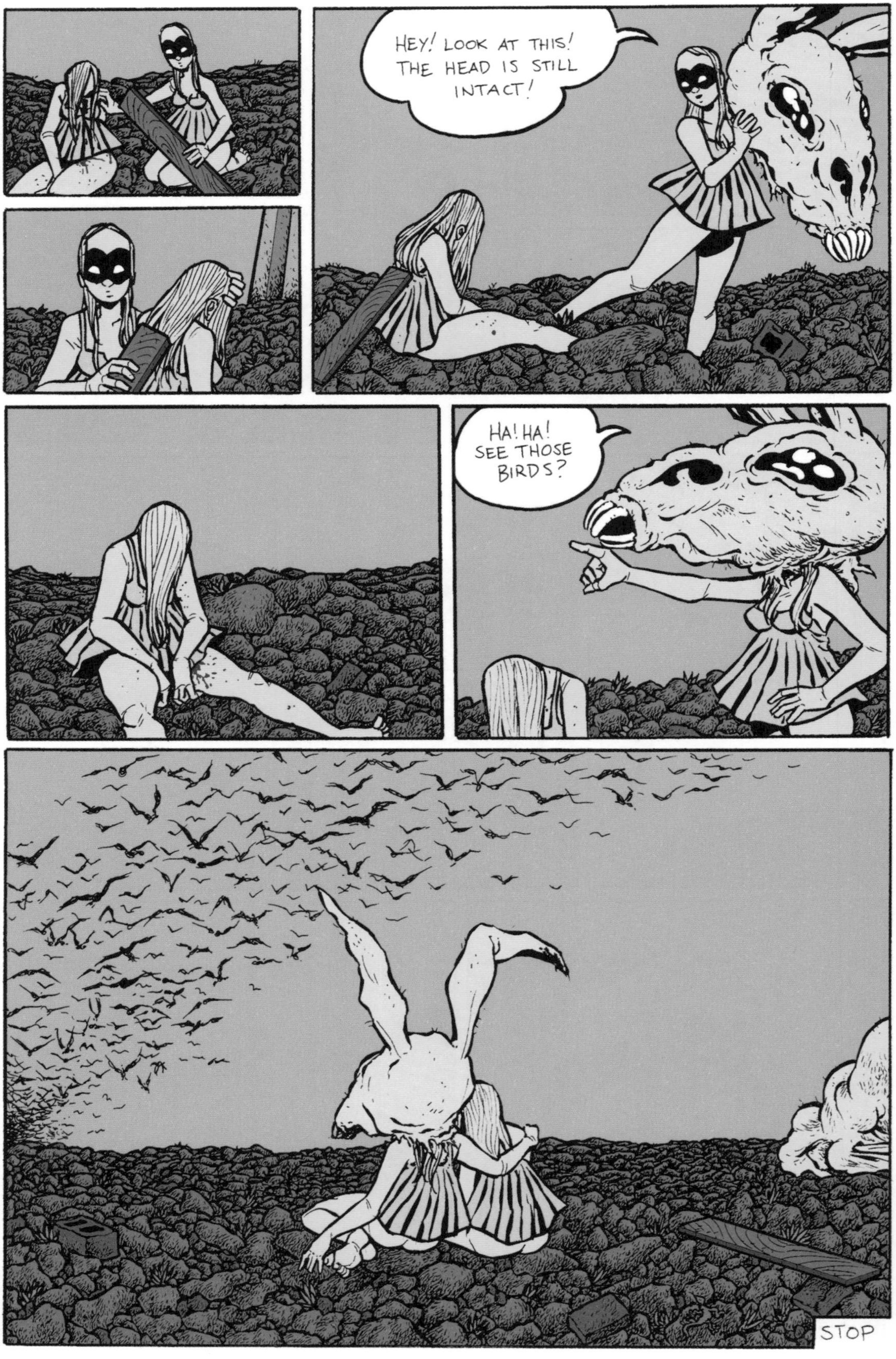
HEY! LOOK AT THIS! THE HEAD IS STILL INTACT!
HA! HA! SEE THOSE BIRDS?
STOP

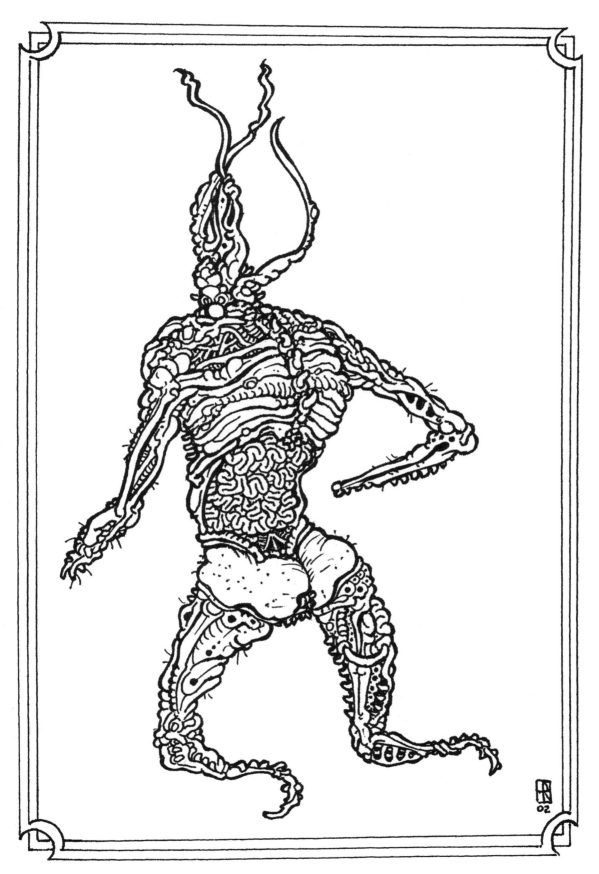

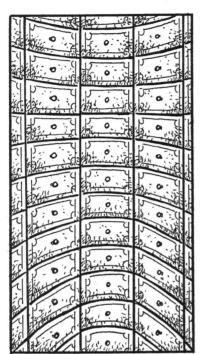
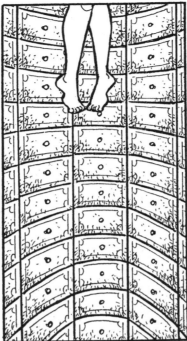

COCHLEA and EUSTACHIA

OKAY! YOU CAN STOP LOWERING ME NOW!

UG...

CREAK

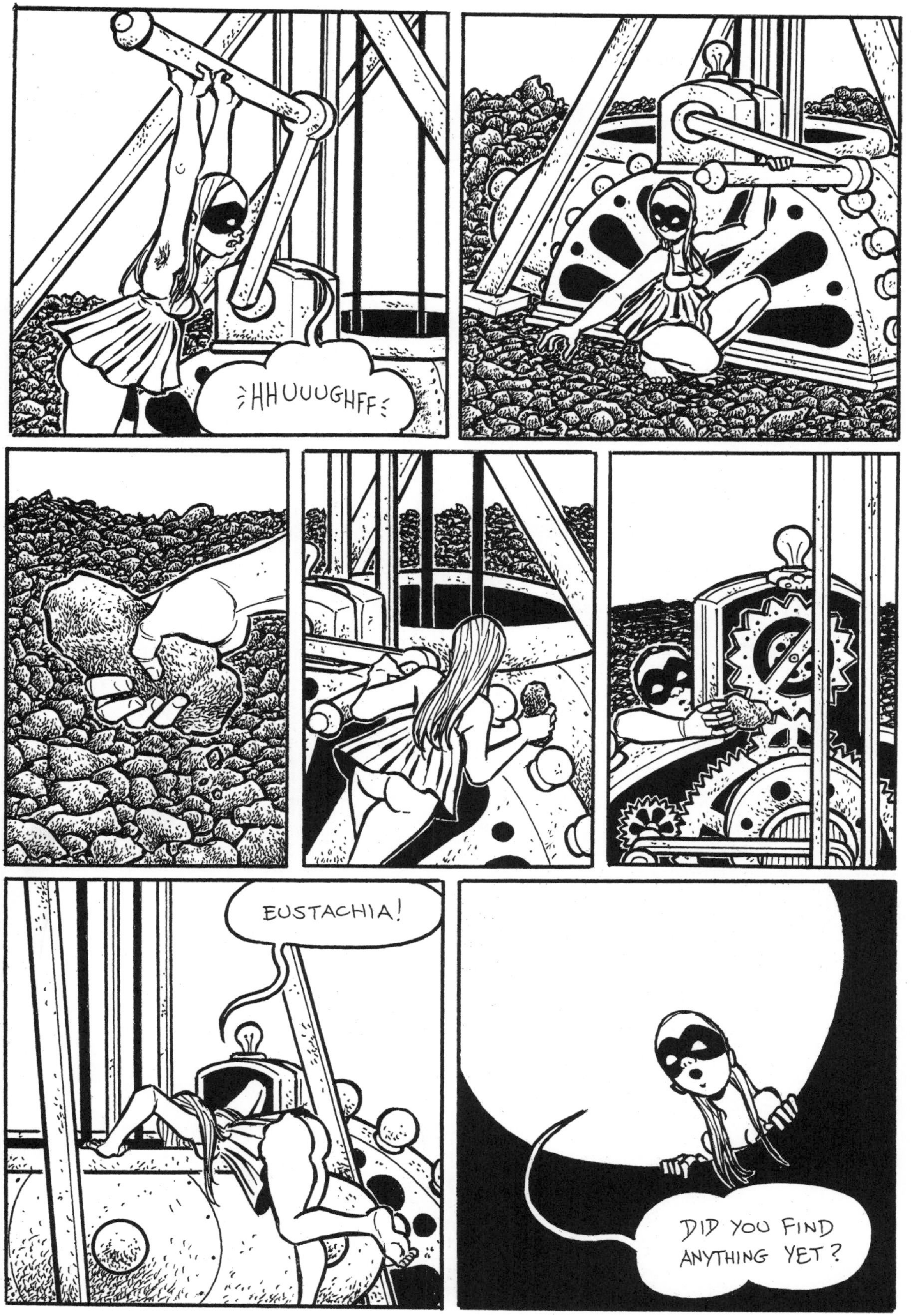
HHUUUGHFF
EUSTACHIA!
DID YOU FIND ANYTHING YET?

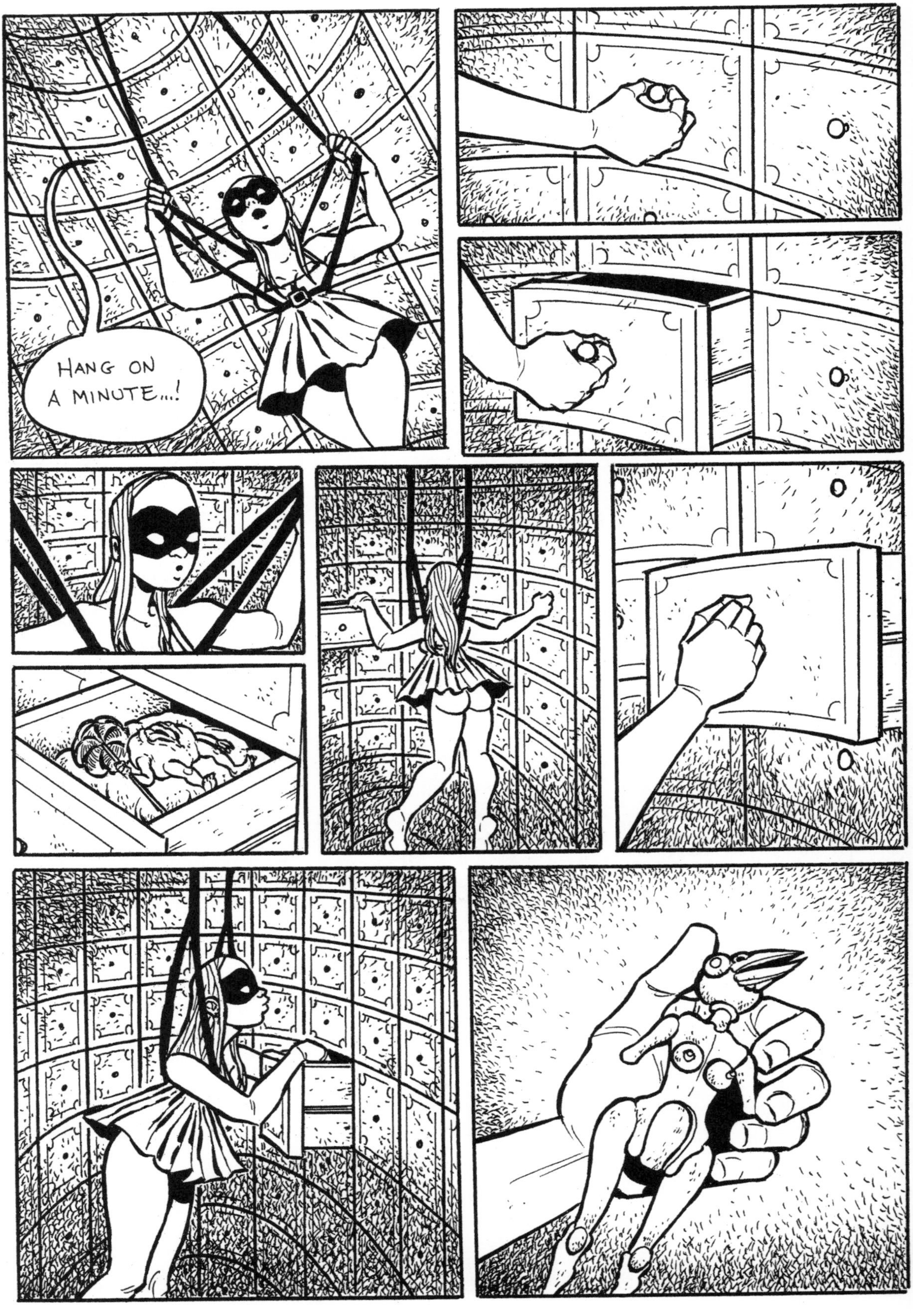
HANG ON A MINUTE...!

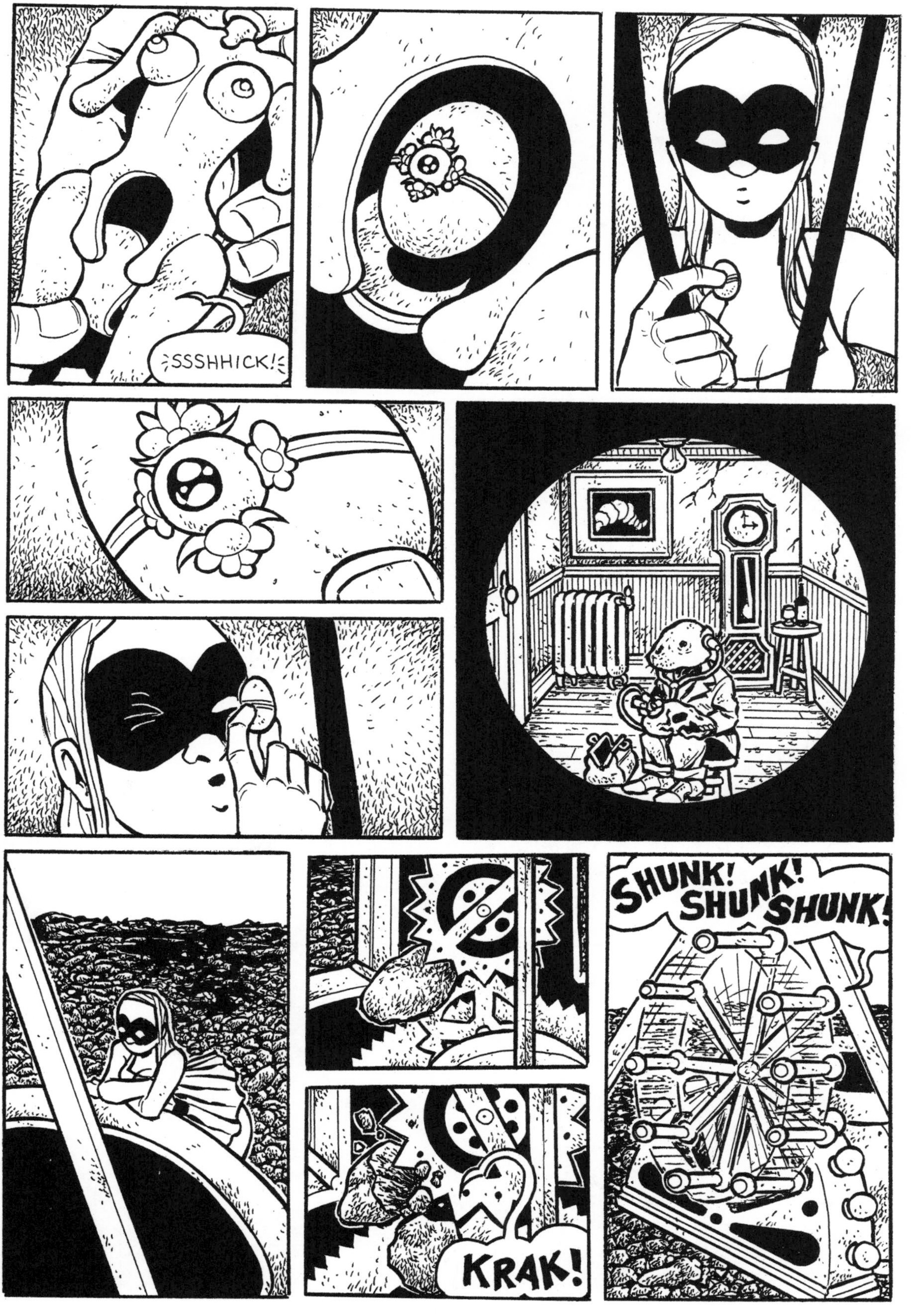
SSSHHICK!
SHUNK! SHUNK! SHUNK!
KRAK!

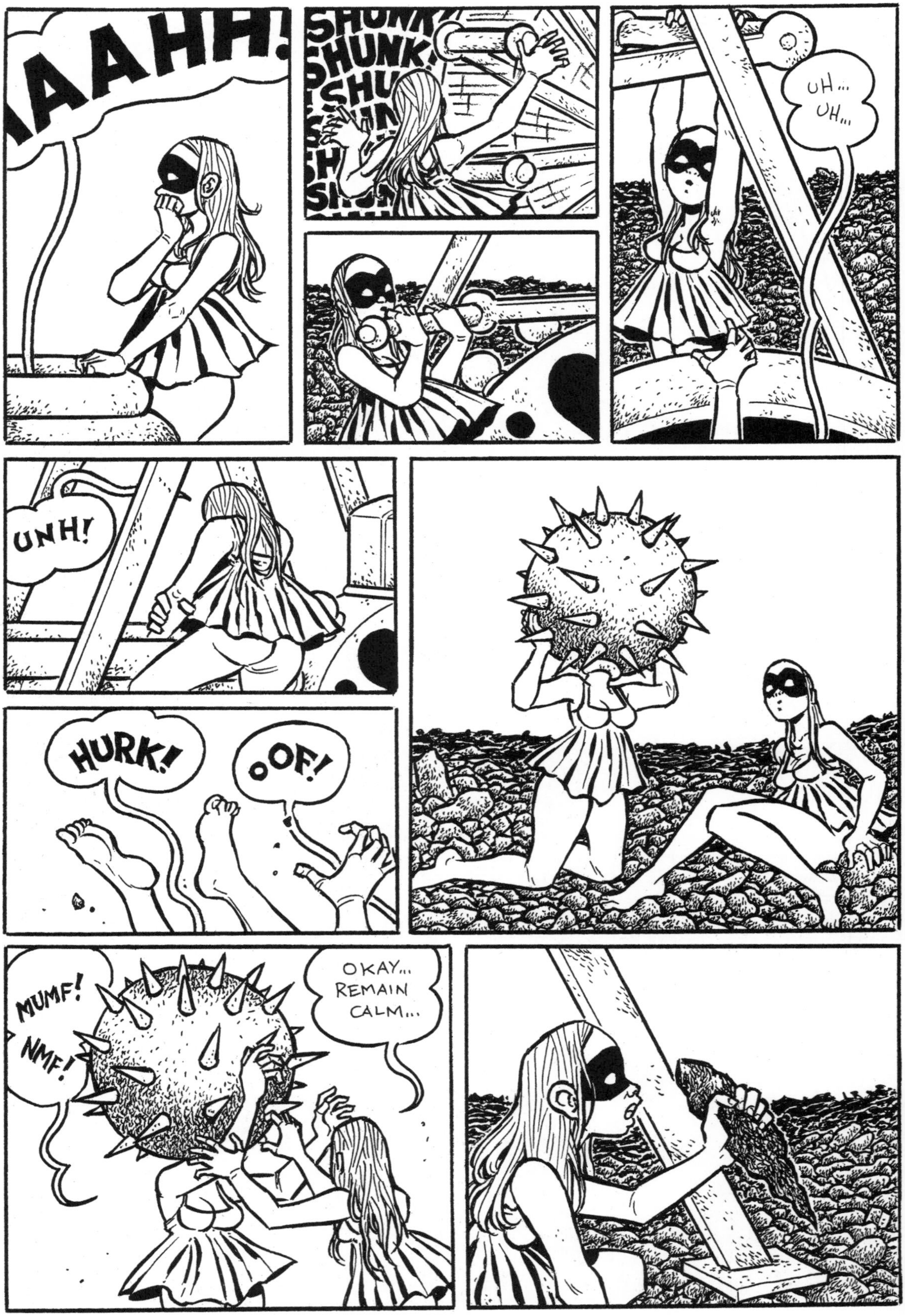
AAHH!
SHUNK! SHUNK! SHU SHU
UH... UH...
UNH!
HURK!
OOF!
MUMF! NMF!
OKAY... REMAIN CALM...

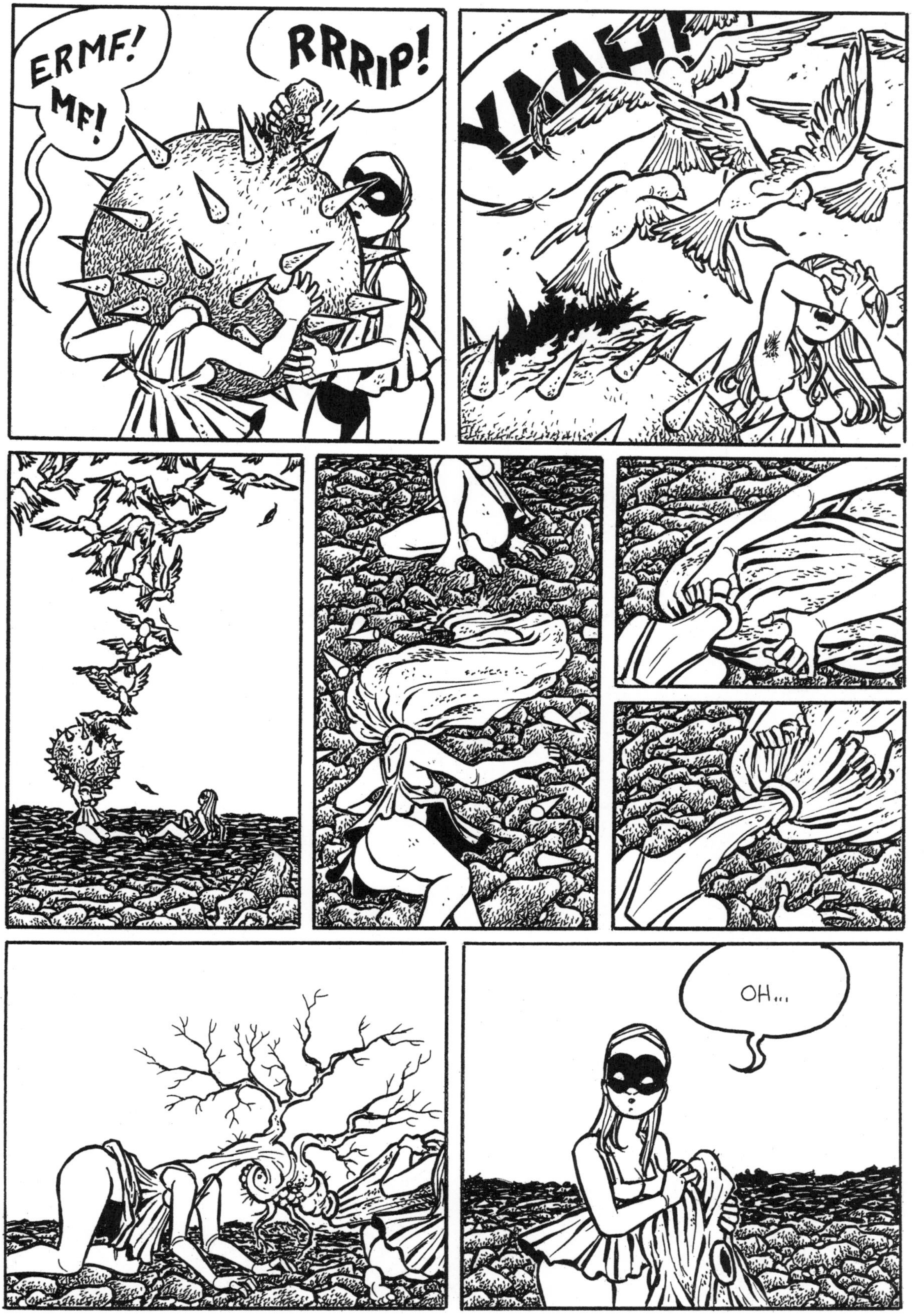
ERMF! MF!
RRRIP!
YAAH!
OH...

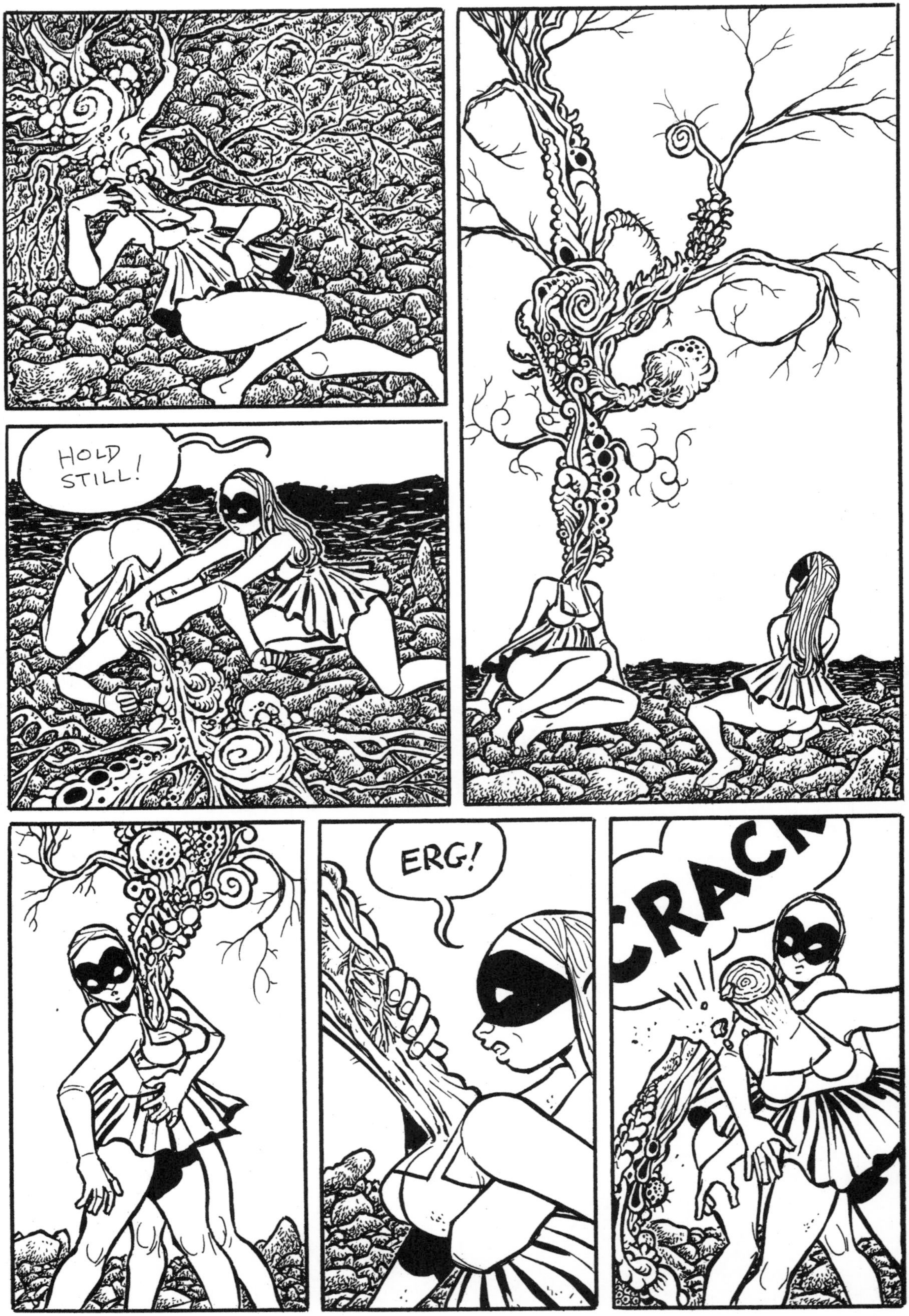
HOLD STILL!
ERG!
CRACK

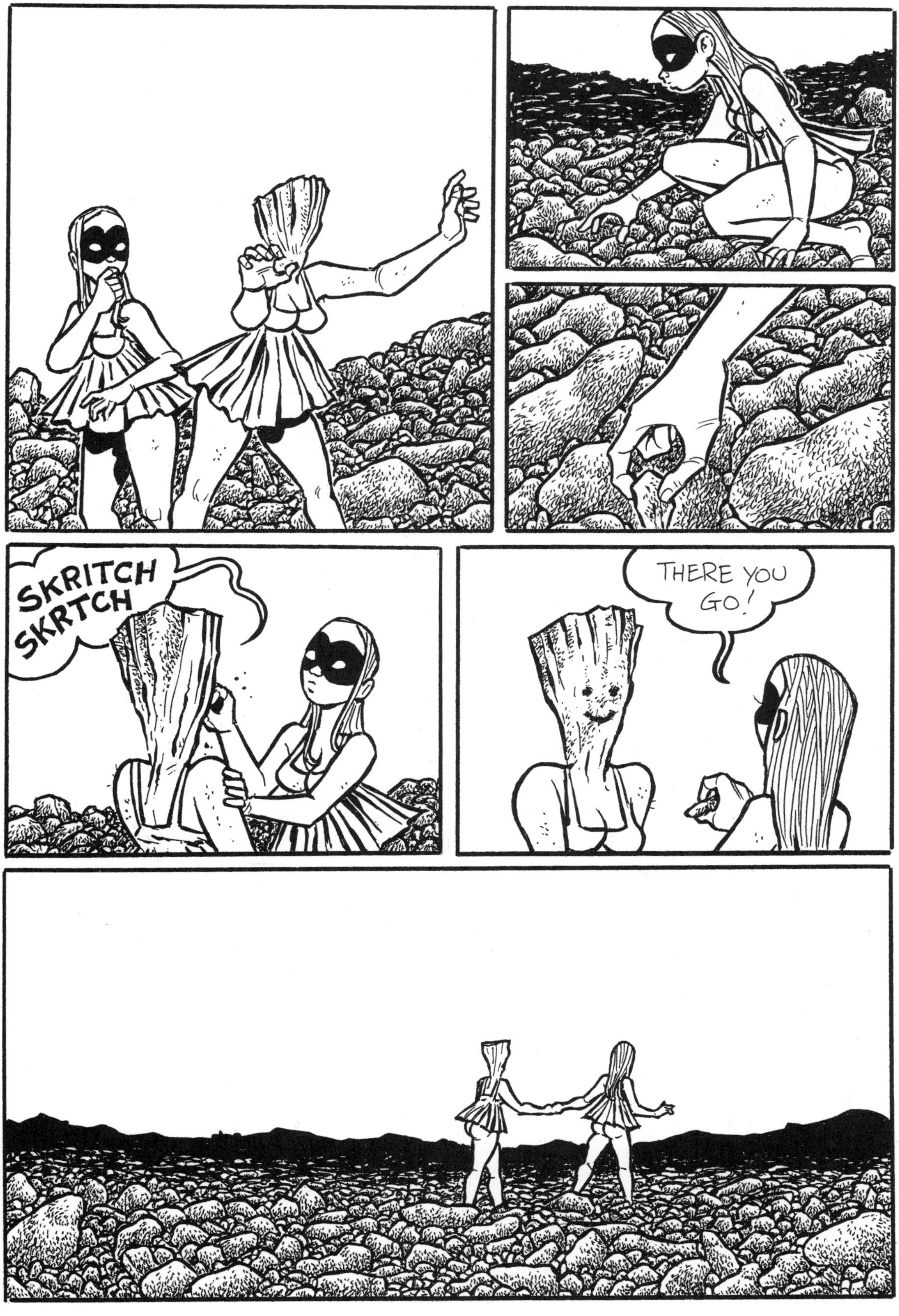
SKRITCH SKRTCH
THERE YOU GO!

CHROME FETUS COMICS

HANS RICKHEIT

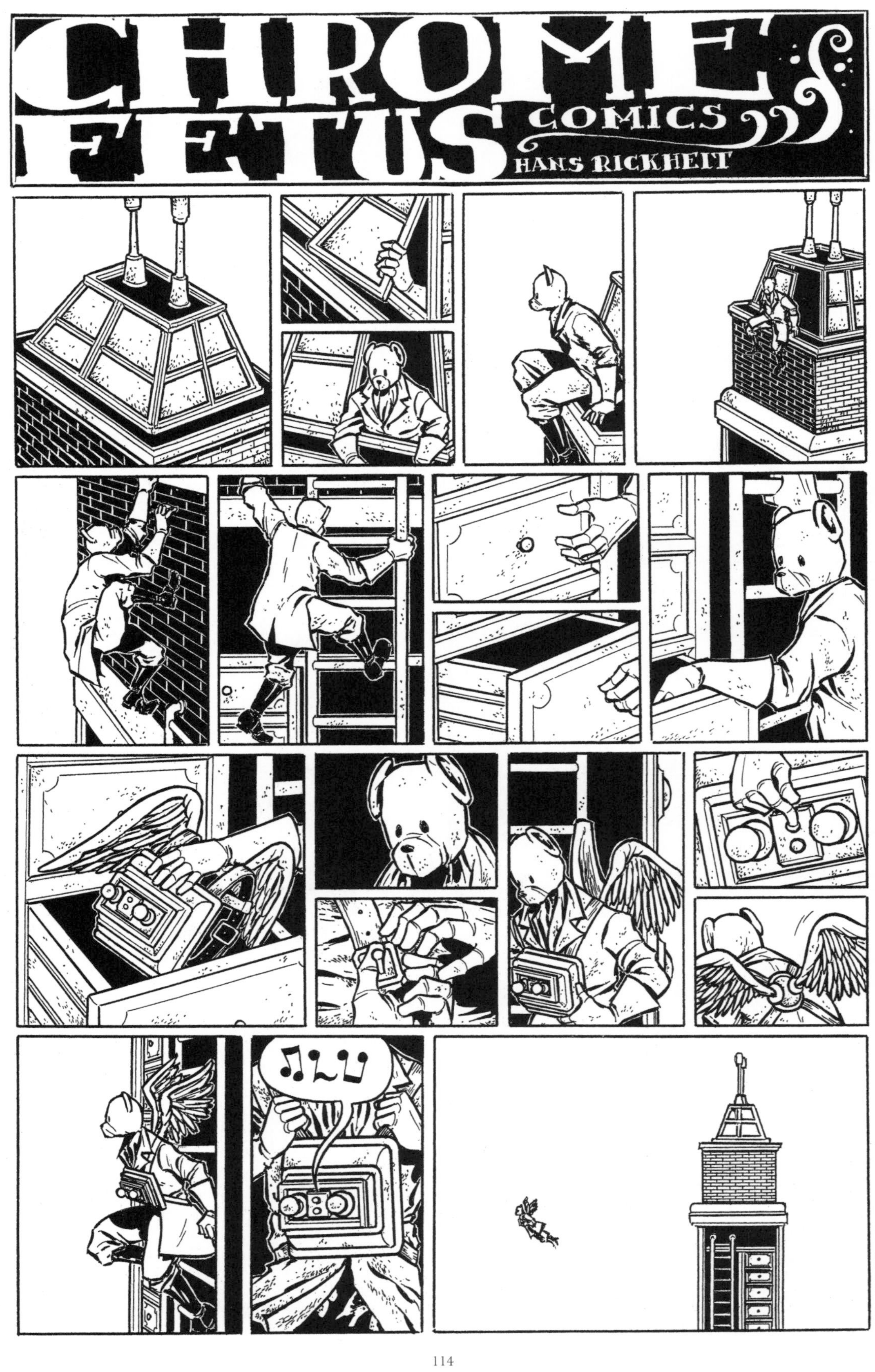

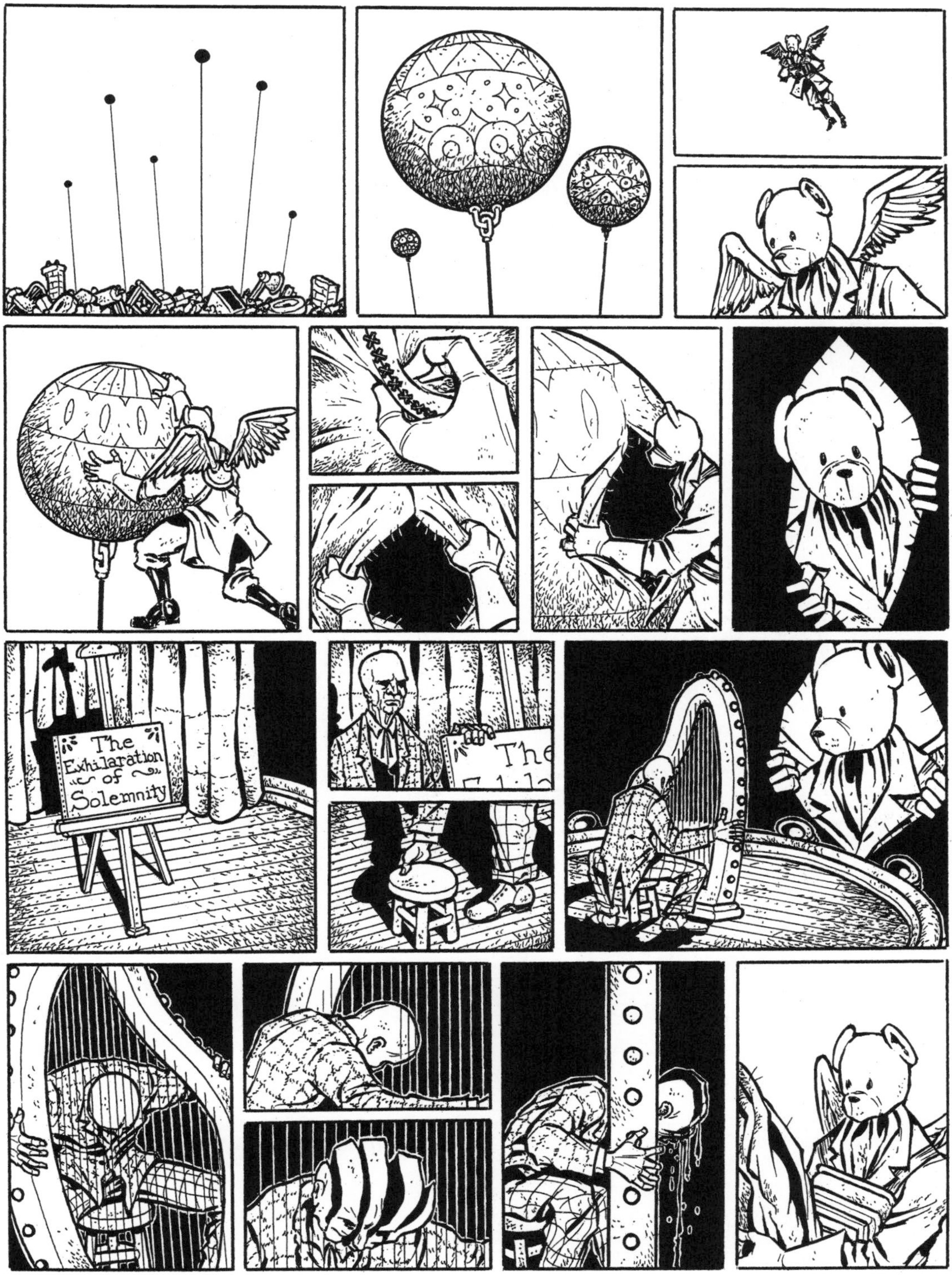
The Exhilaration of Solemnity
The

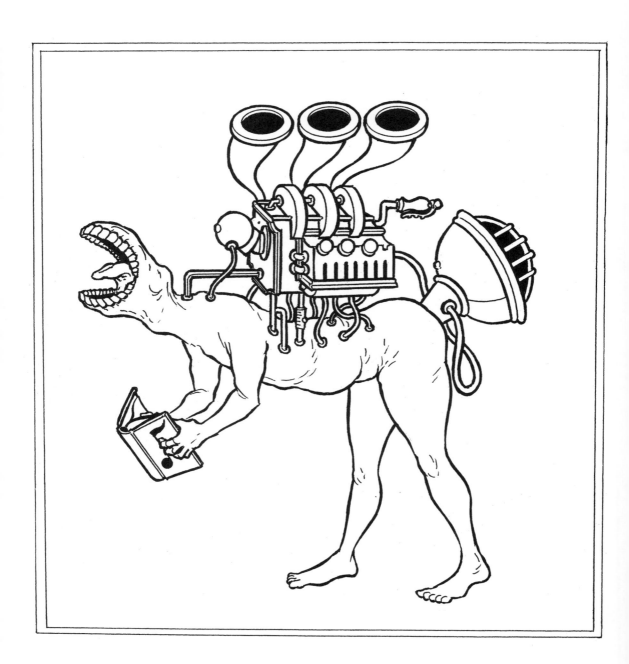

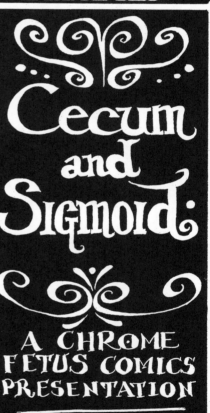

Cecum and Sigmoid:

A CHROME FETUS COMICS PRESENTATION

2006
HANS RICKHEIT

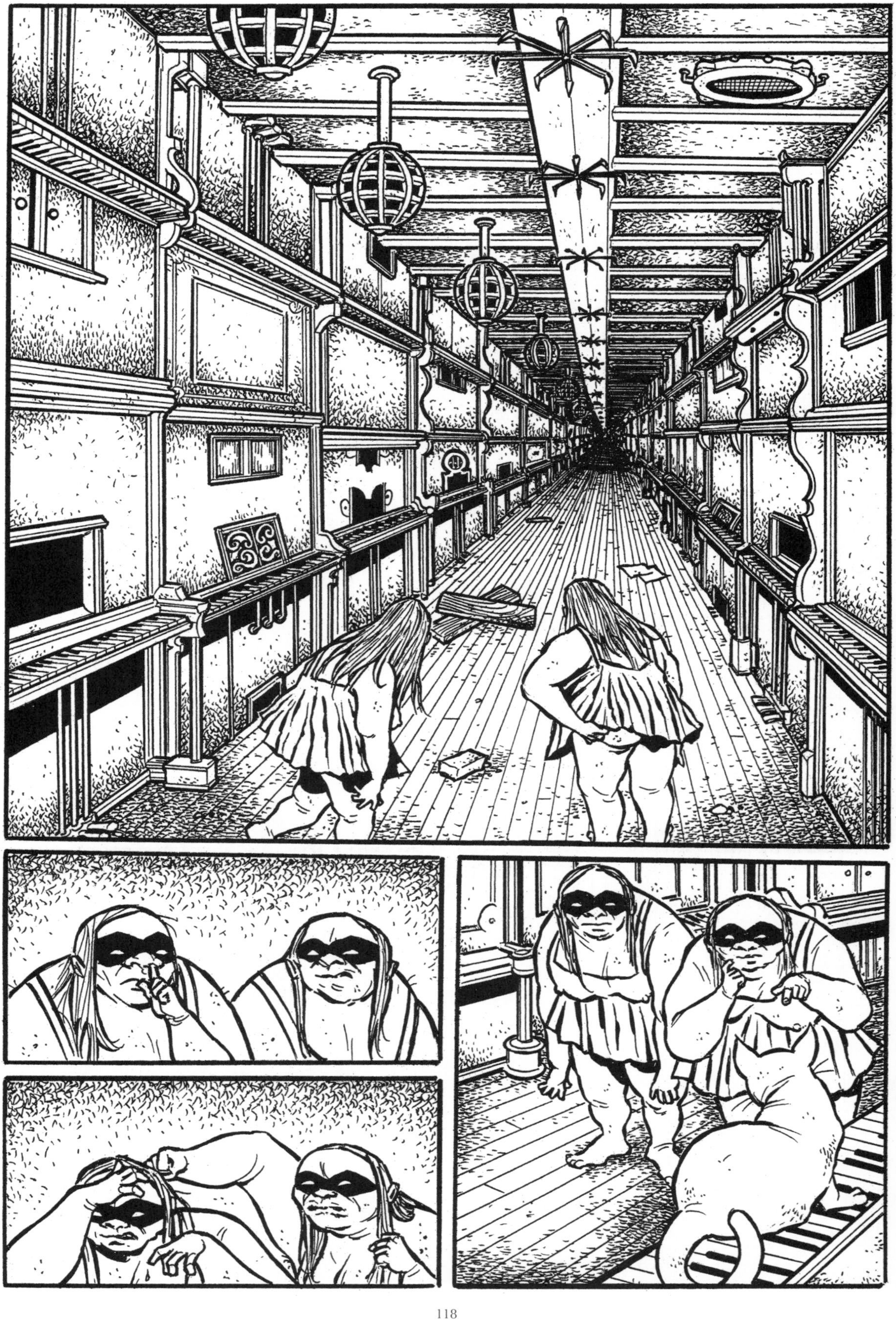

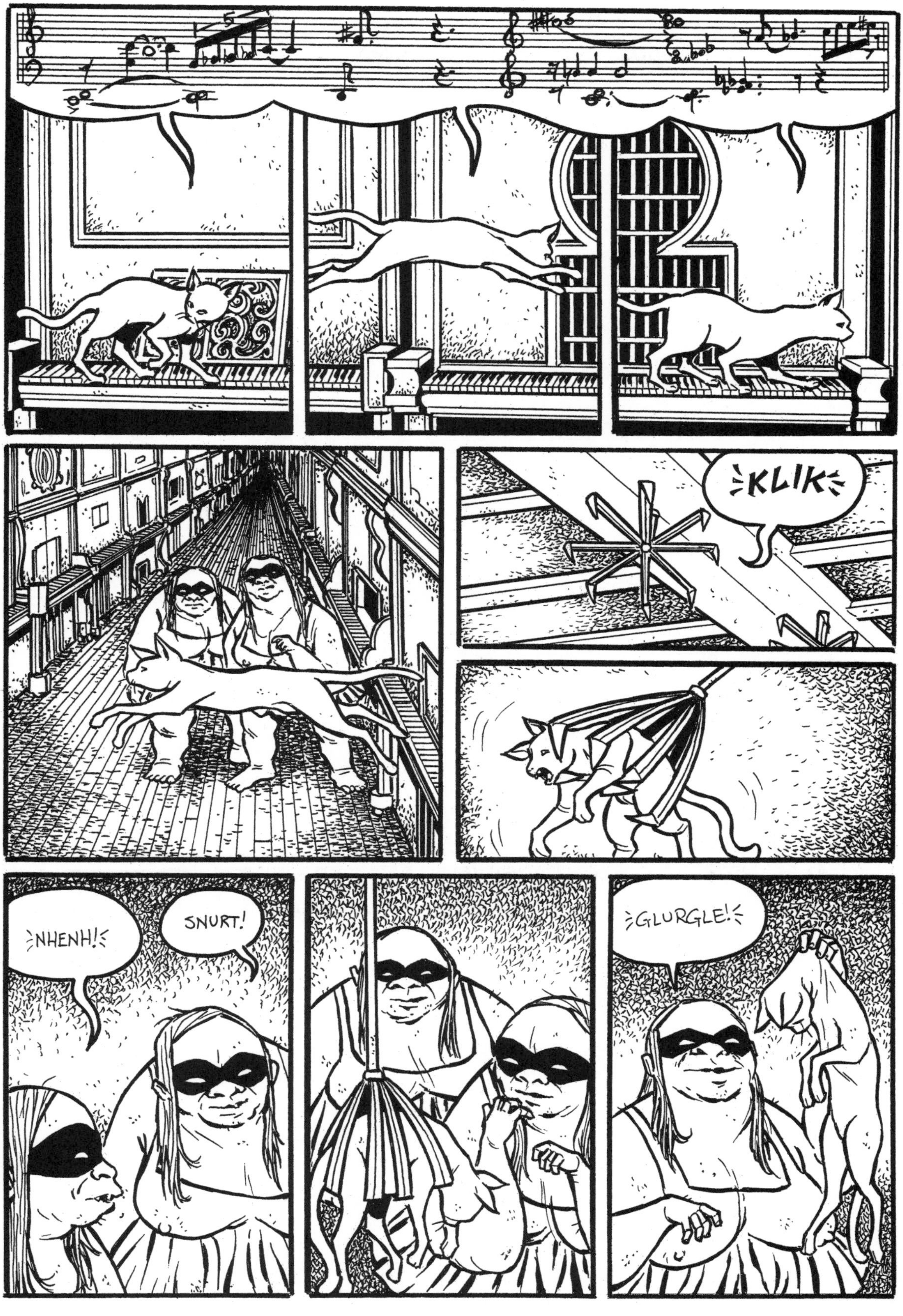
KLIK
NHENH!
SNURT!
GLURGLE!

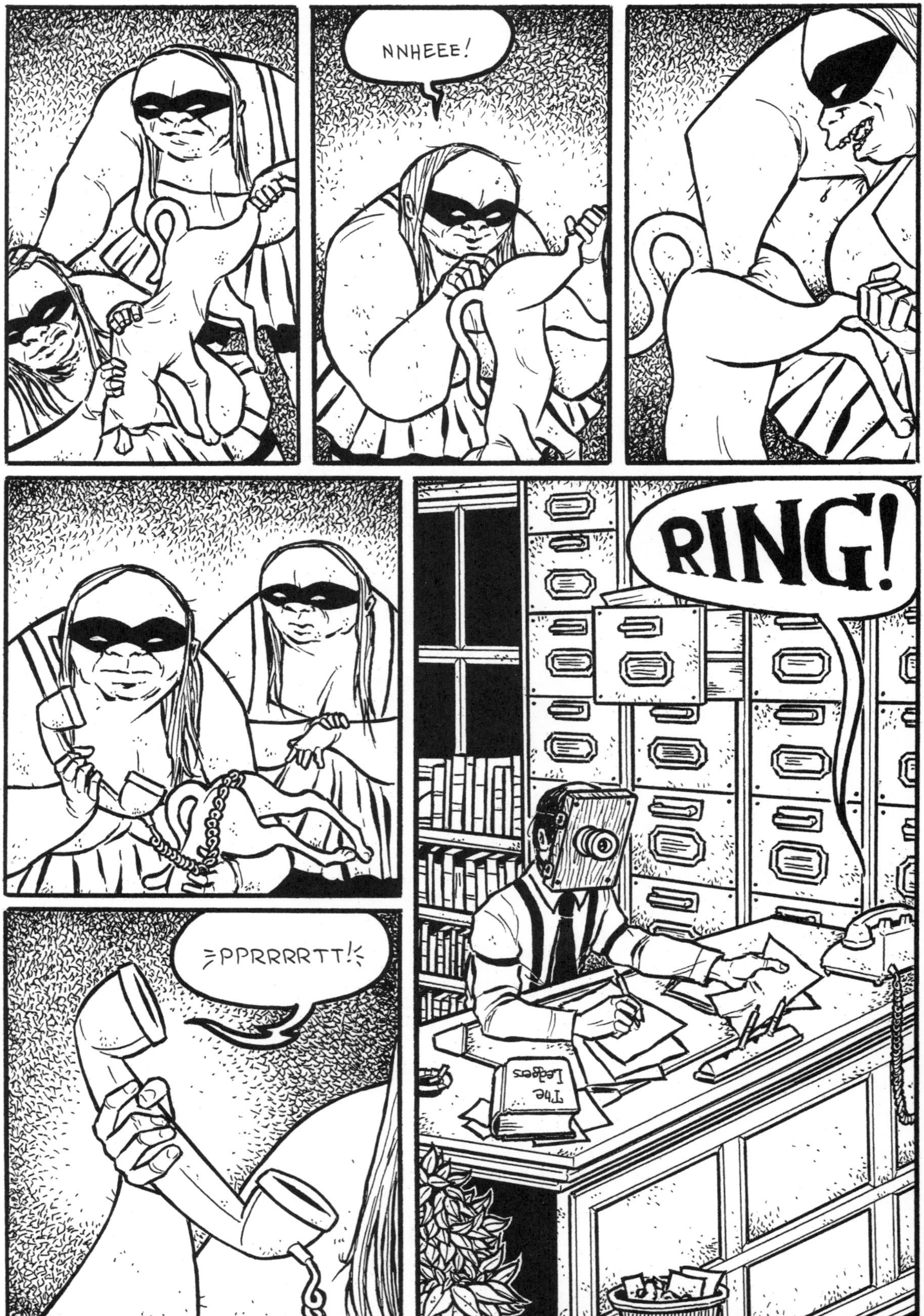
NNHEEE!
PPRRRRRTT!
RING!
The Ledgers

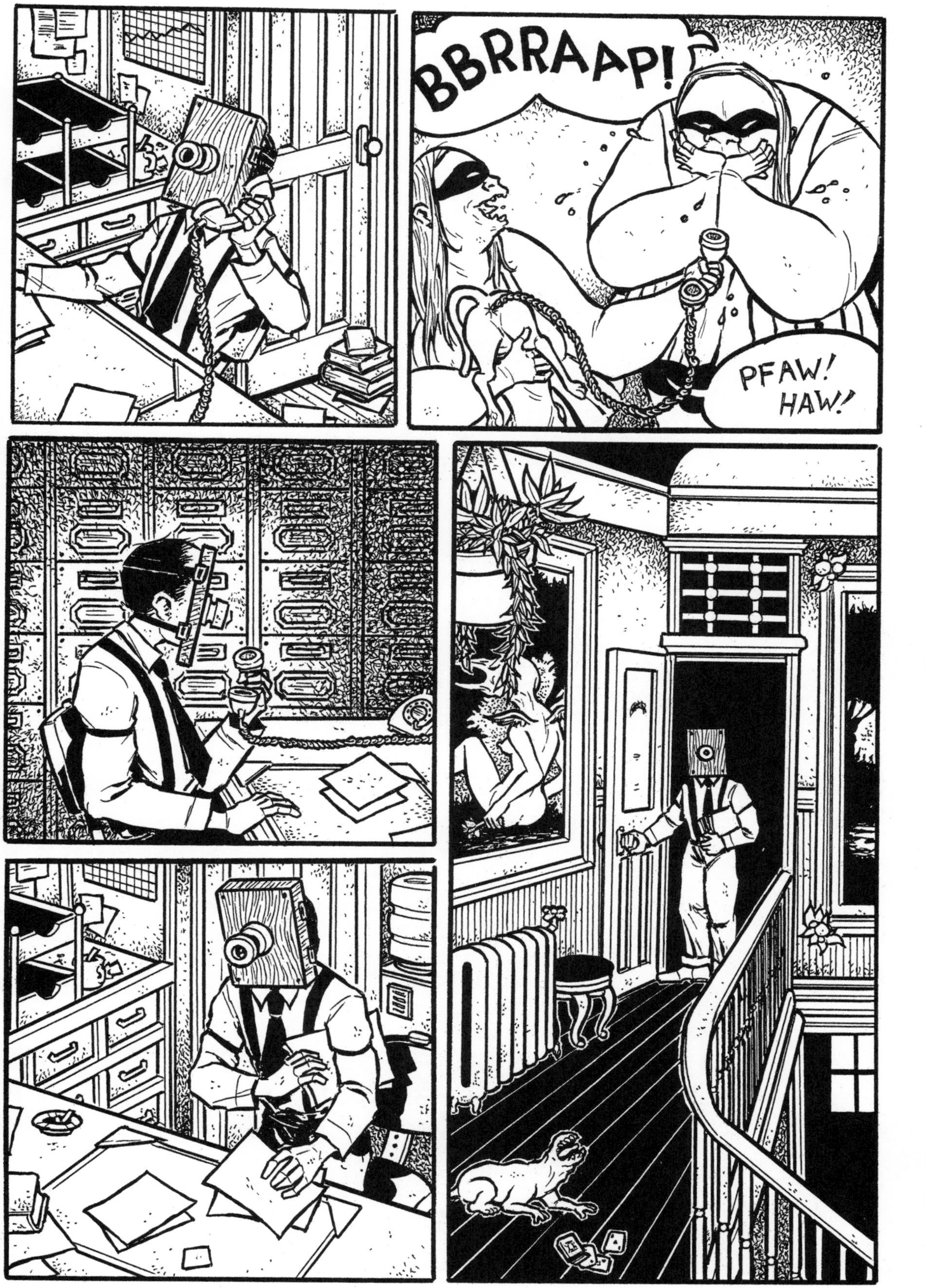
BBRRAAP!
PFAW! HAW!

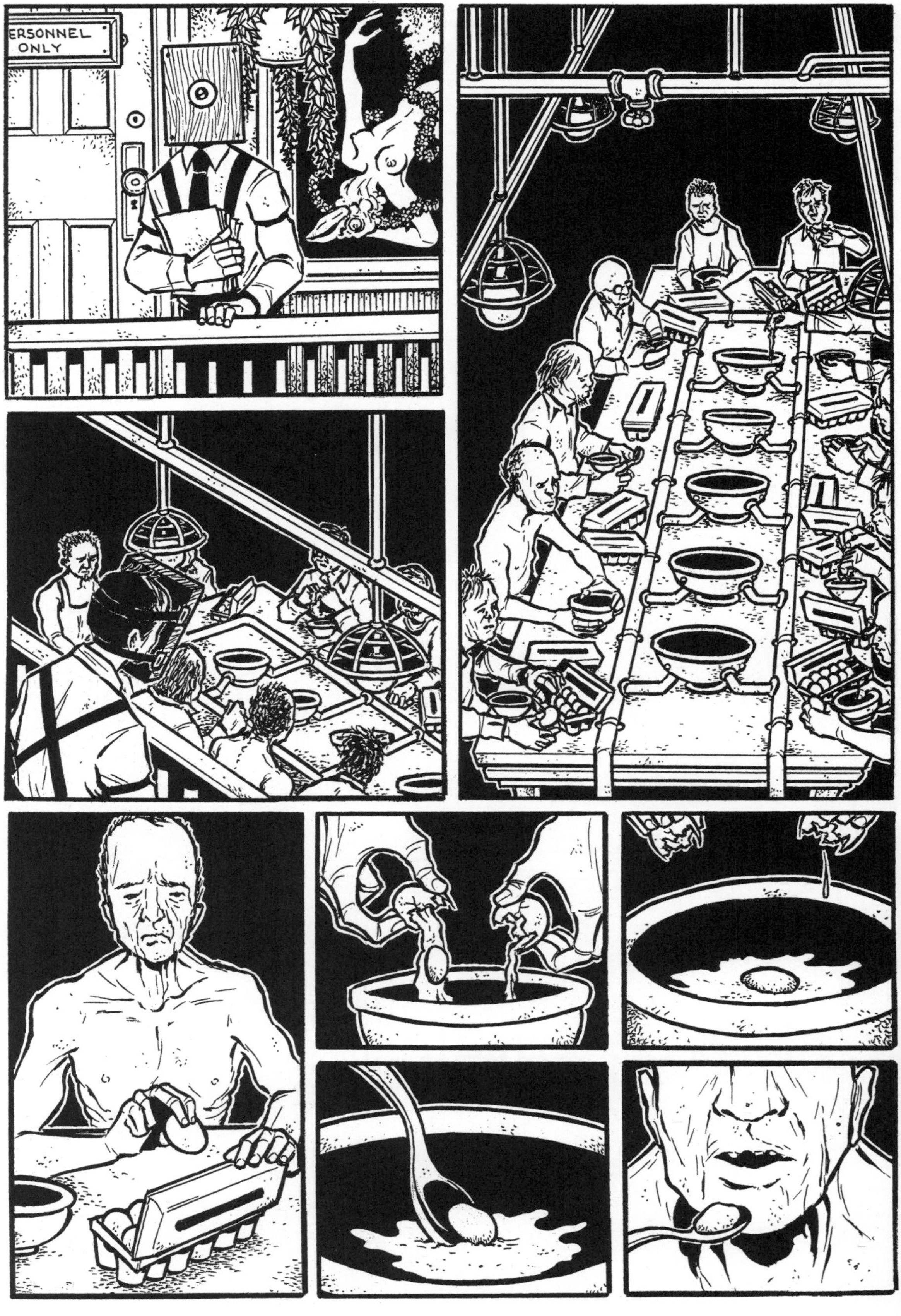
ERSONNEL
ONLY

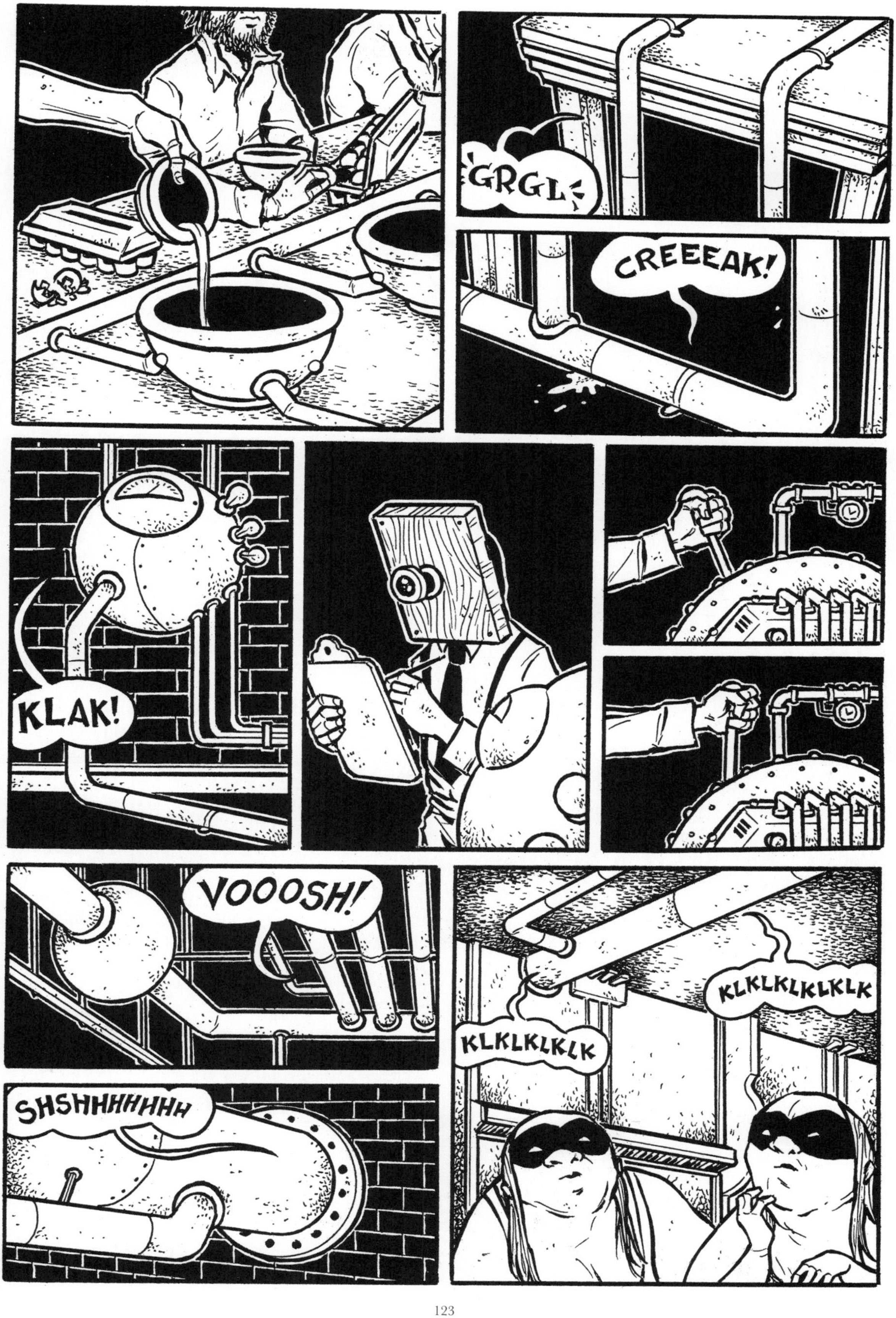
GRGL
CREEEAK!
KLAK!
VOOOSH!
SHSHHHHHHH
KLKLKLKLKLK
KLKLKLKLK

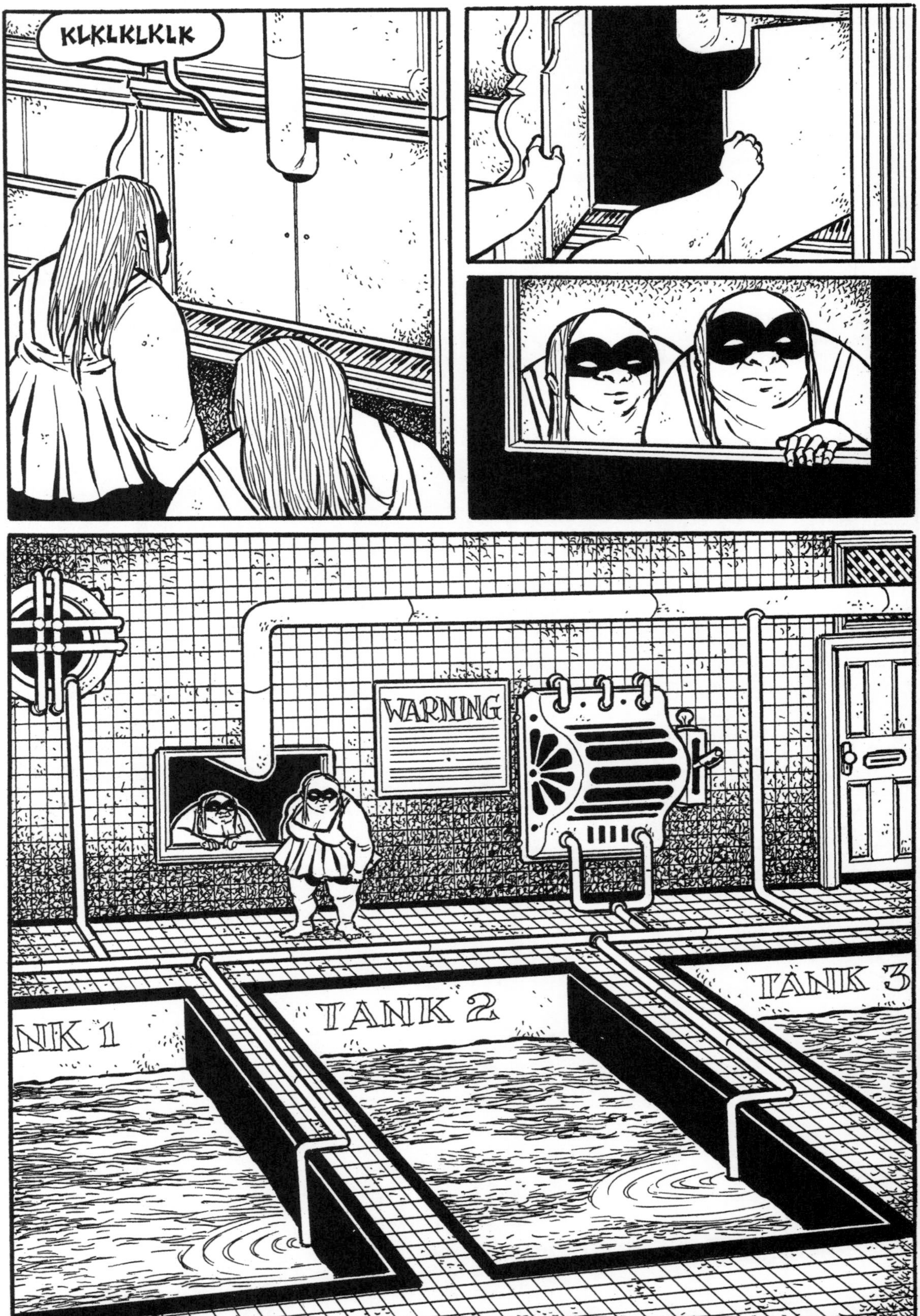
KLKLKLKLK
WARNING
NK 1
TANK 2
TANK 3

TANK 1
NHEH!
SNURK!
NGHEEEE!
GNOM
TAN

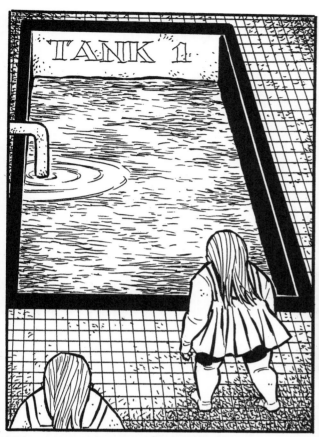

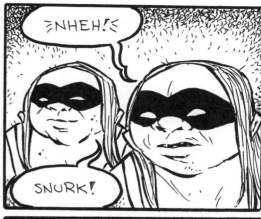

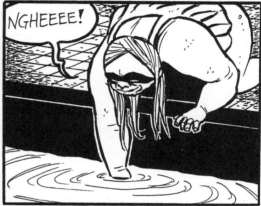

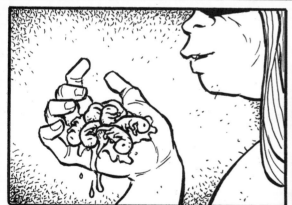

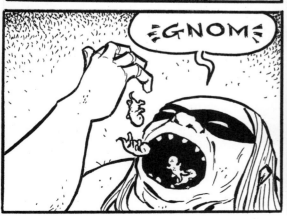

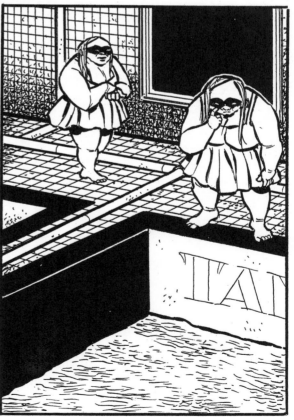

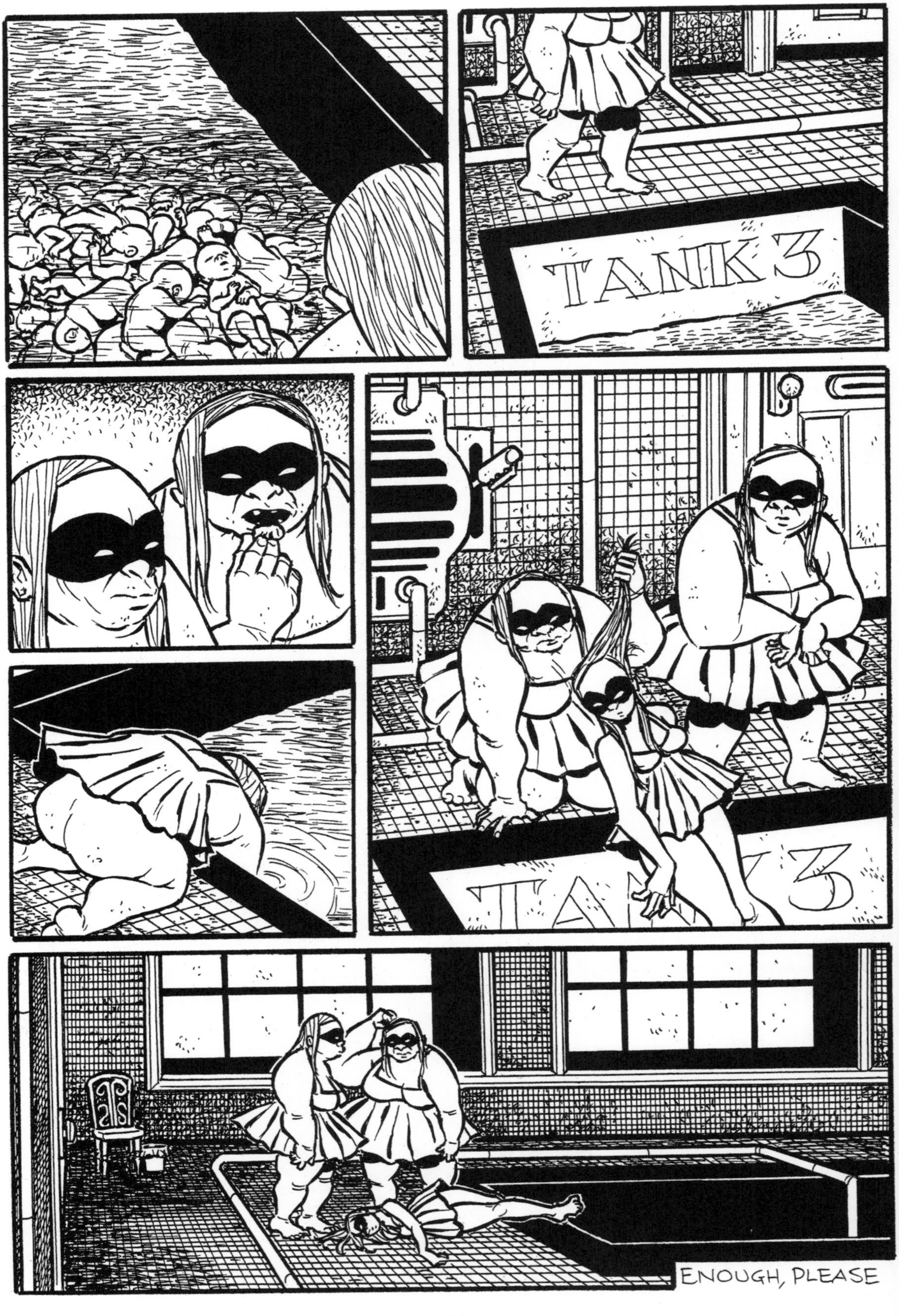
TANK 3
TANK 3
ENOUGH, PLEASE

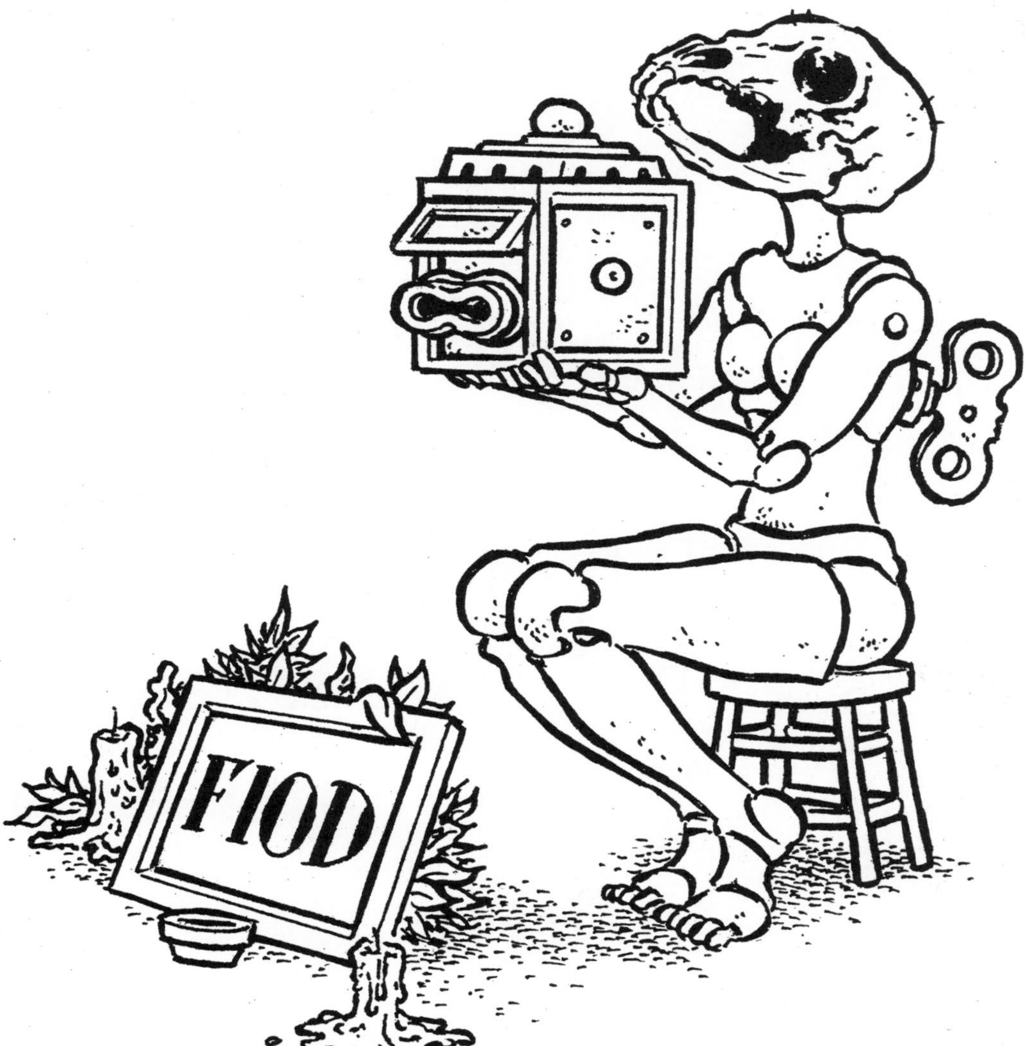
FIOD

CODA

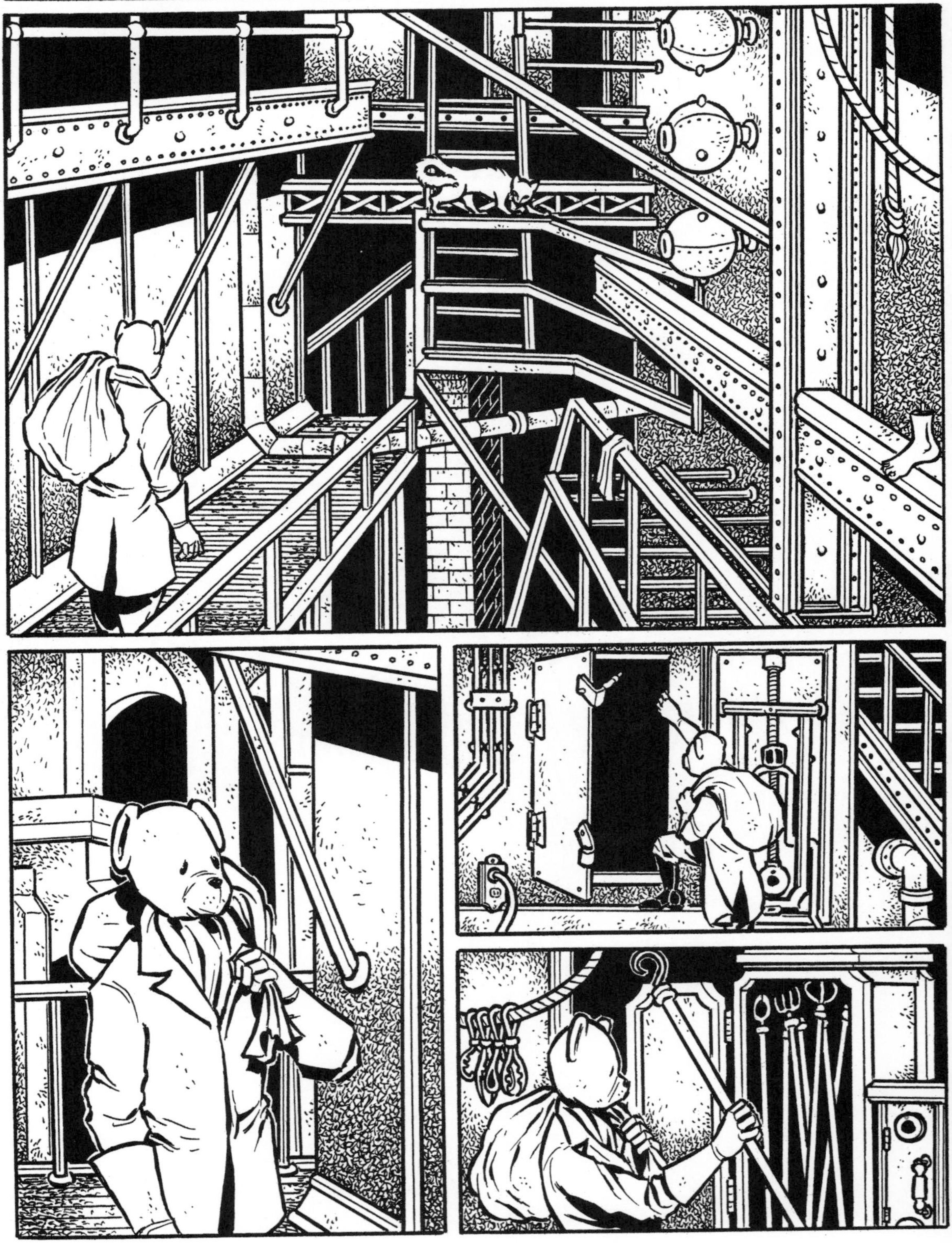

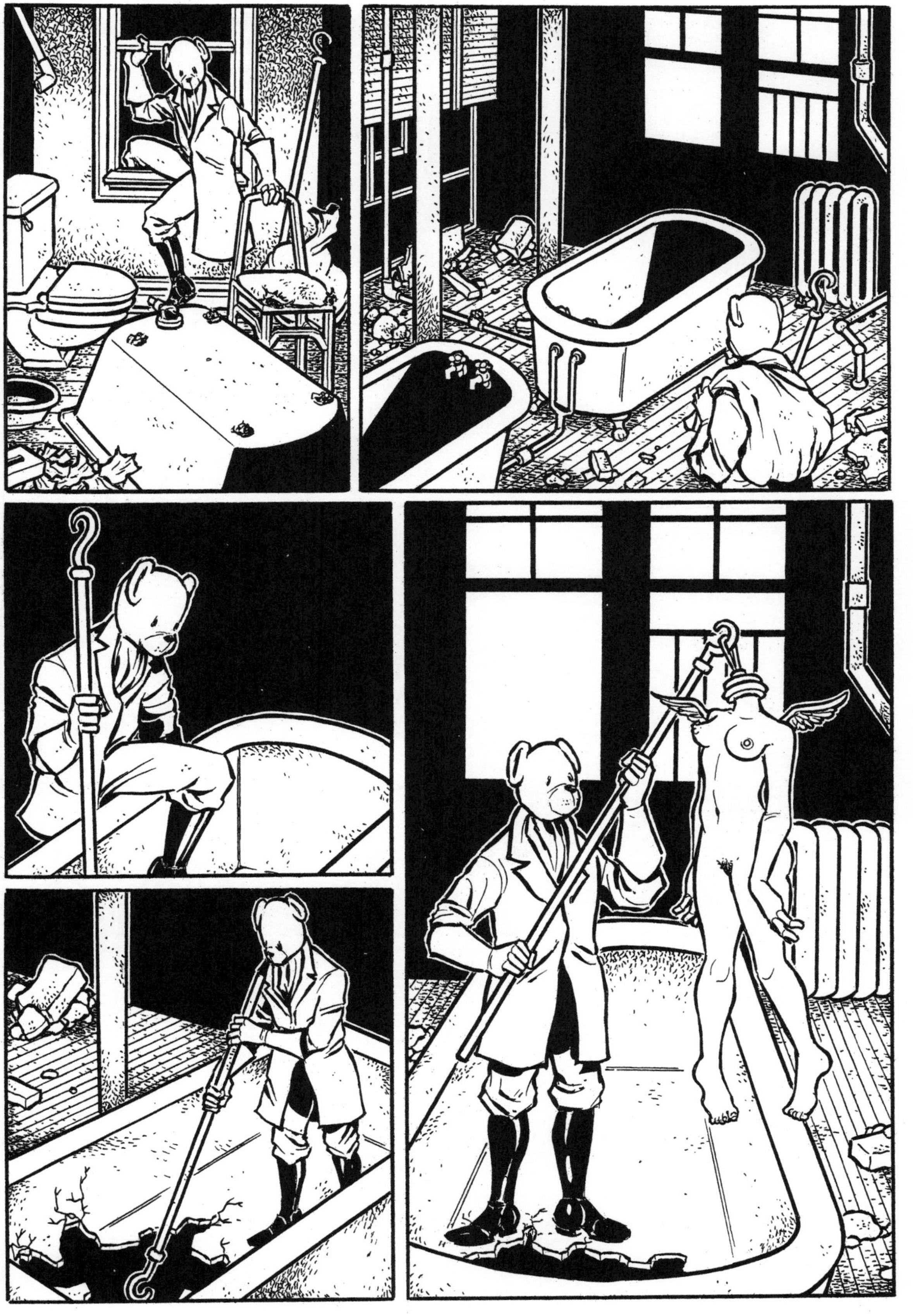

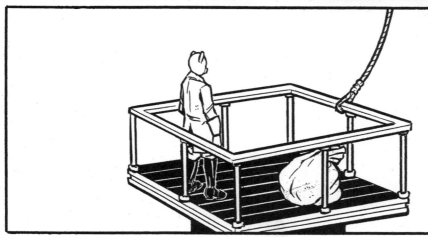

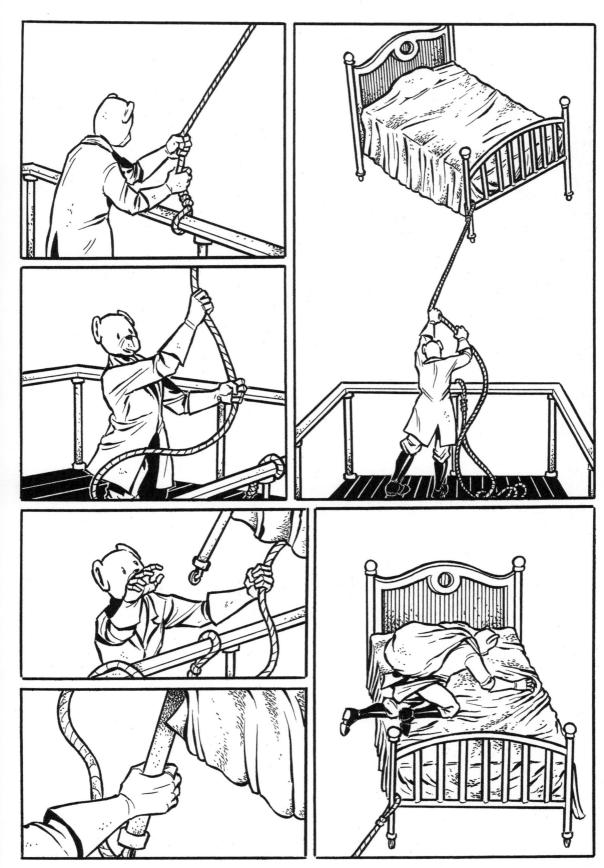

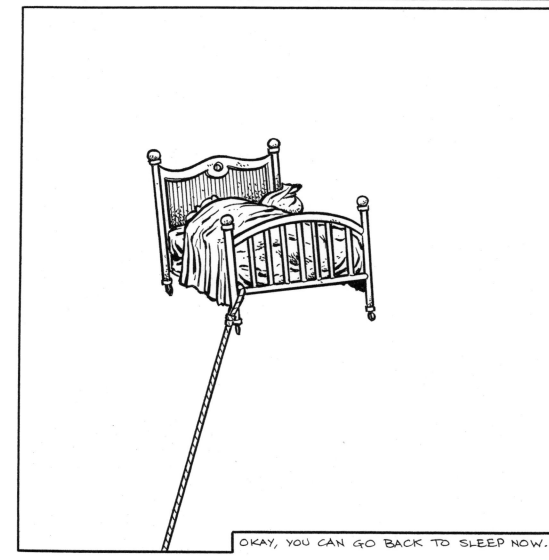

OKAY, YOU CAN GO BACK TO SLEEP NOW.

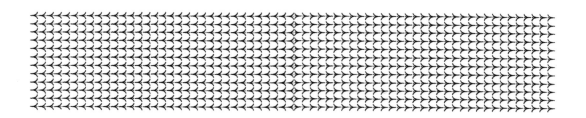

"Perhaps you expect an epilogue, but give me leave to tell you you are mistaken if you think I remember anything of what I have said, having foolishly bolted out such a hodgepodge of words. 'An ape is an ape, though clade in scarlet'; I am no counterfeit. No, I am in every respect so like myself that neither can they dissemble me who arrogate to themselves the appearance and title of wise men and walk like asses in scarlet hoods. And if they want hard words, they run over some worm-eaten manuscript and pick out half a dozen of the most old and obsolete to confound their reader, believing, no doubt, that they understand their meaning will like it the better, and they that do not, will admire it more by how much less they understand it. Nor is this way of ours of admiring what seems foreign without its particular grace; for if there happen to be any more ambitious than others, they may give their applause with a smile, and, like the ass, shake their ears, that they may be thought to understand more than the rest of their neighbors. But to speak of arts, what set men's wits on work to invent and transmit to posterity but the thirst of glory? With so much loss of sleep, such pains and travail, have the most foolish of men thought to purchase themselves a kind of I know not what fame, than which nothing can be more vain. And yet notwithstanding, you owe this advantage to folly, and which is the most delectable of all other, that you reap the benefit of other men's madness. Since then the nature of man is such that there is scarce anyone to be found that is not subject to many errors, add to this the great diversity of minds and studies, so many slips, oversights, and chances of human life, and how is it possible there should be any true friendship? I hate a man that remembers what he hears.

From The Praise of Folly *(more or less...) by Desiderius Erasmus of Rotterdam 1466-1536*

And now tell me if to wink, slip over, be blind at, or deceived in the vices of our friends, nay, to admire and esteem them for virtures, be not at least the next degree to folly? And so, perhaps you'll cry it is; and yet 'tis this only that joins friends together and continues them so joined. These things are not only done everywhere but laughed at too; yet as ridiculous as they are, they make society pleasant, and, as it were, glue it together. Wherefore farewell, clap your hands, live and drink lustily, my most excellent disciples of folly."

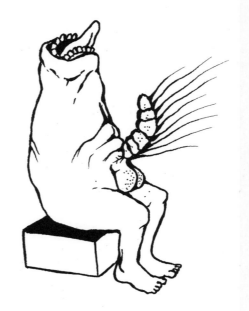